Innovation

The PricewaterhouseCoopers Endowment for

The Business of Government

THE PRICEWATERHOUSECOOPERS ENDOWMENT
SERIES ON
THE BUSINESS OF GOVERNMENT

Series Editors: Mark A. Abramson and Paul R. Lawrence

The PricewaterhouseCoopers Endowment Series on The Business of Government explores new approaches to improving the effectiveness of government at the federal, state, and local levels. The Series is aimed at providing cutting-edge knowledge to government leaders, academics, and students about the management of government in the 21st century.

Publications in the series will include:

2001
Transforming Organizations, *edited by Mark A. Abramson and Paul R. Lawrence*
E-Government 2001, *edited by Mark A. Abramson and Grady E. Means*
Managing for Results 2002, *edited by Mark A. Abramson and John M. Kamensky*
Memos to the President: Management Advice from the Nation's Top Public Administrators, *edited by Mark A. Abramson*

2002
Human Capital, *edited by Mark A. Abramson and Nicole Willenz Gardner*
E-Government 2002, *edited by Mark A. Abramson and Grady E. Means*

Innovation

EDITED BY

MARK A. ABRAMSON
THE PRICEWATERHOUSECOOPERS ENDOWMENT
FOR THE BUSINESS OF GOVERNMENT
and
IAN D. LITTMAN
PRICEWATERHOUSECOOPERS

ROWMAN & LITTLEFIELD PUBLISHERS, INC.
Lanham • Boulder • New York • Oxford

ROWMAN & LITTLEFIELD PUBLISHERS, INC.

Published in the United States of America
by Rowman & Littlefield Publishers, Inc.
4720 Boston Way, Lanham, Maryland 20706
www.rowmanlittlefield.com

12 Hid's Copse Road
Cumnor Hill, Oxford OX2 9JJ, England

British Library Cataloguing in Publication Information Available

Library of Congress Cataloging-in-Publication Data Available

0-7425-2265-2 (alk. paper)
0-7425-2266-0 (pbk.: alk. paper)

Printed in the United States of America

♾ ™ The paper used in this publication meets the minimum requirements of American National Standard for Information Sciences—Permanence of Paper for Printed Library Materials, ANSI/NISO Z39.48-1992.

To our fathers

Louis Abramson
1919–1997

Philip Littman
who brought innovation to
the Department of Treasury
for over 30 years

TABLE OF CONTENTS

CHAPTER ONE

What Do We Know
about Innovation?

Mark A. Abramson
Executive Director
The PricewaterhouseCoopers Endowment
for The Business of Government

Ian D. Littman
Partner
PwC Consulting

Introduction

Innovation is not a new topic. A search on the Barnes & Noble website generates a list of over 2,500 books with the term "innovation" in the title. While innovation has long been an important concept in the business community, the concept achieved attention only relatively recently in the governmental community. It is always hard to date concepts, but innovation in the public sector received a major boost in 1986 when the Ford Foundation created the Innovations in State and Local Government Awards program. Other similar award programs, both internationally and within the United States, were created in subsequent years. During the 1990s, the Clinton administration's National Performance Review encouraged innovative ideas, programs, and approaches in the federal government as a major component of its reinvention initiative.

What do we mean by innovation? There appears be no shortage of definitions concerning what innovation means. In their 1997 book, *Innovation in American Government: Challenges, Opportunities, and Dilemmas,* Alan A. Altshuler and Robert D. Behn devote several pages to the varying definitions of innovation (Altshuler and Behn). In this book, Jonathan Walters and Sandford Borins also enter into the innovation definition discussion. While there are clearly different nuances in various definitions of innovation, there appears to be general agreement that an innovation is "new," usually "novel," and aspires to "change" the way an organization (or part of an organization) operates and delivers service to the public. For the purposes of this chapter, this concept of innovation is used.

There can be little doubt that innovation is now occurring frequently in government at the federal, state, and local level. In chapter three, Sanford Borins demonstrates that innovation is also happening internationally as well. The Ford Foundation's Innovations program, administered by the John F. Kennedy School of Government at Harvard University, has now recognized over 350 innovative government programs as award winners. In 1995, the federal government was added and the program was renamed the Innovations in American Government program. During its nearly eight years, the National Performance Review (renamed the National Partnership for Reinventing Government in 1997) selected over 1,300 government programs and initiatives to receive "Hammer" awards, which recognized innovative activities in the federal government.

So innovation in government does indeed occur and can no longer be viewed as an isolated, infrequent, or anomalous occurrence. The issue is no longer whether innovation in government occurs but how it can be fostered, successfully implemented, and replicated. Today, the public sector has at least 15 years of experience with the concept and practice of innovation. It is thus an appropriate time to reflect on what we have learned about fostering, implementing, and spreading innovation, and about the relationship between innovation and the individual innovator.

Fostering Innovation

We have learned much about how to foster innovation in organizations. While we know that innovative environments can be created, the major challenge for the next decade will be creating such environments in more organizations. Organizations can clearly create environments (or a culture) that encourage and stimulate their employees to seek new and novel ideas to change the way they operate or deliver services. In chapter four, Janet Vinzant Denhardt and Robert Denhardt detail how Phoenix, Arizona, creates its culture of innovation. They describe how Phoenix employees are respected, trusted, and empowered—crucial steps in fostering innovation in any organization. In describing the importance of trust, Phoenix Fire Department Chief Alan Brunacini explained, "The people who have managed this place have done an excellent job in creating systems and processes and experiences where people trust each other, and they're basically willing to change. Because of this trust, change isn't threatening to us. It's just what's next in the process."

At the same time it created an innovative environment, Phoenix also created a strong orientation to serve citizens. Thus, it is often difficult to sort out all the contributing factors to an innovative environment. Phoenix Public Works Director Juan Martin describes the difficulty: "I don't know if our good customer service is a result of our innovative tendencies, or if we've become innovative because we want to provide good customer service." The lesson, however, is that both aspects of their culture—a strong customer orientation and a high value on innovation—reinforced each other. If innovation is to become the norm in any organization, all aspects of an organization's culture must reinforce the drive to innovate.

Lessons Learned from Phoenix, Arizona, on How to Create a Culture of Innovation

- Take pride
- Look ahead and create new challenges
- Build relationships and foster participation
- Serve citizens
- Trust and empower people
- Enact core values
- Respect employees and treat them well
- Take risks and learn from experience
- Recognize and reward people's efforts
- Build a stable foundation and stay the course

From Denhardt and Denhardt, Chapter Four

In chapter three, Sandford Borins describes what individuals at the top of the organization can do to encourage innovation. Borins argues that there must first be clear and active support from the top. In the Phoenix case study, Denhardt and Denhardt attribute much of Phoenix's success to the role played by the city's current city manager, Frank Fairbanks, and his predecessor, Marvin Andrews. In the case study of San Diego County, California, presented in chapter five, William Eimicke also found strong support at the top. Eimicke found, in fact, that the leading driver for innovation in San Diego County was Chief Administrative Officer Lawrence Prior, who served in that position from September 1996 through May 1999 and was strongly supported by the County Board of Supervisors.

Another key factor in creating an environment that fosters innovation is to align an organization's rewards and recognition with the goal of innovation. In Phoenix, both Frank Fairbanks and Marvin Andrews worked hard to create reward and recognition programs that reinforced their quest for innovation. Andrews reflects, "We worked to recognize the efforts of employees.... We set up a quarterly program where outstanding teams were recognized. They were invited to breakfast with their families and it was videotaped and shown on the city's public television station. That went extremely well. I think they are still doing it. Someone dubbed it 'Muffins with Marv.'"

We have also learned that inadequate reward and recognition programs are clearly impediments to fostering innovation in organizations. In chapter six, Scott Tarry presents case studies of innovation in five public airports. Based on his research, Tarry concludes: "The effect of inadequate reward and recognition programs is twofold. First, employees have little financial or professional incentive to innovate. Instead of working to develop new ways of doing business, employees are likely to continue to do their jobs as they were originally construed. Second, those employees who are successful innovators may find themselves frustrated by a system that cannot accommodate significant salary increases and rapid promotions.... In short, public sector reward and recognition programs, as well as traditional approaches to public sector personnel issues, may not prohibit innovation, but they may reduce its likelihood."

While the presence of rewards and recognition are clearly important, Borins also argues that organizational leaders must provide resources for innovation. Innovation is frequently not cost free. Building on research done by David

---

Obstacles to Innovating in the Public Sector

- A public-utility mentality
- A top-down, hierarchical tradition
- Regulatory constraints
- Hesitancy by stakeholders
- Inadequate reward and recognition programs

From Tarry, Chapter Six

Building Blocks for Innovation

Building Block One: The Use of a Systems Approach
Building Block Two: The Use of Information Technology
Building Block Three: Process Improvement
Building Block Four: The Involvement of the Private or Voluntary Sector
Building Block Five: The Empowerment of Communities, Citizens, or Staff

From Borins, Chapter Three

Osborne and Paul Plastrik, Borins argues that central innovation funds are an important tool in creating an innovative environment. Making adequate funds available for innovative activities also sends an important signal to the organization that innovation is valued and deemed important within the organization.

An important finding from the Borins study, supported by the Phoenix case study, is that innovation should be everyone's responsibility within the organization. It cannot just be left to those at the top or the middle. While support from the top is an essential ingredient to fostering an innovative environment, empowerment must be spread throughout the entire organization. Not surprising given the Phoenix experience, Borins' research found that innovation frequently comes from middle managers and from those on the front line. Phoenix City Manager Fairbanks explains his approach: "Part of my leadership role is a responsibility to empower management. The deputies have a sense of empowerment, and through them, the departments have a sense of empowerment. But I really spend a lot of my time communicating this with all the levels by walking around the building talking to people about it. We talk about how it is up to each of us. One of the things we all say to people is that you can't leave it all up to the manager. Each one of us needs to make a difference, and the system has to allow people to make improvements."

Implementing Innovation

After having created a supportive environment in which innovation can be fostered, the next step is to successfully implement innovative ideas and programs. In chapter two, Walters sets forth six elements that contribute to successful implementation. While Walters would probably agree with Borins' contention that organizational leaders need to provide adequate resources for innovation, Walters recommends that innovators keep innovations

Key Elements of Successful Innovation

- Keep It Simple in Concept
- Make It Easy to Execute
- Shoot for Quick Results
- Be Frugal
- Make It Appealing
- Keep It Apolitical

From Walters, Chapter Two

as frugal as possible. But even more important, argues Walters, innovators must keep their innovations simple in concept and make them easy to execute. Complicated programs frequently do not fare well either over the short or long term. Walters also recommends that innovators shoot for quick results and work hard to make their innovations both appealing and likable.

Based on his case study of San Diego County, Eimicke also developed a list of keys to successful implementation. Eimicke found that the need for the innovation must be established and communicated widely and clearly. In his analysis of the first 10 years of the Innovations program, Alan Altshuler recommended that innovators define their mission clearly and in terms of compelling problems (Altshuler).

Innovators, recommends Eimicke, must also make a strong case for their solution. While Walters argues that innovators shoot for quick, demonstrable results, Eimicke ups the ante and recommends that innovations also produce meaningful and measurable outcomes. Anecdotal evidence, however communicable and appealing, does not always carry the day.

An emphasis on outcomes and measurement is also advocated by Scott Tarry. Tarry argues that performance measurement is key to successful implementation. He found that airports, as well as other public sector organizations, are showing increased enthusiasm for benchmarking and performance measurement. It's much easier, writes Tarry, to make the case for an innovation when you are armed with real performance data.

Keys to Successfully Implementing an Innovation

- Be sure the need for innovative change is well established and communicated widely.
- Innovation advocates need to make a strong case for their solution.
- Implementation of the innovation must be accomplished fairly and efficiently.
- The innovation must produce meaningful, measurable outcomes.
- The beneficial impact of the innovative change must be sustained.

From Eimicke, Chapter Five

Ten Lessons from Innovation

1. Define a mission clearly and in terms of compelling problems
2. Define challenging but achievable outcomes against which to measure performance
3. Collaborate with other government agencies whenever possible
4. Build partnerships with the private and nonprofit sectors
5. Respect the talents of "frontline workers"
6. Identify clearly the citizens and groups who are entitled to your services and focus attention as sharply as possible on their needs
7. If your tasks involve regulation, consider working with the regulated parties to meet common objectives through compliance, rather than depending entirely on traditional enforcement
8. Consider how market forces may complement the provision of public goods and services
9. Use information technology to improve services to citizens
10. Be flexible, take risks, don't give up

From Alan Altshuler, "Ten Lessons from Innovation," Innovations in American Government, 1986-1996 (New York: Ford Foundation, 1996).

Borins also reminds us that in implementing an innovation, you need to anticipate a wide variety of obstacles. These include dealing with inadequate resources, building organizational capacity to absorb the change, and responding to the attitudes of the occupational/professional groups that are involved in implementing an innovation. The halls of government are littered with technology changes and new methods of doing work that never took hold because of weak planning. Borins cautions that when you don't spend time anticipating resistance from various places, including your own central office, innovations are less likely to succeed.

Spreading Innovation

Finally, once an organization successfully implements an innovation, how is it spread across more than 38,000 government jurisdictions in the United States? That was one of the issues addressed by Altshuler and Behn in their *Innovation in American Government*. As Paul Berman and Beryl Nelson, contributors to the book, put it, "In our scientific and technological age, we dream of models and technologies that, once invented and proved successful in one place, can be replicated in many others" (Berman and

How to Support Innovation

- Support it from the top
- Provide rewards and awards for innovation
- Provide resources for innovation
- Recognize the importance of diversity
- Learn from the outside
- Make innovation everyone's responsibility
- Experiment and evaluate

From Borins, Chapter Three

Nelson). Oftentimes, a good idea in one place is equally valid elsewhere, but the "not invented here" syndrome is seen as a major inhibitor for the diffusion of innovation. Or is it?

In the 1990s, government innovators were encouraged to clone ideas from whatever sources they could. It was important to reinvent government without reinventing the wheel. Still, questions remained as to whether you can transplant a good idea or whether it has to be homegrown.

Berman and Nelson examined the experiences of one group honored by the Innovations program to see what happened with ideas that were recognized as being among the best. They found efforts to replicate "have often been disappointing" but still found a glimmer of hope—that adaptation is more successful than adoption. Berman and Nelson concluded, "The most important replications in the public sector are those that involve the need for a public organization to change to become more effective." In another chapter in *Innovation in American Government,* Lee Friedman looked at the diffusion of innovations in the public sector and concluded that the following matter: details, leadership, and incentives (Friedman). He found that understanding the details of operating procedures and organizational settings is a very important first step when attempting to transfer a successful innovation to another organization. He observed that managers have a key role in whether an innovative approach is adapted or adopted, based on whether they see it as a help or a hindrance. He also noted that when there is strong positive reinforcement for adopting an innovation (such as personal rewards or increases in budget for the organization), there is a greater chance of rapid adoption.

A key to spreading innovations thus seems to be creating the ability of an organization to adapt. Oftentimes this means leaders giving their "permission" to frontline managers to innovate. Innovation does not always come from the top of an organization, so creating the right environment can be critical to successful innovation. As discussed earlier, such an environment might be stimulated from outside the organization with incentives, such as rewards, awards, or increased resources. Oftentimes it can come from within an organization, but the organization's environment probably matters more than the specific innovation itself.

Innovations and Innovators

We have also learned another important lesson about innovation that is all too frequently forgotten. While we have emphasized key factors in fostering, implementing, and spreading innovation, there is one other major factor in innovation that we need to constantly remember—it is people who innovate, not processes or cultures. Jonathan Walters writes, "It is people who push it [innovation], people often working in dysfunctional organizations under miserable circumstances, and in spite of that, they try to change things."

Innovation is really about the individuals who innovate. In part, the Ford Foundation created the Innovations program to recognize these unsung heroes in government and to give them a very public "pat on the back." While Walters notes that understanding why individuals are driven to innovate may require the work of psychologists, there is much that can be said about the characteristics of these individuals.

As Walters notes, innovators tend to be restless. While this is clearly true, it doesn't present the full picture of their accomplishments. The key to better understanding innovation may lie in understanding the relationship between individuals and their "job" or "position" in an organization. All the innovators discussed in this book and recognized over the years by numerous innovation award programs went "beyond" their "job." In recent years, the concept of "job enlargement" gained some currency in the human resource arena. But the concept of "job enlargement" has largely remained a theoretical concept in the literature. The real "job enlargers" have been innovators in government. They took their "job" and made it larger and into something dramatically different than simply administering bureaucratic routines. They took "risks" by enlarging both their job and the potential impact that their job and the "jobs" of their colleagues might have on the public they serve. In many cases, nobody—including their supervisors—asked them to enlarge their job. Frequently, they received criticism for taking on or pushing new responsibilities that had not been directly assigned to them. In many respects, innovation is about individuals redefining their organizational position into something larger and potentially more beneficial to the public.

In many ways, the desire to innovate is an individual decision made by those who want to do better. Walters

---

What Drives Innovation?

Driver One: Frustration with the Status Quo
Driver Two: Responding to Crisis
Driver Three: Focusing on Prevention
Driver Four: Emphasizing Results
Driver Five: Adapting Technology
Driver Six: Doing the Right Thing

From Walters, Chapter Two

writes that innovation is ultimately "about the direct action of people, people who are tired of being part of systems that are focused on preserving turf, longevity, and resources than on achieving results." Innovators redefine their position within their organization and assume a leadership role (with or without a "leadership" title) as an advocate and implementer of change. Sometimes they are supported, even recognized and rewarded, and other times they are not. But they persevere.

While we have learned much about fostering and implementing innovation in recent years, there is still much to learn about how to encourage and develop more leadership, risk taking, and job enlargement behavior throughout our public sector organizations. The private sector struggles with this same challenge. Thus, the innovation community must now learn more about how organizations can foster and develop more individuals eager to make the personal decision to redefine their jobs and to become leaders seeking new, improved ways of providing services to the public. A better understanding of the human dynamics involved in innovation and risk taking is the next frontier in increasing our knowledge about innovation and innovators.

Bibliography

Altshuler, Alan. "Ten Lessons from Innovation." *Innovations in American Government, 1986-1996*. New York: Ford Foundation, 1996.

Altshuler, Alan A. and Robert D. Behn, eds. *Innovation in American Government: Challenges, Opportunities, and Dilemmas*. Washington, D.C.: Brookings Institution, 1997.

Berman, Paul and Beryl Nelson. "Replication: Adapt or Fail." In *Innovation in American Government: Challenges, Opportunities, and Dilemmas*. Washington, D.C.: Brookings Institution, 1997.

Friedman, Lee. "Public Sector Innovations and Their Diffusion: Economic Tools and Managerial Tasks." In *Innovation in American Government: Challenges, Opportunities, and Dilemmas*. Washington, D.C.: Brookings Institution, 1997.

CHAPTER TWO

Understanding Innovation: What Inspires It? What Makes It Successful?

Jonathan Walters
Staff Correspondent
Governing Magazine

This report was originally published in December 2001.

Introduction:
An Inclination to Innovate

As has frequently been noted by those who follow government, the public sector in the United States has never been known for its inclination to innovate. The list of disincentives to those brave souls who may be tired of the status quo and interested in new ways of conducting the public's business is long and familiar. Items on that list range, on the one hand, from a general culture of risk avoidance and a lack of rewards for those who try to innovate, to the political timelines and political pressures that work against long-range efforts at basic change, on the other. And on and on the list typically goes, and legitimately so to be sure.

Many of those obstacles are discussed in chapter 3, "The Challenge of Innovating in Government." In that chapter, Sandford Borins, professor of public management at the University of Toronto, culls lessons about innovating in the public sector by analyzing winners from three programs set up to recognize government innovators. The one domestic program—the Ford Foundation/Kennedy School Innovations in American Government Awards—is the focus of this chapter; the other two programs are international.

As part of his analysis Borins investigates two aspects of innovation: He looks at the characteristics of innovative organizations and he analyzes the form that innovation takes (more on both of these in a moment). The goal of this chapter is to build on Borins' observations by focusing exclusively on the Innovations in American Government Awards program. The two questions this chapter will delve into based on lessons gleaned from the Innovations award winners are very straightforward:

- What inspires innovation?
- What makes it successful?

The Ford Foundation and Kennedy School's Innovations in American Government program has produced a bountiful list of programs and people who are trying to change what government does and how it does it. Since 1986—with a one-year hiatus in 1989—the program has recognized 150 "winning" programs, which have each been awarded $100,000. In addition, the program has recognized 207 "finalists," which are now awarded $20,000. Winners and finalists come from all levels of government—local, state, federal, and tribal—and across all program and policy areas, from education to criminal justice.

In the process of identifying prize-worthy innovators, the program has sifted through thousands of applications. There have undoubtedly been many innovative programs not selected that were worthy of awards (and many others worthy of being set aside). In 2001, the Ford Foundation endowed an Institute for Government Innovation at Harvard's Kennedy School. The Institute will administer the Innovations in American Government program, as well as serve as the hub of a global network for government innovation, linking the Innovations program with five other Ford-funded award programs for American Indian tribal government and governments in Brazil, Chile, the Philippines, and South Africa. In linking programs devoted to recognizing innovative government, the Institute hopes to become the preeminent portal to information on innovation and innovative programs in government worldwide.

In answering the questions of what inspires innovation and what makes it successful, this chapter focuses heavily on the award-winning innovations themselves; that is, it scrutinizes the ideas that proved to have the power to change government operations for the better. Borins' cut at innovation, on the other hand, focuses more on identifying characteristics of innovative organizations, recognizing pathways to innovation, and investigating where in organizations innovative ideas seem to come from. Specifically, Borins identifies seven characteristics of innovative organizations along with five "building blocks" of innovation. In the "Who Innovates" section of his report, he also uses hard numbers to illustrate what those of us who follow innovation have known for a long time: that innovative ideas spring up from all over the place—both inside and outside of organizations, and from the middle, bottom, and top layers of an organization. Innovation, it turns out, has little regard for title.

It's worth focusing for a moment on Borins' list of the seven characteristics of innovative organizations, however. It's useful because it's not hard to read the inverse into each of those characteristics when thinking about the typical state, local, or federal department (and in considering how remarkable the people who push innovation in government—whatever their title—really are). Innovative public sector organizations, according to Borins, typically evince the following virtues:

- They support innovation from the top (timidity from the top, especially around election time, is all too typical in U.S. government).
- They reward individuals who push change (public sector risk takers are often punished).
- They specifically dedicate resources to innovation (discretionary cash for experimentation is rare in the public sector).
- They harbor a diverse workforce (public sector personnel systems are notorious for their inflexibility in allowing managers to hire on the basis of organizational synergy).
- They evince a basic organizational curiosity ("but we've always done it that way" is the common rallying cry in government).
- Bureaucratic layers are closely connected (an obvious contradiction in concepts in government).

- They exhibit a general inclination to experiment (see all six previous
  parentheticals).

Add to all that the fact that politicians at every level frequently seem
to be enamored of the "solution du jour" versus "what actually works" when
it comes to tackling public problems. Witness the stampede to embrace
military-style boot camps for offending youth, or the universal inclination to
adopt across-the-board hiring freezes and budget cuts as a way to balance
budgets, as evidence of elected officials' remarkable ability to ignore
policy and administrative reality, all the while missing the opportunity to
really innovate.

All that being said, there's clearly something very curious going on in
U.S. government when it comes to innovation, something that has been
going on for a very long time. Despite the formidable forces arrayed in
opposition, there are people at all levels of government—local, state, and
federal—who do figure out new ways of doing things. In fact, given the constraints and disincentives, given the entrenched attitudes and the frequently
countervailing political imperatives and timelines, one could argue that
government in the United States has proved to be remarkably, even
resiliently, innovative. In the face of overwhelming odds, innovative ideas
continue to bubble up out of government—from the smallest local government to the most bloated federal bureaucracy—pushed by everyone from
frontline staff, to middle management, to lofty politicos, to outside agitators.

In going through the list of initiatives identified by the Innovations
program, one could certainly quibble about how innovative some of them
really are. As Borins notes in his paper, real sticklers make a distinction
between "invention," which is the creation of a new idea, and "innovation,"
which is the adoption of an existing idea by a new organization. But while
some of the winners might seem repetitive of previous winners (programs
aimed at early childhood education and alternatives to incarceration, for
example, have been regular staples of the Innovations program), it's impossible to argue that they don't, collectively, represent a rich body of work
worth mining for lessons in new ways of addressing how government does
its myriad and often very difficult jobs.

Borins starts some of that mining in chapter 3. Besides using award winners to pin down key characteristics of innovative organizations, he also
uses them to identify what he calls the "building blocks" of innovation. He
might as easily have called them "modes" of innovation. The five he teases
out are:

- Changing whole systems (federal welfare reform would fall into this
  category)
- Using information technology
- Pursuing process improvement

- Enlisting the help of the private or voluntary sector
- Empowering communities, citizens, or staff

Between the two chapters—this one and Borins'—there is no doubt ample room for multiple alternative analyses of the lessons that award-winning innovation programs in the public sector have to offer; this topic can be sliced and diced in a lot of ways. But together it is hoped the two chapters, as well as others in this volume, will contribute at least a bit more to the understanding of what elements go into creating, sustaining, and replicating innovation in government. In the process, it is also hoped that this volume will inspire those who care about government—both those working inside and outside of government—and who *are* tired of the status quo to perhaps think about pushing government to do the public's business in a new way.

Analyzing Innovations and Innovators: A Note on the "Science" of Change Management

The observations and conclusions in this chapter are based less on the rigorous social-political science of innovation (if a "science" of innovation can even be said to exist) than on observations accumulated through years of close observation of innovation in government. The author has spent more than two decades covering management and change management in government, generally, and 13 years covering the Innovations in American Government Awards program, specifically.

Since 1988, the author has covered the Innovations awards intensively, reading hundreds of applications and site visit reports for programs (more than 200 in the last five years alone), while conducting hundreds of interviews with principals of winning programs, outside experts, critics, and other analysts. Such interviews have been bolstered by numerous visits to the scenes of innovation themselves, ranging from housing projects in Chicago to government office buildings in Atlanta. Sometimes these visits were arranged specifically as part of award-winner coverage; sometimes they were for separate stories on particular state and local programs and initiatives for *Governing* magazine or other publications.

Also contributing to this chapter is a recent set of surveys sent out by the Institute for Government Innovation to all winning programs from the past 15 years asking about program sustainability and replication. Those surveys have also been augmented by follow-up phone interviews with representatives of particular programs.

What Inspires Innovation?

There are good reasons why someone might be reluctant to want to lead change in a public sector setting; it's widely regarded as a high-risk, low-reward enterprise. In her essay, "The Mysteries of Innovative Government," which accompanied *Governing*'s coverage of the 1991 Innovations in American Government award winners, *Governing* founding editor Eileen Shanahan quotes none other than the dark prince of government machination himself, Nicolo Machiavelli, as he muses about pushing change in government. Considering how some of the more creative innovators go about getting the job done, it's probably not inappropriate that Mr. Machiavelli has his say here: *"There is nothing more difficult to take in hand, more perilous to conduct, or more uncertain in its success, than to take the lead in the introduction of a new order of things."*

Why the skittishness around change? There are lots of reasons, but one of the most obvious is that one consequence of trying to do things in a different way is sometimes mistakes and failure. And as William D. Eggers and John O'Leary point out in their book *Revolution at the Roots: Making Our Government Smaller, Better, and Closer to Home* (Free Press, 1995), making mistakes in a public sector setting can have some unsettling consequences. "No public manager," note Eggers and O'Leary, "wants to drink his morning cup of coffee reading a headline describing his latest screwup in 12-point type."

With such perils in mind, the questions are worth asking:

- What triggers innovation in U.S. government?
- Where does it come from?

Don Kettl, professor of public affairs and political science at the La Follette Institute of Public Affairs at the University of Wisconsin in Madison, notes that better ways of doing things don't tend to just spring up in government; they need a push. "New ideas don't tend to get adopted simply because they would be easier, better, smarter, or cheaper," said Kettl. "They almost always need some kind of driver."

In poring over the hundreds of programs recognized by Ford and the Kennedy School through its Innovations awards program, six drivers of innovation ultimately sift out. Some of the programs certainly fit into more than one of the categories, reflecting the complexity of the innovation picture. But in looking at all the winners, each was the result of one or more of the following:

- Frustration with the status quo
- A response to crisis
- A new emphasis on prevention
- A new emphasis on results
- Adaptation of technology
- A moral imperative

The obvious question is the extent to which identifying these categories can help potential innovators get their organizations—or another organization—to start moving off the dime. The hope is that in highlighting what inspired—or allowed—winners to make change, others might more readily identify opportunity when it comes along—or maybe they will flat out try to create it themselves. At the very least, in reading about the origins of innovation, it might bolster would-be innovators' resolve to carry on the good fight, Messrs. Machiavelli's, Eggers's and O'Leary's observations notwithstanding.

Driver One: Frustration with the Status Quo

When Stephen Goldsmith was elected mayor of Indianapolis he posed a straightforward question to his public works department: "How much does it cost to fill a pothole in Indianapolis?" Nobody could answer the question, and that would start the city down a whole new path when it came to delivering city services.

Goldsmith's curiosity was born of a suspicion that certain city work could be done much more effectively and efficiently than it currently was if opened up to competitive bidding. But with Indianapolis being a heavily unionized town, the likelihood that the new mayor would be able to buck entrenched labor interests and start putting things like fleet and street maintenance out to competitive bid seemed highly unlikely.

Competition and Costing Program, Indianapolis, Indiana

It took Goldsmith's resolve, coupled with enlightened—and by no means weak—labor leadership in a fiscally constrained environment, to create the Competition and Costing Program, which netted the city an Innovations award in 1995. Under the program, a host of basic city services—like street repair—were opened up to the bidding process whereby city departments would compete with the private sector for the work. It's worth noting that as part of the deal that Goldsmith struck with his labor unions in pushing the new order, middle management would actually end up taking the hardest hit, not frontline labor. Labor successfully argued that superfluous layers of management would make certain city operating units non-competitive when stacked up against lean, mean private sector outfits. Goldsmith agreed and bureaucracies were flattened.

One might naturally conclude that the Indianapolis example bolsters the "strong leadership" argument as critical to successful innovation. No rational person would argue that strong leadership isn't a huge help when it comes to making big organizational change. But it's not a prerequisite to change; there are ample examples of the same sort of frustration and dissatisfaction exhibited by Goldsmith bubbling up from sources outside of leadership positions and inspiring—even requiring—big change.

Take, for example, Georgia Civil Service Reform, a 2000 finalist. It wasn't David Osborne's observation in *Reinventing Government* that "the only thing more destructive than a line item budget system is a personnel system built around civil service" that inspired Georgia to dump civil service. Nor was it any exhortation by then-Governor Zell Miller to his troops that they should march toward a more private sector model of personnel administration. It was fundamental frustration among the various government departments with the unresponsive, byzantine central personnel office that ultimately led to the change.

Among the most frustrated and least satisfied of the central personnel office's "customers" was the Georgia Department of Transportation (GDOT). GDOT had been unhappy with the civil service system for a while, but one incident in particular sent the department over the brink. To get ready for the 1996 Summer Olympics, GDOT requested some new job titles in areas of transportation that would be critical to the smooth flow of

---

Innovations in American Government Award Winners

To obtain more information about each of the winners profiled
in this chapter, visit the Innovations award site at:
www.innovations.harvard.edu/prog.htm

traffic during the Atlanta games. In particular, GDOT wanted to create a roving band of tow truck drivers who could roam local streets and highways and quickly remove disabled vehicles to prevent traffic backups. When GDOT asked the state civil service department for permission to create the new job titles necessary to do the work, the word came back that it probably wouldn't be able to approve the titles until after the games were over. Frustrated, GDOT officials actually went to the legislature and won a special exemption to state civil service law so they could create the positions without having to go through the central personnel office. It was the hole in the dike that predicted the entire personnel system's eventually being washed away.

There's no arguing that Governor Miller was instrumental in then pushing the plan for dismantling Georgia's civil service system. But his efforts would have gone nowhere had it not been for the deep frustration and eager testimony of disgruntled department officials. A quote in a 1997 *Governing* story on the sunsetting of civil service in Georgia captured the depth and breadth of that grassroots frustration. "My dream is that ultimately there is no position in the department covered by civil service," said Department of Natural Resources Director Lonice C. Barrett. Barrett's dream—shared by many managers in the state—is now coming true: Under Georgia's new system, individual agencies have the sole responsibility for finding and hiring people, and all state employees hired after July 1, 1996, exist outside of civil service as "at-will" employees.

Frustration doesn't only impact governmental systems or departments from the outside. There are dozens of examples from the Innovations program annals where insiders have become so impatient with business as usual that they push change. And as it turns out, insiders as change agents have a special kind of power inasmuch as there are some systems that are so convoluted and complex, only those on the inside really understand what it would take to fix them.

The Child Care Management Services program, a 1993 Innovations award winner from Texas, is a perfect example of that kind of change. The program was an attempt to streamline and coordinate all state and federal child welfare programs, an effort that was pushed by a small handful of persistent inside bureaucrats who were seeing firsthand the dissipated—even harmful—effect that multiple, fragmented services were having on single mothers with kids. It ultimately took five years (and the creative use of technology, it should be noted) to create a more seamless system of one-stop shopping for all child care services. It wasn't perfect, but it was certainly better. It was also prescient. As with a number of Innovations award winners from the late 1980s and early 1990s, the Texas program predicted the wholesale "block grant" approach to social services that would come with federal welfare reform in 1996.

Another 1993 winner, Government Action on Urban Land—from Cuyahoga County in Ohio—was likewise the result of internal frustration, in this case with the long process required to condemn code-deficient and tax-delinquent property. The basic problem: the impact on cities of ram- shackle buildings owned by absentee landlords, which were serving as little more than safe harbors for criminals and targets for arsonists. Such build- ings have long been the bane of urban redevelopers for two reasons. First, they serve to discourage anyone who might actually be interested in pursuing improved housing or commercial life in a blighted neighborhood. Second, they frequently get in the way of urban redevelopment projects that depend on acquiring the large parcels of property necessary for viable redevelop- ment projects.

But, again, it makes sense that it was insiders both in the city of Cleveland and in Cuyahoga County's community development and legal arenas who pushed the change, because they were the ones who really understood the problem in terms of the administrative and legal complexities that had for so long stymied a solution. It took insiders to design a system for quickly *and legally* seizing tax-delinquent or chronically code-deficient property.

"We frequently see innovations being driven by people who've been in a system for a long time," said Gail Christopher, executive director of the Institute for Government Innovation. "They have a drive born of years of frustration, and a wisdom about the complexity of the problems that make them particularly adept at mapping out and pushing change."

Insiders don't always act alone, of course. While taking the clear lead in pushing change, they frequently reach to outside stakeholders to collab- orate in making that change. Those kinds of combinations seem to be par- ticularly important when it comes to dealing with very volatile, emotional, and long-standing conflicts—particularly in the regulatory arena. The 1998 award-winning Northern New Mexico Collaborative Stewardship Project out of the U.S. Forest Service is one where insider frustration with business as usual in combination with stakeholder dissatisfaction finally built to the point where the system moved in a new direction.

The collaborative was inspired by long-standing conflicts around the timber claims of local residents, logging companies, and environmentalists in the Camino Real Ranger District in northern New Mexico. The conflict had resulted in almost complete gridlock around logging, and even threats of violence. And so District Ranger Crockett Dumas quite literally climbed on horseback to begin making door-to-door contact with all the combat- ants. In Dumas's case, he was diplomat enough to bring all the parties together to work out logging plans that satisfied—at least more or less—all parties. And while his brand of multiple-party/combatant collaboration has proved effective in other situations and settings, it is a style of innovation that seems to depend as heavily on the personality of the insider pushing the change as it does any set formula for resolving such long-standing and emotionally charged conflicts.

Massachusetts, which has had three award-winning environmental programs (in 1991 the state won for the Blackstone Project, in 1999 for its Toxics Use Reduction Program, and its Environmental Results Program was a 2001 finalist), frequently employs this insider-outsider approach to resolving long-standing conflicts and to developing more strategic ways to regulate.

The Blackstone Project was initiated by agency insiders in the state's Department of Environmental Protection who were tired of the old-style, fragmented, disjointed, end-of-the-pipe approach to permitting and inspections. The program proved to be a successful experiment in prevention-focused, one-visit, multi-media inspections of companies permitted to discharge pollutants. Using cross-trained inspectors armed with the ability to offer extensive technical assistance in prevention strategies and technologies, the program relied heavily on the regulated community for support and cooperation (and certainly in the business community, Massachusetts environmental regulators had a set of frustrated outside stakeholders). The program even seemed to satisfy its toughest customer, the environmental community. A spokesman for the National Toxics Campaign Fund at the time cited it as a model in the then-incipient national push toward pollution prevention.

It's not uncommon, however, for the dissatisfied party pushing change to come from outside government altogether. In 1999 New Jersey won an Innovations award for developing a new and separate set of more flexible

Rehabilitation Subcode, State of New Jersey

building codes to be applied in the case of rehabbing older structures. The initiative was a direct response to the significant frustration among builders who were interested in rehabbing existing commercial buildings, but who found retrofitting 50- to 100-year-old structures to stringent new codes to be hugely expensive and impractical—and of virtually no added value from the standpoint of public safety. Those builders, not incidentally, had strong allies in the local government officials who wanted to see derelict—and frequently historically and architecturally significant— buildings brought back to life, as well.

Seattle's Community Voice Mail for Phoneless/Homeless Persons, a 1993 winner, was likewise born of outside stakeholder frustration with the status quo. The idea for voice mail for people with no homes or phones came out of a small, not-for-profit social services provider in Seattle that realized homeless people were missing out on jobs because there was no way for prospective employers to reach them. They took their idea to the city, and the city turned it into a formal program.

But probably the best example of the "outside gadfly as change agent" among the Innovations award winners is Norma Hotaling, a former prostitute who had clearly run out of patience with how traditional criminal justice systems were dealing with prostitutes and their customers. To Hotaling, the law enforcement status quo around soliciting amounted to nothing more than a revolving-door world where neither women nor their customers were offered any real positive alternatives other than to go back to the same behavior that had put them in trouble with the law in the first place. And so she approached the San Francisco district attorney's office with an idea: Treat both the women and customers involved in prostitution as people who need help, not as criminals needing punishment.

To its credit, the San Francisco prosecutor's office listened, working with Hotaling on developing the First Offender Prostitution Program, under which men caught soliciting for the first time are offered the chance either to go to court or to attend classes taught by, among others, ex-prostitutes— classes that highlight the fundamental harm that the sex industry has done to women, men, families, and personal and public health. Instead of jail time, prostitutes were offered counseling, medical care, and help getting their lives together. The program proved to be remarkably effective, particularly in getting male customers to stop re-offending. The First Offender program won its Innovations award in 1998.

Driver Two: Responding to Crisis

The change described above tends to be driven by years of pent-up frustration. It's not an acute event that drives such change so much as it is a building realization that a particular way of doing business isn't working very well—and hasn't been for a while. By contrast, there is a whole different class of innovation that is inspired by some acute event that quickly turns people to a new way of doing business.

It's no revelation that crisis creates opportunity to innovate—or in many cases outright forces it. Arguably, U.S. Forest Service Ranger Crockett Dumas's foray into the field described above was in some part crisis driven. Things had gotten so bad in his district that it was clearly time to try something radically different.

In looking over 15 years' worth of innovative programs, it is clear that acute crisis is a powerful driver of fast change. In *Innovating With Integrity: How Local Heroes Are Transforming American Government* (Georgetown University Press, 1998), Sandy Borins cites three Innovations identified programs as having obvious roots in immediate disaster:

- Seattle's comprehensive push toward recycling (the Seattle Recycling Program, a 1990 winner), which had been inspired by environmental conditions at two of its landfills that were so horrendous they had to be shut down.
- An Arizona program to find and close abandoned mines spurred by the accidental death of a young man who'd fallen into a mine.
- The Florida Department of Environmental Protection's adoption of a geographic information system (GIS) to manage environmental crises in its waterways after a disastrous oil spill near Jacksonville in 1987.

As Borins points out in his book, a significant number of Innovations award winners had some element of acute crisis underpinning their creation—in fact, he puts it at as high as 30 percent. It's obvious why crisis is such a powerful catalyst. "People within a public sector organization may know that its performance is not up to par, but this problem becomes a crisis only when it is manifestly visible to the public," writes Borins. The professor is to be credited for his artful understatement. As any good politician who has watched some tale of disaster as it unfolds on the 6 o'clock news will tell you, crisis demands an immediate and highly visible response, whether it's the right response or not.

But in reviewing the Innovations award winners, it's clear that crisis, disaster, and bad news have inspired some fairly creative and coherent efforts to fix things. Without putting too fine a point on it, such programs tend to fall into two categories: programs inspired by crisis and designed to fix a problem, and programs developed to blunt the consequences of inevitable (usually natural) disasters. In fact, a number of the 2001 Innovations program winners fall into these two sub-categories of crisis-driven innovation.

One of them is A Secret Safe Place for Newborns, developed by the Mobile County, Alabama, District Attorney's Office. The Safe Place initiative—a 2001 finalist—came about as the result of truly sad events—a series of six infant and toddler homicides in 1998. Prompted by a local reporter's suggestion that desperate parents—mothers in particular—be offered the option of safely giving a newborn away without fear of prosecution, the DA's office decided to try the idea. While a recent front page *New York Times* article ("Few Choose Legal Havens to Abandon Babies," Aug. 31, 2001) raises questions about the ultimate effect of such programs (35 states now have so-called "safe haven" laws, according to the article), the DA's office in Mobile County, at least, reports no homicides and only one unsafe abandonment since adopting the new policy. Whatever the ultimate effect of the Safe Place program, its intent is clear: to forestall future tragedy.

Likewise, a 2001 award winner, the National Center for Patient Safety, developed by the U.S. Department of Veterans Affairs, was inspired by crisis: Experts estimate that preventable medical errors lead to hundreds of thousands of deaths and injuries a year. In 1997 the VA started encouraging staff at all VA hospitals to voluntarily and confidentially report medical mistakes in order to hone in on possible system flaws leading to injury and death. The theory was that bad systems, not careless people, are mostly responsible for mistakes. As a result, the VA has been awash in new reports of mistakes and near misses, allowing it to adjust and hone a variety of systems to make hospital stays considerably safer.

The Occupational Safety and Health Administration won a 1995 Innovations award for its worker safety pilot program launched in Maine, precipitated by a high per capita incidence of worker death and injury. Under the Maine Top 200 Experimental Targeting Program, especially dangerous industries were targeted for special attention—inspections and cooperative efforts to improve working conditions. Again, the idea was inspired by bad news and aimed at fixing problems once and for all.

It's worth noting that all three programs—A Safe Place, the Center for Patient Safety, and Maine Top 200—have strong elements of prevention and results driving them. Indeed, the VA program could easily fit into the "results-driven innovation" category below because of its wholesale push to change bureaucratic thinking based on improving results. But, clearly, it was a crisis in the medical world that prompted the program.

Then there are those Innovations award programs that were set up to actually blunt the impact of inevitable disaster, similar to the disaster that spurred Florida's GIS system, mentioned above. Oklahoma's 2001 award-winning OK-FIRST initiative fits this model, and also includes a strong element of technology and prevention. OK-FIRST is a weather early-warning system that pulls together a variety of forecasting technologies (some primitive, like human observation, some quite advanced, like Doppler radar) and through a statewide website puts all that information at the fingertips of public safety officials. They can then use it to do things like evacuate towns that appear to be in the path of developing (or developed) tornadoes or close down roads in imminent danger of flash flooding. State officials have credited the system with saving numerous lives already, particularly from tornado damage.

PulseNet, a program developed by the U.S. Department of Health and Human Services and a 1999 Innovations award winner, can also be included in this sub-category of crisis-driven innovation aimed at blunting the impact of inevitable disaster. It's a technology-based system that aims to rapidly identify the type and source of significant food poisoning outbreaks so that those suffering food poisoning can be quickly and correctly treated, and the source of the poisoning identified and shut down. The system was developed in response to the cases of widespread food poisoning—however sporadic—that periodically hit various regions of the country. Since its creation, the system has been credited in several instances with keying in on and closing down the source of potentially serious listeria and salmonella poisoning outbreaks before they caused serious harm.

In 1996, the Federal Emergency Management Agency (FEMA) won an Innovations award for Consequence Assessment Tool Set (CATS): Disaster Damage Prediction and Mapping, a comprehensive system for disaster pre-planning in areas that are at chronic and high risk of trouble at the hands of nature, including earthquakes and hurricanes. It is interesting to note that the essential methodology used by FEMA was adapted from pre-plans it had developed at the behest of the Defense Department for dealing with the aftermath of nuclear war. Call it a peace dividend.

PulseNet, U.S. Department of Health and Human Services

Driver Three: Focusing on Prevention

Change in response to crisis is, of course, all too typical of government, given its reputation for being reactive rather than proactive. Which is why Borins' estimate that 30 percent of all Innovations award winners are crisis inspired isn't all that surprising.

There is another class of Innovations award winner, though, that does have at its core the whole notion of prevention. But even in the case of efforts aimed at nipping some problem in the bud, frequently they're not launched until the problem has first taken a good bite out of government or the public.

Prevention is not an easy track for government to take. As a focus on results has begun to infuse (at least rhetorically, if not always in fact) public policy and administration in the United States, a typical lament among public sector policy makers, budgeters, and managers is that it's hard to measure what hasn't happened. It is, therefore, difficult to justify spending public resources on prevention absent some way to judge the effects of such spending.

It's not an argument that everyone—or even most people—buy, but it still manages to get in the way of funding for preventative programs, nonetheless. It would be much more honest of public officials to simply admit the political difficulty involved in spending money on programs where the goal is for nothing (bad) to happen—a prospective, less-than-flashy, and sometimes downright invisible result.

In *Revitalizing State and Local Public Service: Strengthening Performance, Accountability and Citizen Confidence,* edited by Frank J. Thompson (Jossey-Bass Publishers, 1993), authors Michael Sparer and Lawrence D. Brown spend an entire chapter on one of the most expensive government programs in history—Medicaid, which provides health care to the indigent. It's a program that has long been the subject of heated debate about the value of early intervention as a way to reduce costs. Allowing government to spend hundreds of dollars up-front on something like quality pre-natal care potentially forestalls the need to spend thousands of dollars on intensive—or chronic—intervention later on. Using such an argument, Medicaid money might quite wisely be spent on something like lead paint abatement in apartment buildings. Instead, Medicaid has become one of the most convoluted, rule-bound, and as mentioned above, expensive programs in the history of U.S. government, and costs continue to escalate.

As Sparer and Brown point out, there is a long and impressive list of forces arrayed against innovating in Medicaid, from bureaucratic infighting and paralysis, to political wrangling, to legitimate legal and fiscal concerns. And so far, the whole program has proved so large and politically charged as to defy real reform.

Yet the Innovations program offers numerous, albeit more modest, examples of government willing to invest now to save later, both in the area of health care policy and outside of it.

In 1986, for example, St. Paul, Minnesota, was recognized for its Block Nurse Program, which was designed to provide quality, home-based care to the elderly to avoid much more expensive institutional solutions. In 1996, Florida won for its Healthy Kids Program, an effort to extend health insurance to all children in a single state. Healthy Kids was a clear precursor to the federal Children's Health Insurance Program (CHIP) passed by Congress in 1997, which is aimed at significantly expanding health insurance coverage for youngsters nationwide.

As with health, education has always been a category that invited prevention-based strategies, the prototype probably being Georgia's Voluntary Pre-kindergarten Program, a 1997 winner, aimed at allowing every child in the state access to early education. The approach is based on the long-standing maxim that investing money in education now pays off handsomely in better socialization, higher achievement, and lower costs (indeed, more productive tax-paying citizens) down the road.

Dozens of Innovations winners in other policy areas have prevention at their heart, particularly in the criminal justice and social services areas. Case Management for At-Risk Children, a 1986 winner, takes a comprehensive social services approach to youthful offenders as a substitute for the more typical punitive strategy on the theory that kids sitting in juvenile detention are not getting the kind of help they need to improve their lives. Again, the idea is that investing in an admittedly more expensive range of interventions now will keep troubled kids out of deeper trouble later, which lowers ultimate costs to society, fiscal and otherwise.

In 1987, Illinois won an award for Parents Too Soon, described as "a comprehensive, statewide effort to stem teenage pregnancy through health, social, and educational services for males and females ... to raise awareness about the consequences of becoming parents at a very young age." Efforts aimed at reducing teen pregnancy have since become a staple of state and local government across the United States, and, according to state and national public health statistics, are now paying off in significantly reduced teen pregnancy rates.

The city of Boston won an Innovations award in 1997 for Operation Ceasefire, an aggressive, preemptive approach to gang violence involving a host of players, from the police department to the faith-based community, in an effort to identify and defuse gang trouble before it sparks. The program's focus on stopping trouble before it ever starts proved so effective that Operation Ceasefire programs have sprung up all over the country.

Environmental protection, too, seems to invite a more proactive approach to public policy and administration. In 1999 the Massachusetts

Department of Environmental Protection continued its string of Innovations awards with its Toxics Use Reduction Program, an effort to work with manufacturers on new and creative ways to prevent pollution in the first place, rather than treat it at the pipe during discharge. "Our basic thinking," noted Gina McCarthy, assistant secretary in the state's Executive Office of Environmental Affairs, "was, with all the technology advances and all the Yankee ingenuity at our disposal, is it really necessary to create all this pollution as part of the production process?"

It's a sentiment that sums up the ethic behind quite a few of the Innovations program's prevention-based winners—that is, applying a little inventiveness to treating the problem at the front end is ultimately much cheaper and much more effective than treating it at the back end.

Driver Four: Emphasizing Results

As mentioned above, some argue that prevention-focused programs can be a tough sell because it's hard to measure what hasn't happened (and therefore makes it hard to argue for or justify expenditures). On the other hand, an increasing number of award-winning programs are based on the whole notion that government programs and initiatives ought to be much more soundly based on results that can be measured. Indeed, much of the re-inventing government literature revolves around what advocates describe as a profound new shift in focus for government: from an obsession with process to the pursuit of results.

It's an intoxicatingly simple-sounding approach to doing the public's business. An entire chapter in *Reinventing Government* is devoted to the topic: "Results-Oriented Government: Funding Outcomes, not Outputs." In it, Osborne and Gaebler argue eloquently for this new focus for government policies and programs, and offer a host of examples of results-driven government transformation. The authors predict big changes like welfare reform (based on their observation that the old way of doing the public assistance business wasn't working), and they compliment the Fund for The City of New York on more down-to-earth work like monitoring the Big Apple's spending in relation to its performance in some key and highly visible areas such as street cleaning.

This author argues (less eloquently, to be sure) for the same shift in government thinking in *Measuring Up: Governing's Guide to Performance Measurement for Geniuses and Other Public Managers*. Except that in *Measuring Up*, an entire chapter is devoted to the reasons why government can't possibly shift its focus to results. That chapter, "Eight Reasons Why You Can't Do Performance Measurement and Then the One Reason Why You Have No Choice," outlines a list of excuses that public officials frequently turn to for why they can't pursue results-based government. Those reasons range from a fear of being held accountable for results—bad ones—over which they might have little or no control, to trend fatigue, characterized by a deep cynicism toward any new management bromide being hyped by higher-ups. Both chapters, in their own way, discuss the cluttered path leading to results-based government.

Of course, all the Innovations winners are arguably about "results." In some cases Innovations award winners sell themselves specifically as being exemplary because they have focused government on tracking results, generally. In other cases, winning programs simply represent a new way of conducting business based on that age-old adage: "If the old way of doing something isn't working, then try something new"—preferably something that actually works.

The best example of the former is the Oregon Benchmarks program, a 1994 winner, which represented an ambitious and explicit effort to collect and monitor data on results—the theory being that doing so would then drive policies and programs to change in ways that make them more effective. Under Oregon Benchmarks, the state developed a whole set of measures by which to judge the progress and success of Oregon, its citizens and its government, in a host of socioeconomic, health, and public safety categories—from the health of residents to their annual incomes. The Oregon Benchmarks program has had its ups and downs, but there's no arguing that it helped set off a revolution in how state, local, and even the federal government, at least, talk about what they do.

A couple of other noteworthy Innovations program finalists were also aimed at changing governmental behavior by monitoring results. In 1998 and 1999 Florida was a finalist for its Environmental Performance Measurement System, which collected statewide data on everything from air to groundwater quality as a way to gauge the need for and effect of cleanup efforts, and perhaps retarget resources based on need and impact. Also in 1999— a big year for results-based finalists—Philadelphia was recognized for its Program Development and Evaluation System for Juvenile Offenders, a long title for a program essentially aimed at tracking juvenile offenders to see if any patterns could be deciphered around their individual backgrounds, on the one hand; and which government or government-funded interventions seemed to have the most (or least) success in steering kids straight, on the other. Again, both the Florida and Philadelphia programs were specific efforts to collect data on results that could then be used to assess and presumably steer programs, policies, and resources.

The other subset of results-based award winners are those aimed less at monitoring results than achieving them. The now nationally renowned Project Match, which won its Innovations award in 1988 for its new approach to welfare to work, is the archetype. Project Match is just as much about results as Oregon Benchmarks, just at a different level (call it results with a small "r" versus Results with a big "R").

Project Match, which started out as a demonstration program funded by the Illinois Department of Public Aid, won national recognition for its patient and enlightened—but clearly hard-nosed—approach to breaking the cycle of welfare dependence. The basic motivation for Project Match was the realization that welfare as we knew it wasn't working very well; that moving single women from welfare to independence (or at least less dependence) would take a lot more than simply writing checks and then hoping people would get on their feet. It would take time, considerable effort, repeated failure, and multiple support services.

Project Match was a clear harbinger of the Wisconsin Works program, a 1999 winner, which had its roots in 1987 reforms that essentially took the theories behind Project Match and formed them into a statewide welfare-to-work strategy. Both programs predicted the sweeping 1996 welfare reforms that would come out of Washington.

The 1995 Innovations award-winning Hamilton Terrace Learning Center—an alternative high school for troubled teens and welfare mothers, developed in the Caddo Parish School District in Louisiana—was likewise an experiment in helping break the cycle of welfare dependence inspired by the fact that past strategies to help welfare recipients achieve education-ally just weren't yielding good results.

Environmental cleanup is another area that seems to have inspired a host of small "r" results-based Innovations award winners. In 1994

Wisconsin Works, State of Wisconsin

Minnesota won for its Voluntary Investigation and Cleanup program, through which state officials worked with developers in cooperative, non-punitive ways to get contaminated land cleaned up, back into productive service, and back on the tax rolls. Minnesota's is one of a host of "brown-field" programs that have been recognized by the Innovations program for a shift in focus on (some would say "obsession with") regulation and process toward facilitation and ground-level results.

But, again, every one of the Innovations finalists and winners is ultimately about results. The Innovations application hits hard on accomplishments, asking specifically for the "single most important achievement of your program or policy initiative to date," and then asking for the "three most important measures you use to evaluate your program's success." If you don't have good data on results, it becomes very hard to make the Innovations award cut.

Driver Five: Adapting Technology

A frequently asked question by those observing the results-based governance phenomenon is why a focus on results seems to have all of a sudden infused public sector thinking. What magic has taken hold that now has government obsessing about results? In fact, the idea of applying meaningful performance measures to what government does has been around for generations. What has allowed it to take root so quickly of late is that the technology necessary for comprehensive and thorough tracking and analysis of data on results has only just recently been developed—and is now evolving with incredible rapidity.

But the technology revolution has had a powerful influence across all of government, not just in how it measures what it does, but in how it actually gets its myriad of jobs done. Which is why adapting new technology to old jobs is an increasingly pervasive theme among the applications received by the Innovations awards program. In its own breakdown of categories of winners—including "social services," "environment," and "justice system"—the awards program has created a separate category altogether for "technology."

In fact, these days the program is so flooded with applications that involve adapting technology to the business of government, it's becoming tougher and tougher for judges to sift out real innovation from straightforward—even if appropriate and effective—adaptation of technology to the basic work of government.

It can also be tough to judge whether some innovation occurs because of technology or whether technology is simply part of the new program. Arguably a program like Oklahoma's OK-FIRST could be easily shifted into the "technology-inspired" category of innovator. Yet the program at its core is really about rapidly responding to inevitable crisis.

Which is why the category of technology-driven innovation, like crisis-driven innovation, can also be divided in two. There are those programs, like OK-FIRST and the aforementioned CATS and PulseNet, that represent good ideas that rely on technology to work. Then there are those innovations that are more purely technological in their makeup. Thirteen years ago, the Innovations awards program recognized Vermont for what was arguably one of the earliest attempts at so-called "e-government." The state hooked up hundreds of libraries by computer, allowing single-source electronic access to all their collections—or at least to listings of what materials were in their collections.

Since then the list of technology-specific innovations recognized by the program has been rapidly expanding. Two alone have been handed out in the Los Angeles area, both of them for technology-dependent programs aimed at reducing traffic. In 1992 the city of Los Angeles won an award for its Automated Traffic Surveillance and Control program, a high-tech, sensor-driven system for keeping cars, trucks, and buses moving throughout downtown by altering the pattern of stoplights according to traffic flow and congestion. (The program also contributed one of the more colorful terms of art to the traffic control lexicon. When congestion got particularly horrible on a specific stretch of road, officials would execute what they called "a royal flush"—a string of green lights along a single transportation corridor aimed at emptying out a serious backlog of idling vehicles.) The very next year, Los Angeles County won for its Telecommuting Program, whereby thousands of county employees were granted permission to stay home and work via telephone, fax, and the Internet on days when it made sense.

Among other programs that have technology at their core: In 2000, Perry High School in Perry, Ohio, won for Perritech, a school-based computer repair and consulting firm staffed entirely by students. And in 2001, the ultimate in e-government is recognized as a finalist by the Innovations award program: FirstGov. FirstGov is the U.S. General Services Administration-administered web portal to the world of U.S. government, allowing direct access to federal services and products like tax forms and passport applications, while also providing direct links to state and local government sites.

Needless to say, a string of winners falls into the category of applying technology to long-standing public jobs. In 1986—the first year of the awards program—Rochester, New York, won an Innovations award for using videodiscs to administer its property tax rolls. In 1988, Kentucky won for using video and sound recording in place of court stenographers. In 1990, Ramsey County, Minnesota, won for its use of "smart cards" to dispense welfare cash benefits. In 1991 Kentucky won again, this time for initiating a broadcasting-based distance learning program to remote rural school districts.

Electronic Bond Bidding Initiative, Pittsburgh, Pennsylvania

In 1993, Oregon won for its Vendor Information Program, whereby the state began posting "requests for proposals" and accepting bids over the Internet. New York City won in 1996 for its widely praised and widely replicated "Compstat" program, a tactical policing tool whereby the police use computer-collected data to analyze crime patterns, allowing more effective deployment of resources based on the measurable impact of intervention. And in 1999, Pittsburgh won for its Electronic Bond Bidding Initiative, which allowed the city to cut out the middleman—bond brokers—and sell bonds via the Internet directly to investors, saving the city and investors money.

One Innovations awards winner even applied technology to technology. The Center for Technology in Government, a 1995 winner from the state of New York, was created in part to allow state and local government agencies to experiment with computer-based ways to do the work of government on a small scale before investing big money to roll out such systems for real.

Driver Six: Doing the Right Thing

By direct contrast to those awards driven by technology, there are some that are arguably based on something else altogether: their essential humanity. There is a whole class of Innovations award winners that are hard to explain in any other way than that they are flat out about doing the right thing.

Obviously—as one would hope—all the winners are imbued with a clear sense of positive purpose. But even with such laudably noble efforts as the First Offender Prostitution Program (FOPP) or A Secret Safe Place for

Newborns, there were extenuating imperatives that helped drive the initiatives. In the case of First Offenders, it was clear evidence that the old way of conducting the business of criminal justice wasn't working very well. (Although a strong case can certainly be made for putting FOPP into the "doing the right thing" category, Hotaling was such a force to be reckoned with that it fits perfectly under frustration with the status quo). In the case of the Safe Place initiative, it was a string of shocking headlines that finally moved people to action.

But take a program like Racial Integration Incentives, a 1988 Innovations winner, which sought to actively maintain racial balance in the neighborhoods of three Cleveland suburbs. Absent the program, those neighborhoods would simply follow the same course that had been followed in dozens of neighborhoods for dozens of years: They would naturally segregate. Or why embark on an initiative to offer aid and comfort to lone citizens in the throes of personal tragedy, as the city of San Diego did back in the early 1990s through its Trauma Intervention Program (TIP)? Without such a program, few would be any the wiser and only a tiny handful any the sadder. There would certainly be no front-page news decrying the lack of compassion coming out of city hall if TIP hadn't been invented.

In scouring the literature on innovation, one finds far ranging and detailed discussion of risk taking and rewards, empowerment and flexibility. Hardly anybody talks about innovation in terms of simply doing what's right. Even Daniel Yankelovich's first-rate book *Coming to Public Judgment: Making Democracy Work in a Complex World* (Syracuse University Press, 1991) winds up being more of a technical primer on dispute resolution and collaborative decision making than a disquisition on the Golden Rule.

Yet in 1985, three suburbs outside of Cleveland embarked on a program to fight the "tipping" that social scientists have identified occurs when a particular neighborhood begins to go one way or another in racial makeup. Under the program, local community services offices actively tried to steer whites toward black neighborhoods and blacks toward white neighborhoods, offering various financial incentives to those who agreed to make "pro-integrative" moves. It's no surprise to learn that the Racial Integration Incentives program, which was focused on Shaker Heights, Cleveland Heights, and University Heights, Ohio, is no longer around. And a quote from an interview with one of the program principals back in 1988 was certainly prophetic. "People would rather stick their heads in the sand than take the political heat," said Winston Richie, an African American and executive director of one of the community services groups pushing the program. (We will take up Racial Integration Incentives again in the next section of this paper on survival and replication.)

San Diego's Trauma Intervention Services, meanwhile, was designed to team volunteers with survivors of acute tragedy—most frequently people who'd lost family members to work or traffic accidents. Those volunteers arrived on the scene within minutes to offer emotional comfort to survivors and to help them connect with social services programs when appropriate. But mostly the volunteers simply served as someone to offer comfort and sympathy in the absence of a trauma survivor's own family or friends.

The integration and trauma programs were early examples of Innovations winners that emerged, more often than not, by dint of pure goodwill and willpower by some individual or small handful of individuals intent on doing good. Those types of programs continue to pepper the Innovations awards list.

Not all of them are as emotionally charged as TIP or the pro-integration program. For example, the Department of Defense (DoD) won an Innovations award in 1998 for its Best Manufacturing Practices Program (BMPP). Under BMPP, experts visit willing businesses to analyze best practices—from manufacturing techniques to personnel management. What those teams learn is then posted on a website available to any company interested in improving their own processes. It's tough to explain the program in any other terms than that the Defense Department was simply trying to help companies run better. Arguably there was some enlightened self-interest involved— more efficient companies had the potential to become more reliable, cost-effective suppliers to the DoD. But really the program boils down to simply being a good idea that has the potential to help a lot of people.

More frequently, though, winners in the "right thing to do" category involve much tougher and more emotionally charged issues.

In the year 2000—with Innovations applications based on hard technology pouring into the program—two of the winners that emerged were singled out mostly for their essential human decency. In Hampden County, Massachusetts, Sheriff Michael Ashe bent over backward in arguing the practical public health benefits of Better Inmate Care Improves Public Health, a program that offers inmates comprehensive health care coverage and counseling. Ashe notes that healthier and more health-conscious inmates are much less of a threat to public health when released, and that is no doubt true. But Ashe pushes that argument as hard as he does because he is well aware that any program identified as being humane (read "soft") toward criminals has a high probability of becoming a political target. At the end of the day, though, Ashe is simply doing the right, if less than politically popular, thing.

Pennsylvania, meanwhile, won for its Mental Hospital Seclusion and Restraint Reduction policy, whereby the use of chemical and physical restraints in its nine state mental hospitals has been dramatically scaled back. As in Hampden County, the new policy has paid multiple dividends, not the least of which is evidence of the therapeutic benefits of a more humane approach to restraint. But the program has proved to be expensive to administer and time-consuming to carry out, and no gubernatorial candidate in Pennsylvania is ever going to climb up to a public podium and bellow the praises of the state's efforts to treat a group of virtually invisible, mentally ill constituents in a nicer way.

The Pennsylvania program, like the First Offender program, might also easily be shifted to the category of "frustration with the status quo." The driving force behind the change in policy was a woman named Mary Ellen Rehrman, who says she became a mental health advocate the day she first saw her hospitalized schizophrenic son in a four-point restraint. "It wasn't therapeutic, it was humiliating," said Rehrman. "I thought that enough disability comes with the illness without a patient being left so devalued and vulnerable." So the Pennsylvania program clearly has feet in both the "frustration" and "doing the right thing" categories.

In 1994, the city of Tulsa, Oklahoma, won an award for its Sexual Assault Nurse Examiners Program, which represented a whole new and more humane way to treat victims of rape and other sexual crimes. This program also wound up paying multiple dividends. It turns out, for example, that victims who are led into the warm confines of a counselor's office rather than the harsh spotlight of a police precinct tend to be much more willing to testify against assailants. But at its heart, the program flat out represented a more compassionate way to deal with people who had just been through hell.

Mental Hospital Seclusion and Restraint Reduction, Commonwealth of Pennsylvania

What Makes Innovation Successful?

There are three explicitly stated goals of the Innovations in American Government Awards program:

- To celebrate innovation and innovators.
- To blunt cynicism about and improve the image of government by high-lighting examples of effective government.
- To help sustain innovation and replicate it in other jurisdictions.

Clearly the program does a good job of celebrating innovation and innovators. Finalists are invited to Washington, D.C., where they enjoy the heady surroundings of the National Press Club's storied briefing and conference rooms. There they make their final oral presentations to a national selection committee. The awards are presented the next day at a festive luncheon, attended by a who's who of public sector change management experts. Winners are sometimes even accorded visits to the White House. A special supplement covering the finalists and winners is published in subsequent issues of both *Governing* and *Government Executive* magazines (a supplement that, by way of full disclosure, has for the past four years been written by this author). So, from the standpoint of celebrating innovators, the program seems to hit the mark.

As for the program's goal of reducing cynicism about and boosting confidence in government, even the program's most ardent supporters will admit that that's a hard one to measure. It is taken on faith that the program will have some positive impact. There is a measurable flurry of media coverage of the finalists and winners immediately after their designation, usually by local market newspapers, television, and radio. Judging by the responses to the questionnaire recently sent out to all winning programs by the Institute for Government Innovation as part of the Innovations' 15th anniversary activities, quite a few of the programs have received extensive media coverage. Being named by the Kennedy School and the Ford Foundation as an innovator no doubt has helped many of them in that regard.

But the real hope of the Innovations program is that it supports both the survival and the dissemination of good ideas. Both the Innovations program application and the grilling that finalists take from the national selection committee during oral presentations hit hard on each. The aforementioned survey recently sent out to every winning program focused extensively on program survival and replication, as well as the extent to which being recognized by the Kennedy School and the Ford Foundation had some positive influence in each regard.

It's understandable that the Innovations program would be curious about its own impact on innovators and the seeding of good ideas around the country and world. But trying to decipher cause and effect in that regard is an uncertain proposition, and it's probably better left to the Institute to make its own calls about its impact as it sees fit. The more profitable line of inquiry for the purposes of this chapter is to look at those programs that have been "successful"—that is, they have survived and perhaps been replicated elsewhere—and try to figure out the characteristics of those programs as a guide to others who might want to follow on the innovation path.

To do that, this chapter examined the list of 30 programs that the Innovation Program identified as having particular staying and multiplying power. But this section doesn't restrict itself to those 30 by any means. It will consider a much wider range of programs based, again, on the author's personal knowledge and extensive coverage of the award winners and also on other writings about successful (and unsuccessful) programs. This section also relies on follow-up phone calls to program principals and stakeholders, close observers of the Innovations program, and those who follow innovation in the public sector more generally.

One of the most remarkable statistics associated with the Innovations in American Government awards program is the number of winning programs that are still around. Of 150 winners identified by the Innovations program between 1986 and 2001, only 14 are defunct, and seven of those date back to pre-1990. Meanwhile, scores of those winning ideas have been picked up and replicated nationally and even internationally. And so clearly the programs identified by the Ford Foundation and Kennedy School offer solid lessons to would-be innovators when it comes to designing successful—that is resilient and replicable—innovations.

For those contemplating joining the ranks of innovators, the lessons that sift out in looking at both "winners" and "finalists" come through quite clearly. When designing a program it's best to:

- Keep it simple in concept
- Make it easy to execute
- Shoot for quick results
- Be frugal
- Make it appealing to the widest constituency possible
- Keep it apolitical

Keep It Simple in Concept

Innovations award winners can be divided into two categories: the ones that are easy to explain and the ones that are hard to explain. There are far more in the former than the latter category, to be sure. But it's clear from looking at those programs that have caught on and those that haven't, that the more straightforward the concept, the better a program's chances of sticking around and being adopted by other jurisdictions.

Take, for example, Compstat, the New York Police Department's high-profile and widely replicated effort to turn information technology to the task of mapping crime trends. Compstat has received so much attention, people are probably sick of hearing about it. Well, from the standpoint of replication, that's a good thing. Jurisdictions from Los Angeles to New Orleans have adopted the Compstat approach. Indeed, it represents such a basic idea—tie resources to results—that the "stat" suffix is now being affixed to a wide range of other policy and program areas, from finding welfare recipients jobs—"jobstat" (also in New York City)—to a host of city functions. Mayor Martin O'Malley has launched "Citistat" in Baltimore, which applies the "stat" concept across city functions, from law enforcement to building code enforcement, from street sweeping to restaurant inspections. Of course, the idea of using results to drive resource deployment is hardly a new one, but it's possible to argue that the specific use of "stat" to identify the practice has been a catchy, simple, and powerful way to drive the idea into government.

Take, on the other hand, a program like "Here, Thayer and Everywhere," a 1994 winner out of the Winchester, New Hampshire, School District. It was an effort, according to a description in the October 1994 issue of *Governing,* to "help other schools grapple with issues raised by such practices as team teaching, mixing students regardless of ability, scheduling subjects in blocks, orienting learning around projects, and finding ways to ensure that teachers get to know their students as fully as possible." It was also meant to take on such topics as how to assess students and "personalize the learning process," and to do all that through workshops to be broadcast via satellite at 500 registered sites around the country and over some cable and public television stations. Without denigrating one iota the school's sincerity about the program, it's easy to see where such a diffuse plan of action to be delivered in a way that would require such extensive planning, marketing, and organization was not destined to either survive or thrive, and indeed the program is now defunct.

North Carolina's Smart Start, a 1998 winner, has a catchy title, but when one digs into the guts of implementation, it's a pretty complicated program, requiring counties to come up with elaborate action plans to coordinate a host of educational and social services to compete for the millions of state government dollars the program offers. To date, Smart Start survives, but it hasn't proved to be a popular selection at the innovations replication vending machine.

One of the more perplexing characteristics of the 2001 award-winning Mathematics, Engineering, Science Achievement initiative is that while it seems to have been wildly successful in California—helping push thousands of minority kids into higher education—very few other states have seen fit to adopt similar programs. One explanation for that might be the tough-to-explain system of parental, mentor, tutor, corporate, and teacher relationships on which the program's success depends; it's a hard initiative to sum up in a sentence.

On the other hand, 1987 winner Parents as Teachers from the state of Missouri was as fundamental an educational concept as has ever been identified by the program: Train parents in some basic techniques for boosting their kids' learning skills. The program didn't merely survive, it spread like wildfire, even going overseas.

Bill Parent, former executive director of the Innovations awards program, points out that many of the innovations that show strong replicative powers are in program or policy areas where there "are established, strong national networks of practitioners." And so good ideas that spring from the education and social services world tend to spread quickly through what are traditionally fairly cohesive networks, whereas initiatives in an area like environmental protection—a notoriously fragmented policy area, both from the standpoint of programs and jurisdictions—don't spread so quickly.

As a purely mechanical matter, it's a point worth emphasizing: Communication networks are clearly important to program replication, and the larger and more established those networks the better. But regardless of how well developed the communication network, complicated ideas just don't seed well. Parents as Teachers and Here, Thayer and Everywhere were both educational initiatives, yet one became an international phenomenon while the other disappeared. The only explanation for why that happened is that one was a very simple idea; the other wasn't.

Make It Easy to Execute

Programs that seem to have natural powers of survival and replication don't require major legislation or huge administrative rule changes to create or implement, nor do they force participation. That is, stakeholders can choose to be part of a new way of doing business of their own free will.

Operation Ceasefire, the preemptive approach to gang violence out of Boston and a 1997 Innovations award winner, wasn't predicated on the permission of—or any official action by—the Boston City Council. Furthermore, the program doesn't force anybody to do anything. It's based on a voluntary and collaborative approach to diffusing tension among gangs, essentially by trying to get people in a room to talk. In fact, in Operation Ceasefire's case, a large part of its effectiveness is clearly because at-risk youth are asked to participate rather than ordered to fall into line. (To be accurate, the program does have a "stick" component: If gangs don't decide to ease up on their own initiative, the police promise a swift crackdown.)

The program is a strong survivor and has been replicated in cities from Birmingham, Alabama, to Wilmington, Delaware.

Project Match, the ground-breaking welfare-to-work program out of Chicago, was a new strategy in helping break the welfare dependence cycle that, likewise, required no one's permission to try and didn't mandate participation. The program did benefit from money set aside by the Illinois Department of Public Aid for pilot projects. But because Project Match wasn't created by legislation or administrative rules, and because clients were coming to the program voluntarily, it evinced a staying and replication power that has allowed it not only to survive right through federal welfare reform, but also to serve as a model for all of the mandatory programs aimed at moving people off welfare and into jobs that operate today.

Likewise, the long-running and 2001 Innovations award-winning Mathematics, Engineering, Science Achievement program out of California was not the result of any lengthy hearings or detailed change in laws or rules, and it does not mandate participation. The program simply offers students the opportunity to get some extra help in studying science and math in order to move forward academically. In 30 years the program has expanded from one school to more than 450 schools. And arguably, it is because of the program's voluntary nature that it continues to thrive even after California's sweeping anti-affirmative-action ballot initiative, Proposition 209, which specifically prohibits the state from establishing programs or policies that make choices based on race.

On the other hand, Georgia's successful effort to sunset its civil service system was directly dependent on legislation, legislation that, not incidentally, required a once-in-a-generation alignment of some very state-specific political stars, along with the solid backing of the system's (former) internal "customers"—those state agencies the civil service system was supposed to be helping. The initiative survives in Georgia because it is now the law, but don't look for many (if any) states to follow Georgia's lead. In fact, as close as any state has come to doing what Georgia has done is Florida, which recently put a large number of its management positions outside of its merit system. Putting all employees outside of the merit system proved to be too tough an initiative to push through the legislature.

Similarly, Child Care Management Services, Texas's effort to offer one-stop shopping for a variety of child welfare programs, was heavily dependent on the permission of government officials—federal government officials, in particular. In fact, the program finally was created only after a five-year fight with the federal government over regulations and waivers. For that reason, the whole effort became as much a cautionary tale about tangling with the federal welfare bureaucracy as it did a model for how to do child welfare services more intelligently. According to the survey returned by the Texas program to the Institute for Government Innovation, only four other states have followed Texas's lead. Despite that, there were and continued to be sporadic attempts (pre-1996 welfare reform) to integrate and streamline a variety of social services programs in states and counties around the country, and some of those efforts were subsequently recognized by the Innovations program. But each seemed to have its own tale of woe about bucking entrenched interests in finally developing more integrated programs and systems.

Shoot for Quick Results

Many of the Innovations award winners that have gone on to be widely copied have another thing in common: They yield measurable results in a very short period of time. David Osborne puts it another way: "They have a good story to tell." And in the innovations business, a good story revolving around quick, easily communicated results is priceless.

The Oregon Vendor Information program, the 1993 winner mentioned earlier that allowed the state to put up requests for proposals and to accept bids for materials and services over the Internet, is a perfect example of not just a good story but a great one. The Oregon program yielded its results almost instantaneously. Virtually the moment Oregon started posting RFPs on the Internet, it started hearing from far-flung vendors ready to compete. It was a twin win for the state. First, the new program was a huge money saver just from an administrative standpoint. According to Oregon officials, the program paid for itself within one year just in the reduced costs of doing RFPs the old-fashioned, paper-driven way. (The state was actually spending nearly $150,000 a year in postage under the old paper-driven system.) Second, state officials estimate they saved $17 million the first year and a quarter from enhanced competition injected into the purchasing process by electronic bidding. In fact, the electronic bidding process was such a good idea that had Oregon not gotten there first, someone else clearly would have. The electronic bidding process is how hundreds of jurisdictions nationally and internationally now do business.

That same sort of instant success helped Community Voice Mail for Phoneless/Homeless Persons root and flourish, having been adopted by dozens of other jurisdictions since the program won its Innovations award in 1993. Besides being relatively easy to implement—it was a simple matter of setting up phone mail accounts for clients—it yielded results almost immediately. As reported in *Governing's* coverage of the program in November 1993, one unemployed power plant worker had six job offers within four days of the program's initiation—job offers that would have never found him absent the voice mail. Within a week the unemployed worker had a job. One month later, fully employed and getting back on his feet financially, he moved into his own apartment. Now that's a fast-acting program—and a great story.

A winner from 2000 that's generating a lot of interest is Perritech, the high school-based computer consulting firm run and staffed by students that was also mentioned earlier in this chapter. The company was mostly set up to trouble-shoot and service the school's new computer system, but students—who get advanced training and certification in a host of computer software, hardware, and networking systems—are now actually consulting to local businesses, including, of all places, the local nuclear power plant. There students helped set up hundreds of new desktop and laptop computers. "You have this image of typical fly-by-night teenagers who can't even make change without using a calculator," said Bob Kundrat, supervisor of client services for the plant. "These kids were really professional. They knew they were there to do a job and they did it well."

One of the Perritech's first alumni, a 19-year-old named Chris Hanus, is now working for one the state's largest law firms as its network analyst. Talking to Hanus on the phone is a joy; he's smart, personable, and full of entertaining tidbits, including the fact that he recently bought a house. Meanwhile, the program itself is developing partnerships with several other schools interested in starting similar programs, including an alternative school in Georgia for young offenders. Those are all great stories.

Perritech, Perry Local Schools, Ohio

Be Frugal

As many have noted, one of the organizational imperatives damping down innovation in the public sector is a general disinclination to spend new money on untested ideas, even ones ginned up by seasoned veterans who might know what they're up to. This rule holds even for programs that extensive research indicate are probably going to be a worthwhile investment—eventually.

That would explain why a perfectly fine idea like Georgia's Voluntary (note the "voluntary") Pre-kindergarten Program hasn't been widely replicated. The price tag in Georgia of $200 million a year is clearly what's keeping other states from embarking on similar initiatives, even though it's axiomatic that dollars invested in a child's education early on pay dividends in educational achievement and social adjustment down the road. An innovation like the Trauma Intervention Program, on the other hand, is never going to get derailed due to lack of funds; it relies heavily on volunteers and costs relatively little to operate.

Kentucky's massive educational overhaul, Recreating Public Education for Results, a 1997 winner, has proved to be a virtual one-of-a-kind effort. Although pieces of it have been adopted in other states, no state has undertaken a similarly comprehensive reengineering of an entire educational system. And it's actually dubious whether the state itself would have undertaken the multibillion-dollar restructuring and reinvestment program had it not been for the fact that the Kentucky State Supreme Court had ordered it to do so.

Any program that is flat out dependent on a regular check from a legislative body is always going to be at risk. The Work Force Unemployment Prevention Program—a 1990 winner out of Cambridge, Massachusetts, which placed inner-city youngsters into after-school white-collar job settings—was heavily dependent on a regular state stipend. Before the program could even begin developing a Perritech-like track record, it was summarily de-funded by the state legislature.

This truth—that innovation's replicability is frequently tied tightly to cost—seems so deeply imbedded in the innovation ethic, it's actually hard to find many Innovations award winners that involve huge investments of money. This holds true even for the high-ticket world of health care. Indeed, many of the health-related programs identified by the Innovations award program have been picked specifically for the fact that they extended health care to some previously uncovered population and did it without significantly increasing a jurisdiction's costs. For example, Medical Care for Children, a 1990 winner out of Fairfax County, Virginia, was chosen in large part because it was a very successful effort to get medical and dental care to indigent kids without a huge influx of new county money. Likewise, Buncombe County

Medical Society Project Access, a 1998 winner out of Buncombe County, North Carolina, won its award in part because it succeeded in expanding the delivery of quality primary care to uninsured adults countywide without a huge investment of new dollars. On the other hand, few jurisdictions have followed the lead of Hillsborough County, Florida, which tacked a half a cent on to its sales tax to fund managed health care for the poor, an idea that netted the county an Innovations award in 1995 for the Hillsborough County Health Care Plan.

One of the most likable of the 2001 Innovations award finalists was Chicago Fitness Plus, an initiative aimed at getting older folks into the habit of regular exercise as a way to promote independence and general well-being. When asked what was holding the obviously incredibly popular program back from expanding into more health and elder care centers, program officials cited that old refrain: money. If it costs a lot of money, survival will always be a struggle and the idea will always be a hard sell.

Make It Appealing

One of the really interesting features of the Innovations award program is that it clearly doesn't tend toward political pandering. Of course, it shouldn't. But still, what easier way to recognize replicable programs than to stick one's finger in the air, see which way the political winds are blowing, and then choose an early "three strikes and you're out" initiative knowing that 49 of them are bound to follow in rapid succession. In fact, the awards program tends to attract—and reward—those who buck conventional political "wisdom" and eschews the quick fix of the day.

This characteristic of the Innovations awards is particularly notable in the whole area of criminal justice. For example, a string of programs have been recognized for a focus on alternative ways to deal with criminals. The first was Alternatives to Incarceration, a 1987 program out of Georgia that emphasized probation over incarceration for non-violent offenders. And most recently, Reparative Probation, a 1998 winner from Vermont, was chosen for its emphasis on community service over probation—again, for non-violent offenders. But while both might be considered trend-buckers at first glance, it turns out that one has actually tapped into deep community sentiment, while the other really hasn't. In other words, to put it most simply, one has proved readily likable, the other less so, and the proof is in the replication.

If anything, the Georgia program preceded a wave not of alternatives to incarceration but of unprecedented "get-tough-on-criminals" laws, including boot camp and mandatory sentencing initiatives. Needless to say, states haven't fallen over themselves in following Georgia's lead, although there is—and recently has been—a good deal of discussion and debate nationally about alternatives to jail time for non-violent offenders. California's recent ballot initiative requiring that non-violent drug offenders do counseling rather than hard time is evidence that, at least in some places, people are climbing on this bandwagon. Still, few politicians seem very interested in getting out in front on the alternatives to jail platform. Nor does there seem to be enough of a groundswell of support for such ideas that Georgia's or California's efforts will be broadly replicated. New York has been mired in a debate about easing up its tough drug sentencing laws for years now; there's no evidence that the legislature or governor is getting anywhere near enough grassroots pressure to move them.

On the other hand, Vermont's Reparative Probation program seems to have struck a real populist, community chord. Through the program, communities set up citizen boards to consider community service sentences for non-violent offenders who've committed crimes against that community. Offenders have the option of pleading guilty and opting for alternative service (graffiti artists might be required to paint the trim on city hall, for example) over a trial that would then risk fines, jail time and/or probation. Not only has the program grown within the state, but more than a dozen other states and localities have started similar ones, according to Vermont officials.

The difference between the Georgia and Vermont initiatives, and the lesson for would-be innovators: To survive and thrive the innovation doesn't have to pander, but it does have to, at some level, be one that people can connect with. At the very least they have to be ideas that don't draw sustained, focused opposition in the absence of widespread community or stakeholder support.

For example, politically dicey programs like Sheriff Ashe's jailhouse health campaign can probably survive as long as they skim along below the radar. But the Hampden program doesn't fall into the "likable" category, especially when compared to a host of other Innovations award winners. Take, for example, the Police Homeowner Loan Program, a 1993 initiative out of the capital city of Columbia, South Carolina, aimed at encouraging city police officers to move back downtown and into distressed neighborhoods. While it took some persuading and real sweetening of the financial home purchase and employment packages to get police officers' attention, as a program there's nothing not to like about it. And that's clearly one of the reasons that it has been picked up in dozens of other communities. Such programs, it should be noted, have been dogged by charges of fraud in some places. An innovation lesson for another day is that even the best ideas can be abused by creative thieves, but that shouldn't stop people from pursuing good ideas.

In looking at the broad swath of Innovations programs, a bunch of them are flat out likable. Gallery 37, a youth-focused program out of Chicago and a 1997 winner, pairs kids in paid apprenticeships with accomplished, professional artists. The kids' work is then displayed in various public places all over the city. It's such a likable idea that it's been picked up in more than a dozen jurisdictions, from Tuscon, Arizona, to Toledo, Ohio, and even Adelaide, Australia, according to Gallery 37 officials. Likewise, who is going to squawk about a program like the aforementioned Perritech, a natural for replication? And chances are that even Chicago's Fitness Plus program will start to seed itself in other cities, even if it does cost a little money. It will likely do that because there's another kind of math that enters into the replication equation here: an aging voter population looking to government for likable ideas. Fitness Plus is one that older folks seem to like a lot.

Likable, though, can be tough to predict at times. One program that seemed like it couldn't possibly lose a civic popularity contest wound up sinking out of sight anyway. California's much hyped and publicized Info/California, a 1993 winner, with its fleet of publicly placed touchscreen, interactive kiosks, fell flat on its face. The state had plans to buy and locate 100 of the terminals at $30,000 a pop, but those plans were scrapped. It wasn't that people necessarily hated the things, they just didn't use them.

Meanwhile, those programs that touch off basic and sustained (or very effective acute) opposition are obviously not destined for bright futures. Take, for example, Maine Top 200. Given the Occupational Safety and Health Administration's remarkable and measurable success in reducing worker injury and death in key industries in Maine, OSHA decided to take the program national. Its reward for its ambitious push was to be sued by the National Association of Manufacturers, which claimed that recordkeeping requirements under the new initiative amounted to new "rules." The manufacturers argued that all such rules must go through the usual process of public hearings and comment, which they hadn't. The manufacturers won their lawsuit, effectively killing the program. (To be accurate, the program lives on in a way: After its success in Maine, OSHA continues to use data on deaths and injuries to target enforcement nationally. What was lost in the wake of the manufacturers' lawsuit, ironically, was the working-cooperatively-with-industry component of the program.)

But of all the programs handed an Innovations award, there was probably none so doomed as Racial Integration Incentives, that star-crossed 1988 award winner mentioned earlier. Dedicated to creating and maintaining racial balance in the neighborhoods of three Cleveland suburbs, it did have the fierce support of a handful of both whites and African Americans. But it was also fiercely attacked from both sides. Even the U.S. Justice Department under Ronald Reagan investigated it for charges of "racial steering" in real estate sales (nothing came of the investigation). In the end, the program was as unpopular as it was honorable. Unpopular prevailed.

Keep It Apolitical

A small handful of the initiatives identified by the Innovations program have "star power" because they're closely identified with a high-level elected or appointed public official.

Wisconsin Works (W2), which presaged federal welfare reform by almost 10 years (it was launched in 1987), was the hallmark of Governor Tommy Thompson's long reign as governor, and probably didn't hurt him when it came to winning his new job as Secretary of the U.S. Department of Health and Human Services. Replication of W2 was swift and pervasive; at least a dozen states pursued waivers similar to those granted Wisconsin under W2. And when Wisconsin finally won its Innovations award in 1999, the whole country was already three years into federal welfare reform. But even if W2 could be credited with having a huge influence over other states—and even the 1996 federal welfare reforms—its survival and replication would be the exception to the rule as far as innovation's longevity is concerned.

Typically programs recognized by the Innovations program that have close connections to a politician or political regime end up being swept out with a change of administration. Two in particular are representative. Minnesota's Strive Toward Excellence in Performance (STEP) program, a 1986 winner aimed at improving state administrative services, was tightly connected to political appointee Sandra Hale. When Governor Rudy Perpich's administration went, Hale and STEP went with it. It's worth noting, though, that Minnesota continues to be a leader in performance-based governance, and it's reasonable to argue that many of the ideas behind the STEP program live on in other incarnations. At the same time, programs similar to STEP have proliferated, although results-based governance is clearly one of those broad trends whose origins are really tough to pinpoint.

Maryland's Smart Growth initiative, recognized in 1999 as a finalist and in 2000 as a winner, will be interesting to watch in this regard. Tightly tied to the administration of Governor Parris Glendening, the sweeping sprawl-slowing initiative hasn't been picked up by any other state, and there is plenty of speculation about the program's survival once Glendening moves along. If he is succeeded by a fellow Democrat, then the program will probably continue to have the high-level support it needs to maintain its integrity and impact. Moreover, the fact that it is embedded in legislation gives it a better chance of survival. But sweeping land use regulations and policies in other states—like Vermont and Oregon—have become targets for steady chipping away by opponents. If there is a change in party in Maryland, look for Smart Growth's profile as a target to rise considerably.

While Oregon Benchmarks was closely tied to Governor Barbara Roberts, it was, in fact, a legislative initiative, which is one of the main reasons why it manages to stay alive through continuing legislative appropriations.

Smart Growth and Neighborhood Conservation, State of Maryland

Its survival is a matter of constant vigilance, to be sure, because it does rely directly on the munificence of the state legislature. But because Roberts won the buy-in of key legislators in pushing the program, it wound up with a more solid foundation of support than if it had been simply identified as a product of the Roberts administration.

All in all, though, one of the interesting and fairly consistent characteristics of the programs highlighted by the Kennedy School and the Ford Foundation is that they very rarely rely on star power or get tangled up in politics. For the most part, they are born quietly, and are pushed by people who weren't famous when they stepped into the innovations limelight and who haven't become famous after they stepped out of it. And that, as it turns out, is a pretty good foundation for successful innovation.

Personal Observations:
13 Years of Chronicling Innovators

For all the millions of words written about innovation in government (and the private sector), and for all the long-winded attempts to analyze the alchemy of change management in government—this tome included—innovation, at the end of the day, is a pretty straightforward proposition: It's a people-driven business. And the people behind innovation are a fascinating group.

It's easy to attach to them all the typical adjectives: creative, persistent, even courageous. But those words are used so often they've lost a lot of their punch, as accurate as they might be. Besides, what I've noticed about those who've been identified through the Innovations awards is something a little subtler: They are restless.

When it comes to how public jobs get done, there's a group of people (many, to be sure, who've never been recognized by any awards program and who never will be) who just seem, like the mythical Prince Valiant, to be perennially dissatisfied. Which is why no change-management recipe book in the world is ever going to capture the magic of innovation in the form of some immutable quasi-political or social-scientific math equation. In the end it's actually more of a nurture-nature question best left to psychologists—who, by the way, don't really have any answers, either.

Still, "experts" have been analyzing innovation in the public (and private) sector for eons. Whether it's Borins, Osborne, Light, Peters, or Walters, dozens have gone through the exercise of putting innovative organizations and programs under the microscope in hopes of finding that magic bit of genetic material that will allow innovation to be cloned.

It's not an easy thing to do. Yes, organizations can be structured in a way that will encourage innovation. And certainly it helps to understand the inspiration behind certain types of innovation so that when opportunity visits it can be turned to action. Characteristics of sustainable and replicable programs are worth identifying so that once-and-future innovators at least have the benefit of knowing some tricks of the trade as they embark on the frequently frustrating adventure of pushing change.

But if innovation were a matter of organizational dynamic or just the right opportunity, it would hardly ever happen in the public sector, or probably anywhere else, for that matter. It is people who push it, people often working in dysfunctional organizations under miserable circumstances, and in spite of that, they try to change things.

Which is why in the 13 years of closely following the Innovations in American Government program, what I have seen collected is as much a gallery of good people as it is a database of good ideas. As mentioned in the previous section, very few of the programs recognized have been pushed by high-level, well-known public sector all-stars. For the most part, the programs are the product of inside and outside stakeholders who are simply tired of doing something one way when they suspect—or know— there's a better way; who are tired of chronic mediocrity (or outright failure) when they know government should and could do better.

Trying to list all the people I've met and/or interviewed in the course of those 13 years who've impressed me with their dedication and creativity (not just from the standpoint of the idea, but also from the standpoint of getting the idea implemented) is a hazardous enterprise only because there have been so many who stand out. I will mention a few; but I could easily list many more.

Let's start with Donald L. DeMarco, one of the first award winners I ever met. He's one of the principals behind the ill-fated program aimed at maintaining racial balance in Shaker Heights, Cleveland Heights, and University Heights, Ohio. Even to a green reporter (at least when it came to covering innovations), it was obvious that DeMarco's quest was pure Don Quixote. Here was a guy who, in essence, was trying to buck the most fundamental forces of social and economic behavior in our nation—if not the world. What was the payoff? Besides an Innovations award (much appreciated, certainly, but no antidote for the inevitable), DeMarco got nothing but resistance and attack from all quarters. He was even harassed by his own government in the form of the U.S. Department of Justice. What DeMarco had going for him was this startling, fearless, bulldog tenacity when it came to doing what he thought was right. It wasn't until I met DeMarco that I fully understood the single-minded dedication of purpose, the capacity for action, and the courage of those who had pushed for civil rights in the 1950s and '60s. It was an eye-opener.

Or consider a guy like John Baldwin, principal of the Hamilton Terrace Learning Center, the 1995 award-winning program aimed at helping shepherd troubled teens and welfare mothers into higher education and toward independence. He commandeered an empty school building (he talked a custodian out of his keys). He then won over his superintendent by promising to deliver an education program that would become the "crowning star" of the district. Then—and on his own—he lined up the financial support needed to create the program. And, finally, he developed a whole new curriculum aimed at this jumbled-up and challenging student mix. Keep in mind that Baldwin had no other ambition here. He wasn't running for anything. The work he did wasn't going to make him wealthy (to say the least). He was never going to be on the cover of any national magazine recognizing him for his fine work and dedication. There was no large cash "genius" prize in his future that would allow him to live easily for a while. All he got was the satisfaction of knowing that in the face of chronic failure, he was trying something different to help a specific group of people who needed that help.

Norma Hotaling

Photo: Andy Kuno

Two women, likewise, immediately come to mind when I think about the activists I've met or talked to who had some connection to the Innovations awards. Norma Hotaling, who pushed the First Offender Prostitution Program in San Francisco, is, to put it mildly, intimidating. She is an ex-prostitute with an attitude. Not only did she pull herself out of a life on the streets, she's now trying to make a real difference in other people's lives by championing a much more compassionate and common sense approach to the all-too-human problem of sexual exploitation of women and children. Largely because of her work and the work of like-minded activists, the ideas she supports do slowly seem to be working their way into the law enforcement policies of other localities both here and overseas, in spite of frequently running up against political brick walls.

Where Hotaling is a steamroller, Mary Ellen Rehrman is a tough, wise-cracking lobbyist with a huge heart and the ability to work with government insiders to make big change. Rehrman, like Hotaling, is also fueled by hard firsthand knowledge of public sector policy failure. After just a few minutes on the phone with Rehrman—who now runs a Philadelphia-based clearinghouse advocating more enlightened treatment for people in mental hospitals nationwide—it became quite clear why it is that her home state of Pennsylvania has come to lead the country in its highly evolved restraint and seclusion policies for its public mental hospitals. Rehrman flat out wouldn't have it any other way. Most simply put, people like Hotaling and Rehrman are the status quo's worst enemies.

Joe Dear

Photo: Carl Cook

By contrast, but just as effective, is a chronic innovator like Joe Dear, who has bagged two Innovations awards. He is one of those quiet, behind-the-scenes types who evinces a constant restless energy that is focused on analyzing government activity in relation to desired results. Where the two don't seem to be matching up, Dear starts asking hard questions. He was behind OSHA's Maine Top 200 initiative, which looked at death and injury rates in that state in relation to types of work and then focused preemptive safety efforts on the appropriate industries to remarkable effect. He also pushed an award-winning initiative to overhaul Washington State's dysfunctional worker compensation system. Bespectacled and diminutive, Dear will chew over a question you've asked him about public sector management in Austin, Texas, in April and will continue his answer when you bump into him a month later in Olympia, Washington. He's very smart. Unfortunately for the public sector, Dear is now working for a private business. But I predict he'll be back at some point; he seems to have too much fun doing public policy.

Just as restless and smart is someone like Mary Ellen Skinner, one of the driving bureaucrats behind the Texas Child Care Management Services initiative, the effort to knit together diverse programs aimed at helping kids in

Texas. It goes without saying that persistence had more than a little to do with pursuing her *five-year* fight to bring some rationality and cohesiveness to social services delivery there. But what she actually taught me was the value of a (very wry) sense of humor when it comes to surviving that kind of grinding campaign against institutionalized irrationality. In a soft, Southern, almost whimsical lilt, she can deliver some wicked one-liners aimed at federal child care policy—and they are frequently right on the mark.

Then there's a guy like Redlands, California, Chief of Police James R. Bueermann, who is simply way ahead of the game. His program—Risk-Focused Policing—is a community health approach to crime prevention and was a 2000 Innovations award finalist. The chief was clearly disappointed that his program didn't win. That's understandable, but I was happy just to meet the brains behind the effort. Even in this day and age of community policing, top cops tend to come from the old-fashioned "bust heads" school of law enforcement. But Bueermann is a thinker, someone who really understands and can articulate the value of prevention when it comes to keeping communities safe. If more in law enforcement thought the way he did, governments would be spending much more money on housing and community development and a lot less on high-powered handguns and bulletproof vests for police officers.

Again, it's not just Innovations award winners who deserve to be mentioned here; I could continue on with dozens of people I've interviewed in the last 20 years who embody all the same qualities and who've never been formally recognized by anyone for their achievements, large and small, and who probably never will be. Government is no different in that regard from the private sector; it harbors the hapless and the wonderful alike. But I believe being wonderful is considerably harder in the public sector, and it really means something.

A perennial and probably futile hope is that the mainstream press will start recognizing this; that it will shake its obsession with disaster and celebrity and tune in more carefully to those in the public sector who are out on a limb, trying to get something good done, often against fierce odds and occasionally failing spectacularly. Probably the most haunting thing ever told to me by an Innovations award winner was when I asked Don DeMarco what it was like to be pushing change on such a deserted, controversial, and unpopular frontier: "For so long we've been the test," said DeMarco, "and it's lonely out here." Short of the popular media figuring out who the real heroes in this world are, such award programs as that funded by Ford and run by the Kennedy School are at least, I hope, making it a little less lonely.

Finally, if pressed to come up with my own formula for how all this should work, and to borrow from the contemporary political lexicon, maybe we need to institute some sort of "two strikes" rule for innovation based on Mary Ellen Rehrman's observation: If some policy or program is not humane and it's not therapeutic (or, more broadly, if its not morally defensible and it's not working), then it's a signal to everyone that it's time for change. Or maybe it ought to be a "one strike" rule. But either way, it's going to be people who decide that.

Bibliography

Articles/Reports:

Innovations in State and Local Government 1986, Ford Foundation, 1986
Innovations in State and Local Government 1987, Ford Foundation, 1987
Innovations in American Government, 1986-1996, Ford Foundation, 1996
Achieving Excellence, Building Trust, Ford Foundation, 1997
"Government That Works," *Governing,* October 1988
"The Innovators Revisited," *Governing,* October 1989
"Innovators: The Year's Best," *Governing,* October 1990
"The Mysteries of Innovative Government," *Governing,* October 1991
"Renewing Government," "The Best of '92," *Governing,* October 1992
"The Best of the Best," "More Programs that Work," "Masters of Public Innovation," *Governing,* November 1993
"The Best of the Best," "More Programs that Work," *Governing,* October 1994
"The Innovators, 1995," "More Programs that Work," *Governing,* October 1995
"So Long Civil Service," *Governing,* August 1997
"Innovations 98; Achieving Excellence, Building Trust," *Governing* special section, December 1998
"Innovations in American Government 1999," *Governing* special section, December 1999
"Innovations in American Government; Creative Solutions to Public Concerns," *Governing* special section, December 2000
"Politics of Impatience," *Governing,* April 2001

Kennedy School of Government Case Studies:

"Finding Black Parents: One Church, One Child," 1988; "'Integration Incentives' in Suburban Cleveland," 1989; "The Electronic Benefits System in Ramsey County, Minnesota," 1991; "The Ladder and the Scale: Commitment and Accountability at Project Match," 1992; "Community Voice Mail for the "Phoneless": Starting Up in Seattle and Minnesota, 1993; "Preventing Pollution in Massachusetts: The Blackstone Project," 1993; "A Community Responds: Boston Confronts an Upsurge of Youth Violence," 1998

Books:

Ammons, David N., ed. *Accountability for Performance: Measurement and Monitoring in Local Government.* International City/County Management Association, 1995.

Borins, Sandford. *Innovating With Integrity: How Local Heroes Are Transforming American Government.* Georgetown University Press, 1998.

Dilulio, John J., Jr., ed. *Deregulating the Public Service: Can Government Be Improved?* Brookings Institution Press, 1994.

Eggers, William D. and John O'Leary, eds. *Revolution at the Roots: Making Our Government Smaller, Better, and Closer to Home.* Free Press, 1995.

Kettl, Donald F. *The Global Public Management Revolution: A Report on the Transformation of Governance.* Brookings Institution Press, 2000.

Kettl, Donald F. and John J. Dilulio, Jr., eds. *Inside the Reinvention Machine: Appraising Governmental Reform.* Brookings Institution Press, 1995.

Koehler, Jerry W. and Joseph Pankowski. *Continual Improvement in Government: Tools and Methods.* St. Lucie Press, 1996.

Osborne, David and Ted Gaebler. *Reinventing Government: How the Entrepreneurial Spirit is Transforming the Public Sector From Schoolhouse to Statehouse, City Hall to the Pentagon.* Addison Wesley, 1992.

Osborne, David and Peter Plastrik. *The Reinventor's Fieldbook: Tools for Transforming Your Government.* Jossey-Bass, 2000.

Thompson, Frank J., ed. *Revitalizing State and Local Public Service: Strengthening Performance, Accountability, and Citizen Confidence.* Jossey-Bass, 1993.

Walters, Jonathan. *Measuring Up: Governing's Guide to Performance Measurement for Geniuses and Other Public Managers.* Governing Books, 1998.

Yankelovich, David. *Coming To Public Judgment: Making Democracy Work in a Complex World.* Syracuse University Press, 1991.

CHAPTER THREE

The Challenge of Innovating in Government

Sandford Borins
Professor of Public Management
University of Toronto

This report was originally published in February 2001, revised December 2001.

Introduction: The Case for Change[1]

With the rapid development of information technology driving one of the strongest periods of economic growth in American history, it is not surprising that management practitioners and scholars have become very interested in innovation. In recent years, gurus such as Rosabeth Kanter and Tom Peters have written on the subject, while the latest in a long line of best-sellers about business innovation is Gary Hamel's *Leading the Revolution* (2000).

Interest in public sector innovation has also grown substantially in the last 15 years. The origins of this trend are very different, however, with the launch of major public management innovation awards by a number of non-governmental organizations being the important catalyst. These awards shared two key objectives: countering media criticism of and political hostility to the public service and encouraging the development and dissemination of innovations within the public sector. The best known award in the United States is the Ford Foundation's Innovations in American Government program, administered by Harvard University's Kennedy School of Government (Ford-KSG awards). It was initiated in 1986 for state and local governments, and included the federal government for the first time in 1995.

What follows is a set of recommendations for aspiring public management innovators, practical advice for practitioners based on extensive research regarding the best applications in both the Ford-KSG awards and a major award program for countries in the Commonwealth. We'll consider the implications of rigorous statistical analysis and look in detail at a range of exemplary international cases. While this body of research focuses on individual initiatives, it also reveals a number of organizations producing a steady stream of innovations. How did they do it? We'll analyze their key features to define the characteristics of an innovative public sector organization.

We begin by clarifying our central term. Academic literature on innovation has traditionally distinguished between invention, the creation of a new idea, and innovation, the adoption of an existing idea by an organization. Strictly speaking, an invention would be patentable whereas an innovation would not. Increasingly, both popular and academic usage elides the distinction between the two terms. In a business context, it is not uncommon for one firm to modify another's invention or to come to market later with a more user-friendly product. The follower may even become more popular than the leader: VHS has long since pushed Beta out of the market. Is the more successful follower, then, an invention or an innovation? More and more, the term "innovation" is being used to refer to *all* creative activity undertaken within organizations.

How do the public and private sectors compare in their attitudes toward creativity? In many countries government and business are working together to build institutions that encourage private sector innovation, especially in

areas like information technology. Mechanisms to protect intellectual property rights such as patents, copyrights, and the registration of web addresses
are designed to enable innovative firms and individuals to profit from their
creativity. Venture capital provides a dynamic and readily available source of
funding to seed innovative initiatives, while compensation through share
ownership enables startup firms, their investors, their employees, and,
increasingly, their suppliers to reap large financial rewards from this activity.

Contrast this with the traditional situation in the public sector. Innovations
developed by public servants in the employ of government are generally
government property. Public sector organizations are funded by legislative
appropriations; there are no venture capitalists to seed public management
innovations. There is no share ownership in the public sector, and public
servants are paid fixed salaries, with bonuses that, at best, are minuscule in
comparison to those in the private sector. In other words, the rewards for
successful innovations in the public sector are meager.

On the other hand, the consequences of unsuccessful innovation are
grave. The media and opposition parties are always eager to expose public
sector failures and pillory the public servants involved, with potentially disastrous effects on their careers. Additionally, the stringent central agency
controls that governments put in place to minimize corruption and ensure
due process also serve to constrain the innovativeness of public servants.
Taken together, these asymmetric incentives and external constraints make
the public sector a far less fertile ground for innovation than the private.
And they further compound the problem by leading to adverse selection—
that is, to innovative individuals rejecting careers in the public sector pre-
cisely because of its hostility to change.

Jones and Thompson (1999) make a similar point applying Peter Senge's
(1990) model of the learning organization to government and showing that
government is a flawed learning organization. Extensive and inflexible rules
and regulations, an unwillingness to empower employees, complicated and
rigid pay and classification systems, and a distaste for risk taking all undermine public servants' initiative and innovativeness.

In all likelihood, we as a society do not want a public sector that is as
unrelentingly innovative as the private sector, nor one that displays the
volatility of an Internet startup. Yet it is equally likely that we do want the
public sector to be more innovative than it traditionally has been. There are
change factors affecting organizations everywhere—advances in information
technology, changes in the nature and preferences of the workforce, more
demanding customers, and increased global competition—and citizens
expect a public sector that can transform itself in response. The question is,
how can the public sector be made to do so?

I answer that question first by discussing some results of my research
about individual public management innovations, in particular the charac-

teristics of successful innovations and the process by which they were implemented. This information will improve the chances that initiatives will succeed. I then turn from individual innovations to consider how public sector organizations can be induced to deliver more such innovations.

Finding the Best: A Note on Methodology

How were the research results on innovations generated? A brief outline of methodology will explain. Three award programs for public management innovation were used as the source for large research samples that were then subjected to coding and quantitative analysis, described in more detail in Appendix II. Do these samples represent the best innovations? Encompassing awards in the U.S. (Ford-KSG awards), Canada (Institute of Public Administration of Canada, or IPAC, awards), and the countries of the Commonwealth (Commonwealth Association for Public Administration and Management, or CAPAM, awards), the source programs are all well-known in their respective jurisdictions. They are defined broadly and encourage applications from all policy areas. Expert panels judge on the basis of novelty, impact, and replication or replicability.

The Ford-KSG awards yield the most varied sources of information, including initial questionnaires, a more detailed semifinalist questionnaire, a site visit report by an expert, and an interview. A questionnaire virtually identical to the semifinalist version was sent to applicants to both the CAPAM and IPAC awards programs. To avoid overweighting Canadian responses in the Commonwealth sample, this study uses the statistical results of the Ford-KSG and CAPAM samples only. It quotes completed questionnaires and, for the U.S. sample, expert evaluations of the finalists.

Studies of innovation in both the public and private sectors have generally relied on individual or small sample case studies, or small samples of innovations in a particular region or a specific policy area. In contrast, the research cited in this study uses large samples, many regions of the world, and many policy areas. It is truly representative of the best public management innovations.

Five Innovation Building Blocks

All the applicants in our samples were asked to define what was innovative or distinctive about their initiative. Their responses were varied and multiple, frequently identifying more than one key feature. Quantitative analysis of these responses reveals five building blocks of innovation, proven tools for change. Table 3.1 presents the characteristics of the innovations as identified by the applicants. The table entries indicate the percentage of the sample displaying a given characteristic in their program. Where responses are closely related, the percentage of the sample displaying one or more related responses (e.g., total systems approach) is provided. Five characteristics stand out as appearing most frequently in the U.S. and both CAPAM samples:

- the use of a systems approach, appearing in approximately 70 percent of the samples in advanced and 60 percent of the sample in developing countries
- the use of new technology, usually new information technology, appearing in between 29 and 57 percent of the samples
- process improvement, appearing in between 35 and 66 percent of the samples
- the involvement of organizations or individuals outside the public sector to achieve public purposes, appearing in approximately 30 percent of the samples
- the empowerment of communities, citizens, or staff, appearing in between 14 and 30 percent of the samples

Building Block One: The Use of a Systems Approach

The systems approach theme became apparent in my original study (Borins 1998, 19-22 and 26-29). I approached the data with my own classification scheme for the characteristics of the innovations, one component of which was partnerships. In coding the applicants' own testimony about what made their programs innovative, I noticed that, while some programs were formal partnerships, other applicants were often referring to a wider range of inter-organizational arrangements. Applicants, particularly in social service programs, often described their innovations as dealing with the whole person, rather than any one problem a person faced. Finally, a third group of applicants emphasized that their programs focused on developing a systemic analysis of how the problem they were attempting to solve interacted with other problems and programs. Thus, the overarching category of systems approach was introduced to encapsulate the three concepts applicants most often expressed. This finding is consistent with contemporary research and practice. For example, Bardach (1998) examined a sample of successful interagency collaborative programs to deduce smart practices in developing and maintaining such arrangements. The Blair government in the United Kingdom has been espousing "joined-up government," which refers to both integrated frontline service, often facilitated by information technology (IT), as well as interdepartmental policy development to respond to interrelated social problems.

Table 3.1: Characteristics of Innovations (percent)

Characteristic	U.S., 1990-98	Commonwealth, Advanced	Commonwealth, Developing
Systems analysis	39	25	37
Coordinates organizations	38	41	22
Multiple services	27	36	7
Total systems approach	**69**	**68**	**59**
Use of information technology	**29**	**57**	**37**
Faster process	32	59	33
Simpler process	7	25	11
Total process improvement	**35**	**66**	**37**
Uses incentives, not regulation	10	20	11
Uses private, voluntary sectors	21	16	22
Uses volunteers	7	4	7
Total non-gov't involvement	**30**	**29**	**33**
Empowerment	**28**	**14**	**30**
New management philosophy	15	18	30
Changes public attitudes	11	14	19
Total (percent)	217	266	245
N	321	56	27

Notes:

N = number of observations.

Table entries are the percentage of a given group displaying a particular characteristic. For example, the "39" in the first cell of the first column means that in 39 percent of the 321 innovations in the U.S. sample from 1990 to 1998, the innovators claimed that one of the characteristics of their program was that it was based on a systems analysis of a problem. Totals add to more than 100 percent because some innovations had several characteristics.

Total systems approach *= uses a systems analysis of a problem or coordinates organizations or provides multiple services to clients.*

Total process improvement *= faster process or simpler process*

Total non-governmental involvement *= uses incentives, not regulation or uses private or voluntary sectors or uses volunteers.*

Because a single response to the questionnaire might include several of the responses in a group, group totals are less than the arithmetic sum of the responses in the group (e.g., total systems approach is less than systems analysis + coordinates organizations + provides multiple services).

The terrorist attacks on the United States on September 11, 2001, also illustrate how a new priority requires collaboration among existing agencies and the creation of new mechanisms of coordination such as the Office of Homeland Security. Other governments are also developing integrated responses to terrorism.

This pattern is also evident in the literature on private sector innovation. In her review article, Rosabeth Kanter (1988, p. 171) concluded that one of the distinctive characteristics of private sector innovation is that

> the innovation process crosses boundaries. An innovation process is rarely if ever contained solely within one unit. First, there is evidence that many of the best ideas are interdisciplinary or interfunctional in origin.... Second, regardless of the origin of innovations, they inevitably send out ripples and reverberations to other organizational units, whose behavior may be required to change in the light of the needs of innovations, or whose cooperation is necessary if an innovation is to be fully developed or exploited.

Three international examples illustrate the varying levels of complexity and comprehensiveness of the samples' organizational partnerships and cooperative arrangements. The first example shows a program that crosses organizational boundaries, while the second and third illustrate more ambitious attempts to deliver a wide range of services through a single portal.

- South Africa's **Working for Water** program combines environmental protection with employment creation. The program's objective is to clear 25 million acres (over 8 percent of the country) that are covered by invasive non-native plants. The work is very labor-intensive, and has been used to create jobs for marginalized groups such as the rural poor, women, the disabled, youth, and ex-offenders. Managing the program requires a partnership among the Departments of Environmental Affairs, Agriculture and Land Affairs, and Water Affairs and Forestry, all responsible for the program's technical base; the Departments of Education and Welfare, responsible for program participants; and a variety of community organizations and entrepreneurs who serve as contractors. This program brings into contact departments that normally have few dealings with one another (South Africa Department of Water Affairs and Forestry, 2000). Working for Water won one of two silver awards in the 2000 CAPAM awards program.
- In April 1999, the government of Singapore launched **eCitizen** (www.ecitizen.gov.sg), its comprehensive website for the delivery of public services online. The site is organized around life events, rather than the current departmental structure. Thirty agencies are now offering a total of over 100 services through this site, which receives

100,000 visitors per month, approximately 10 percent of potential clientele. The United States Office of Intergovernmental Solutions has cited eCitizen as a leader in integrated service delivery, and eCitizen won one of three bronze awards in the 2000 CAPAM awards program (Infocomm Development Authority of Singapore, 2000).

- **Centrelink** is an agency of the Australian federal government with a mandate to provide a wide variety of services (income support, job training, pensions, student grants) on behalf of nine government departments. It serves 6 million of Australia's population of 19 million and pays A\$45 billion (US\$25 billion) in benefits. It has an operating budget of A\$1.6 billion (US\$.9 billion), and 24,000 staff in 400 locations. Establishing Centrelink was a key ministerial priority of the current government, which wanted to separate policy making from operations to allow the operational agency to focus on increasing efficiency and improving service delivery. Centrelink is funded on the basis of partnership agreements with its client departments, and its chief executive reports to a board of management with representatives of industry and of its two largest client departments (Centrelink, 1999). With a clear service delivery mandate, Centrelink has produced an efficiency dividend of approximately A\$100 million in 1998-99, while enhancing customer satisfaction. It is also in the process of implementing one-to-one service, with each customer assigned to a specific service officer (Centrelink, 2000). It was a finalist in both the 1998 and 2000 CAPAM awards program.

Centrelink and eCitizen present two very different starting points for large-scale service integration. The Australian government established an integrated service delivery organization by undertaking a major departmental reorganization. Centrelink's focus on service delivery and producing efficiency dividends drives it to make increasing use of information technology. On the other hand, Singapore began service integration by establishing a comprehensive website, and gave departments the option of buying in. A large number of departments have already done so. The open question is whether technology will then drive organizational structure and lead to reorganization.

Building Block Two: The Use of Information Technology

Information technology (IT) innovations appeared in the 1990 to 1994 U.S. and Canadian samples as ingenious applications devised by middle managers with technical backgrounds who saw opportunities of which politicians and agency heads were unaware. Consider an Australian example. A decade ago, the government of New South Wales set up a judicial commission to investigate inconsistencies in sentencing. As a result, a database operating on mini-computers was established, but it proved to be both cumbersome and unreliable. In late 1994, an information systems manager, an analyst, and a programmer at the judicial commission came up with the idea of moving the database to an intranet. Using a very early version of Netscape as their browser, they programmed the original system; its successor is widely used and has had a significant impact on the sentencing practices of Australian judges and magistrates (Judicial Commission of New South Wales, 2000).

Awareness of IT's potential has became more widespread in the last five years, especially at the senior level. This change likely explains why the U.S. sample, two-thirds of which consists of innovations from 1990 to 1994, contains a smaller percentage of innovations involving IT than the CAPAM sample, which was taken in 1998 and 2000. For example, the 2000 CAPAM sample included 13 responses from Singapore, almost all of which used IT as a major component.

The later technology-based innovations are large projects that entail extensive transformation of the manner in which agencies conduct their business. Some involve the creation of new information systems that have a powerful impact on how an organization does its work. Three of the winners of the 1996 Innovations in American Government Awards demonstrated this transformative effect.

- The **New York Police Department** began producing comprehensive crime statistics on a precinct-by-precinct basis in a timely manner. This geographic information system is used in regular meetings in which the department's senior managers ask precinct commanders to explain recent trends. Precinct commanders are being given increased autonomy to develop local solutions and are being held accountable for local results (New York Police Department, 1996).
- The **United States Department of Housing and Urban Development** consolidated and rationalized the management of a wide variety of community development management programs. Underlying this reform is the development of geographic information system (GIS) mapping software that enables the department and its clients to see the interaction of programs and projects locally, with the objective of improving planning and decision making (U.S. Department of Housing and Urban Development, Office of Community Planning and Development, 1996).
- The **Federal Emergency Management Agency**, as part of a management turnaround in the early 1990s, developed its Consequences Assessment Tool Set (CATS), a set of computer models and databases that can be used to predict the impact of disasters, determine the appropriate response needed, and set in motion the logistics of the response (Federal

Emergency Management Agency, 1996). The site visit report concluded that "one could almost say that CATS is to emergency management what radar is to flying" (Smith, 1996).

Websites did not feature as prominently in the samples of IT innovations as might have been expected. The explanation for their absence is simple. The spread of Internet technology virtually overnight in 1994 and 1995 meant that it became standard practice for departments to establish informational websites. The websites that did win awards were those that pushed forward the boundaries of integrated service delivery, such as Singapore's eCitizen, or those that reached out to communities in unique ways.

An example of the latter is Canada's SchoolNet (www.schoolnet.ca). This site provides content to accompany a joint federal-provincial initiative that connected all 16,500 Canadian schools to the Internet by 2000. SchoolNet is also used by educators and students throughout Canada to disseminate Internet-based educational resources they have developed (Industry Canada, Information Highway Applications Branch 1998). It was chosen as one of the two winners of the CAPAM bronze award in 1998. SchoolNet is supported by Industry Canada's Computers for Schools Program (www.schoolnet.ca/cfs-ope) that funds the refurbishing of surplus government and other computers for use in schools. The program has benefited from the contributions of numerous partners, such as the Telephone Pioneers, an organization of retired telephone company employees who do much of the work; Microsoft, which provides free software; Sears Canada, which solicits private sector donations of computers; and Canadian National, which does the shipping (Industry Canada, Computers for Schools Program, 2000).

Information technology projects in developing countries often involve "leapfrog" technologies, a signal example being Grameen Telecom, one of two bronze prize winners in the 1998 CAPAM awards. The Grameen Bank received a license from the government of Bangladesh to develop and operate a cellular telephone service in rural villages. Cellular telephones—operated on a pay-phone basis by local women—are provided for villages that previously had no telephone service at all. Establishing a cellular phone system is much less expensive than building land lines. It delivers numerous benefits such as information for farmers about market prices for their crops, contact with the outside world in the event of natural calamities such as floods, employment for the women operating the pay phone, and communication with relatives working overseas (Latif, 1999). Grameen Telecom may well be a model for the provision of wireless Internet access to villages in the developing world.

Information technology systems in government are large and expensive, and experience has shown that some systems have been costly and disastrous failures. As a consequence, we can expect to see meta-innovations, namely innovations in the management of the public sector's information technology. One early example is New York State's Center for Technology in Government, a research center based at the State University of New York at Albany, with a mandate to study what does and doesn't work and to develop low-cost prototypes of high-cost systems (State University of New York at Albany, 1995). It was a winner of the Innovations in American Government Awards in 1995.

Building Block Three: Process Improvement

The third characteristic frequently observed—process improvement— refers to innovations designed to make governmental processes faster, friendlier, or more accessible. These initiatives often involved applications of the Pareto rule (20 percent of the cases are responsible for 80 percent of the workload, and conversely) to separate the few complicated cases from the many uncomplicated ones; separation of high and low value users through user pay mechanisms such as electronic toll roads; voluntary compliance, especially in the regulation of business; and alternative dispute resolution. Voluntary compliance and alternative dispute resolution initiatives start with a recognition that judicial processes are expensive, adversarial, and time-consuming, and look for ways to streamline or circumvent them.

The Ford-KSG awards provide many examples of process improvements.

- **Applying the Pareto rule.** The Pension Benefit Guaranty Corporation has the mandate of insuring private pension plans. In allocating its limited staff resources, the corporation set a priority of monitoring most closely the largest underfunded pension plans—one percent of the plans in its pool that were responsible for 80 percent of its exposure. These plans received intensive monitoring, involving research on corporate performance and frequent contact with senior financial officers. Smaller and fully funded plans are monitored less frequently. This Early Warning Program won an Innovations in American Government Award in 1995 (Pension Benefit Guaranty Corporation, 1995; Donahue, 1999).

- **User pay mechanisms.** Information technology has made it possible to charge user fees with minimal transaction cost. An example is the use of electronic toll mechanisms (onboard transponders and electronic readers) for highways. Tolls enhance economic efficiency by allowing those users most willing to pay to reduce travel time, and provide revenues to cover the toll roads themselves and/or fund other improvements in the transportation system.

  California's State Route 91, a finalist in the 1997 awards, is a 10-mile, four-lane, electronic toll road built in the median of the Riverside Freeway in Orange County. It is restricted to vehicles using transponders (California Department of Transportation, Office of Public/Private

Partnerships, 1997). The Canadian province of Ontario built a technologically more sophisticated toll road, Highway 407, on the outskirts of Toronto. Unlike State Route 91, which runs for 10 miles and has entrances and exits only at the ends, Highway 407 is 40 miles long, with entrances and exits every mile or two. If cars do not have transponders, the license plates are video-imaged and the bill sent to the owner. Highway 407 was privatized in 1999.

- **Voluntary compliance.** The U.S. Department of Labor has too few inspectors to enforce minimum wage and labor standards legislation in the thousands of garment factories throughout the country. In the mid-'90s, it adopted a different strategy, namely pressuring the large retailers to ensure that their subcontractors were following the law. The department did this by calling retailers' attention to a clause of the Fair Labor Standards Act prohibiting interstate commerce in goods made in violation of labor laws, then signing agreements with retailers who were willing to monitor the wages and working conditions of their suppliers, and publicizing which retailers were in compliance. This campaign to eradicate sweatshops by using an understanding of the dynamics of the fashion industry to develop a voluntary compliance strategy won an Innovation in American Government Award in 1996 (U.S. Department of Labor, Wage and Hour Division, 1996; Donahue, 1999).

Building Block Four: The Involvement of the Private or Voluntary Sector

The fourth characteristic of the innovations—using the private or voluntary sectors to achieve public purposes—included initiatives opening up some public sector activities, such as municipal services or military supply, to private sector competition; partnerships entailing private sector delivery, particularly in the area of technology; the use of voluntary or non-governmental organizations for program delivery; and, occasionally, the involvement of individual volunteers in public sector programs. The following are a few among many possible examples:

- **Opening up the public sector to private sector competition.** As a result of shortcomings in the military supply system exposed during the Gulf War, the U.S. Department of Defense decided to give all branches of the military increased discretion over their purchasing decisions. The threat of private sector competition was taken seriously by the Defense Logistics Agency's Defense Supply Center, which previously was a monopoly provider of support services such as food, clothing, and medicine. As a result, the agency underwent a complete reinvention, with innovations being driven by frontline staff and middle managers.

Its initiatives included online ordering, faster delivery, purchasing in bulk, benchmarking private sector retailers, partnerships with the private sector, and elimination of rigid military specifications (Defense Logistics Agency, 1995; Donahue, 1999). This transformation won an Innovations in American Government award in 1995.

- **Partnerships involving private sector delivery.** The Province of Ontario has used private sector delivery extensively in the last decade. This is due in part to fiscal necessity (the province was running substantial deficits for most of the decade) and because many of its innovations involved leading-edge information technology. The technology for Highway 407 was supplied by a consortium of companies including Hughes Aerospace, which provided the transponder reading and video-imaging hardware; Bell Canada, which provided the billing software; and two transponder manufacturers. The province developed a system of electronic kiosks for automobile-related transactions such as renewing licenses and paying fines. The kiosks are provided and serviced by IBM, which is compensated by a $1 fee for every transaction. Ontario is also developing a leading-edge geographic information system for its land titles system in a joint venture between the government and several software companies (Ontario Public Service, Restructuring Secretariat, 1999). This package of innovations, under the rubric of "Ontario Delivers," won one of two CAPAM gold awards in 1998.

- **Involving volunteers.** As noted earlier, retired telephone company employees have played a major role in refurbishing computers for use in Canadian schools. One of the applications to the 2000 CAPAM awards receiving an honorable mention was Project Ilima, an initiative to repair schools in the Pietermaritzburg Region of the South African province of KwaZulu-Natal. Ilima is a Zulu term, referring to a traditional custom of voluntary community help for those in need. Because the government had no funding available for school repairs for at least three years, communities volunteered labor and materials to repair schools. The program also solicited private sector donations of materials in major cities, and the South African Air Force delivered the materials to remote schools (Province of KwaZulu-Natal, Pietermaritzburg Region, 2000).

Building Block Five: The Empowerment of Communities, Citizens, or Staff

Empowerment, the fifth of our tools for change, may take a number of forms. Initiatives directed at community groups or citizens involved consulting with them in policy making or inviting them to play a role in policy implementation. Staff empowerment involved encouraging frontline staff to take the initiative for change and showing greater tolerance for risk taking. The "new management philosophy" category in Table 3.1 encompasses initiatives such as participatory management, continuous improvement, and restructuring. It has some overlap with staff empowerment. We'll look more closely at this issue in our consideration of innovative public sector organizations.

The CAPAM awards demonstrated numerous community empowerment initiatives in developing countries. The Education Guarantee Scheme in the Indian state of Madhya Pradesh was the other gold award winner in 1998. The objective of the scheme is to provide schooling for children of socially underprivileged groups in one of India's poorest regions. As soon as a village demonstrates that it has a group of at least 25 children who do not have access to a school within one kilometer, the state government will provide a salary and training for a local teacher as well as educational materials. The village's responsibility is to provide a facility, mobilize t he children to attend school, and manage the school, for example, by establishing a school year consistent with local agricultural practices. This educational partnership between the state government and local communities rapidly expanded access to schooling in Madhya Pradesh, and became the model for a national program (Rajiv Gandhi Shiksha Mission, 1999). In April 2000, the program established a website called www.fundaschool.org, which enables people throughout the world to support one of the program's 26,000 schools for a year at a cost of US$400.

The initiators of the program were two younger officers in the elite Indian Administrative Service (IAS). Members of the IAS spend their first developmental assignment as senior administrators at the local level (Borins, 1999). A number of other applications from India were also initiated by IAS members in such positions, suggesting that these assignments give them the latitude to innovate.

These characteristics of public management innovation should be thought of as building blocks for public management innovators to use in designing their programs. Mathematically, there are a very large number of ways that the five building blocks and their subcomponents can be arranged. Many of the most interesting innovations came about when the originators were faced with a complicated problem and then fashioned a multi-faceted response.

A systems approach, new technology, process improvement, external involvement, and empowerment—these are the conceptual tools for innovation revealed by my large sample of international studies of successful public sector innovations. As tools, they are both flexible and scalable, transcending particular policy areas and even national public service structures and cultures. They offer public management innovators a framework for thinking about change, as well as a repertoire of techniques for effecting it, independent of the particular problem, challenge, or opportunity faced.

Winning Hearts and Minds: Implementation Techniques

Obstacles to Innovation

Designing an innovation is only the beginning. Securing its implementation can be no less challenging. In this section, we'll examine in detail the range of obstacles our sample of innovators encountered and the means they used to overcome them. The U.S. and CAPAM questionnaires also asked the innovators who their strongest supporters were, while the CAPAM questionnaire asked what they had learned from designing and/or implementing their program and what advice they would have for those who follow in their footsteps. We'll consider the implications of this data, too. Table 3.2 outlines the obstacles that were identified, and compares the relative frequency of occurrence for the total U.S. and total Commonwealth samples. The two Commonwealth sub-samples (especially the 27 cases in developing countries) were too small to be presented separately.

The obstacles reported were divided into three groups. The first, consisting of barriers arising primarily within the bureaucracy, included hostile or skeptical attitudes, turf fights, difficulty coordinating organizations, logistical problems, difficulty maintaining the enthusiasm of program staff, difficulty implementing a new technology, union opposition, middle management opposition, and public sector opposition to entrepreneurial action.

The second group identified obstacles arising in the political environment, for example, inadequate funding or other resources, legislative or regulatory constraints, and political opposition. One obstacle with both bureaucratic and political aspects is inadequate resources, which can result from funding decisions made at either the bureaucratic or political levels.

The third group addressed obstacles in the environment outside the public sector, such as public doubts about the effectiveness of the program, difficulty reaching the program's target group, opposition by affected private sector interests, public opposition, and opposition from private sector entities that, as a result of the innovation, would be forced to compete with the public sector.

The three groups of obstacles appear with similar frequencies in both the U.S. and Commonwealth samples. The largest number of obstacles arose *within* the public sector, reflecting the tendency of these innovations to change standard operating procedures, occupational patterns, and power structures. Many instances of obstructive attitudes were cited, particularly on the part of occupational or professional groups. Police officers were sometimes opposed to a community policing initiative because it required them to do what they considered to be "social work." Health

Table 3.2: Obstacles to Innovation

Obstacle	U.S. 1990-98, Occurrences	U.S., % of total	Commonwealth, Occurrences	Commonwealth, % of total
Bureaucratic attitudes	66	9.2	16	9.6
Turf fights	12	1.7	5	3.0
Other resistance	50	6.9	11	6.6
Total bureaucratic	**128**	**17.8**	**32**	**19.3**
Coordination problems	66	9.2	18	10.8
Logistics	66	9.2	24	14.5
Burnout	38	5.3	2	1.2
Implementing technology	39	5.4	15	9.0
Union opposition	13	1.8	5	3.0
Mid-mgt. opposition	11	1.5	4	2.4
Opposition to entrepreneurs	6	.8	4	2.4
Total Internal	**367**	**50.9**	**104**	**62.7**
Inadequate resources	113	15.7	32	19.2
Laws, regulations	48	6.7	7	4.2
Political opposition	21	2.9	6	3.6
Total Political	**182**	**25.2**	**45**	**27.1**
External doubts	70	9.7	9	5.4
Reaching target group	49	6.8	2	1.2
Affected interests	28	3.9	2	1.2
Public opposition	13	1.8	2	1.2
Private sector competition	12	1.7	2	1.2
Total External	**170**	**23.6**	**17**	**10.2**
Total	**721**	**100**	**166**	**100**

Note: Each occurrence is unique, so each subtotal is the sum of previous elements and the total percentage is 100. Total includes total internal, total political, and total external.

professionals opposed initiatives that employed community health workers or advocates in outreach programs. A voluntary action-learning based network of teachers in Singapore has been resisted by officers in the Ministry of Education, who consider it a challenge to their authority (Singapore Ministry of Education, 2000). To generalize, programs requiring professions normally having little contact to work together; programs requiring professions to do something not traditionally viewed as within their scope; and programs using volunteers, community workers, or para-professionals have often been opposed by professional groups (Borins 1998, 67 and 288). Surprisingly, given the traditional barriers to innovation in the public sector, the internal obstacle encountered least frequently was opposition to acting entrepreneurially, which constituted less than one percent of the occurrences in the U.S. sample and 2.4 percent of the occurrences in the Commonwealth sample.

Under political obstacles, the one most frequently appearing was lack of resources. This can be explained by the fact that many of the innovations studied were pilot programs that were looking for additional resources to increase their scale of operations. Legislative or regulatory constraints occurred when an innovator was hampered by existing legislation or regulations that had been enacted previously, for other reasons. The least frequently appearing political obstacle was opposition from elected politicians. The infrequency of political obstacles may mean that bureaucratic innovators are working far enough from the political level that their work largely escapes notice by politicians. Jerry Mechling, the director of the Strategic Computing Program at the Kennedy School of Government, recognized the significance of initiatives below the political level in a site visit report to a program involving optical imaging technology in the City of New York:

> Significant reforms in government often begin as 'middle out' initiatives—that is, as agenda items that are not at the very top in terms of public discussion and controversy, but ride just below and, due to the persistence of managerial leadership, create major benefits. The 'middle out' approach is not as threatening as more visible and aggressive reforms, but in some cases it can be extremely effective on a cumulative basis (Mechling, 1997).

On the other hand, if these innovations are noticeable at the political level, the innovators may understand what is and is not politically feasible and gauge their actions accordingly, forestalling political intervention or obstruction. The U.S. sample examined the frequency with which those political obstacles that were experienced were overcome, and found, encouragingly, that they were overcome approximately 70 percent of the time (Borins 1998, 67).

The third set of obstacles—external obstacles—includes difficulties reaching the program's target population, public doubts about a program, and more active public opposition. The U.S. sample showed that external doubts were overcome 90 percent of the time and public opposition approximately 60 percent of the time (Borins, 1998, 67). These numbers tell us something very important about the social context for public sector innovation. The infrequency of both political and public opposition—and the substantial frequency with which any that did arise was overcome—suggests that the public recognizes that the performance of the public sector can be enhanced and that policy outcomes in many areas can be improved. It further indicates that the public is not wedded to existing policies or procedures, and is receptive to innovation and change.

Overcoming Obstacles

Table 3.3 shows various tactics that were used to overcome the obstacles to innovation and the number of times each was cited for both the U.S. and Commonwealth samples. As was the case for the obstacles themselves, the tactics appear with similar frequencies in both samples. The tactics most commonly used could be described broadly as *persuasion*—showing the benefits of an innovation, establishing demonstration projects, and social marketing—and *accommodation*—consulting with affected parties, co-opting affected parties by involving them in the governance of the innovation, providing training for those whose work would be affected by the innovation, compensating losers, and making a program culturally or linguistically sensitive. The innovators took objections seriously, and attempted either to change the mind of opponents or skeptics, or to modify the innovation so that opponents or skeptics would be more comfortable with it.

It is instructive that the tactic used least frequently in both the U.S. and Commonwealth samples was something that might be considered a "power politics" approach—changing the manager responsible for program implementation. The innovators usually attempted to persuade or accommodate their opponents, rather than to appeal to the authority of superiors simply to stifle them. These successful change agents overwhelmingly employed consensus building rather than strong-arm tactics.

For both the U.S. and Commonwealth samples, obstacles identified were matched with the tactics reported for overcoming them. The results are presented in Table 3.4, which indicates up to five tactics used most frequently to respond to each obstacle. The Commonwealth results are not always presented because some obstacles appeared very infrequently. As in the previous two tables, the responses to each obstacle are similar in both samples. The most frequent responses to bureaucratic opposition in the U.S.

Table 3.3: Tactics to Overcome Obstacles to Innovation, Total Frequency Used

Tactic	U.S., number of cites	U.S., percent of total	Commonwealth, number of cites	Commonwealth, percent of total
Show benefits of program to opponents	73	9.6	34	16.8
Social marketing	52	6.8	4	2.0
Demonstration project	41	5.3	2	1.0
Total persuasion	**166**	**21.8**	**40**	**19.8**
Training affected parties	76	10.0	16	7.9
Consultation with affected parties	75	9.9	9	4.5
Co-optation (opponents become participants in program)	60	7.9	18	8.9
Program design made culturally or linguistically sensitive	16	2.1	1	.5
Compensation for losers	11	1.4	1	.5
Total accommodation	**238**	**31.3**	**45**	**22.3**
Finding additional resources	72	9.5	19	9.4
Persistence, effort	69	9.1	8	4.0
Logistical problems resolved	52	6.9	11	5.4
Other	36	4.7	44	21.8
Gaining political support, building alliances	36	4.7	3	1.5
Focus on most important aspects of innovation, have clear vision	27	3.6	5	2.5
Modify technology	26	3.4	20	10
Legislation or regulations changed	20	2.6	6	3.0
Provide recognition for program participants or supporters	9	1.2	0	0
Change managers responsible for program implementation	8	1.1	1	.5
Total	**759**	**100**	**202**	**100**

Note: Each occurrence is unique, so each subtotal is the sum of previous elements and the total percentage is 100.

Table 3.4: Tactics Most Frequently Used to Overcome Each Obstacle to Innovation

Obstacle	Sample (n)	Tactic 1 (%)	Tactic 2 (%)	Tactic 3 (%)	Tactic 4 (%)	Tactic 5 (%)
Total Bureaucratic	U.S. (128)	Consult, Co-opt (37)	Training (26)	Effort (24)	Show Benefits (21)	Demo. Project (15)
	CAPAM (32)	Consult, Co-opt (31)	Show Benefits (21)			
Coordination	U.S. (67)	Consult, Co-opt (52)	Focus (15)	Training (12)		
	CAPAM (18)	Consult, Co-opt (25)				
Technology	U.S. (39)	Modify (29)	Training (31)			
	CAPAM (15)	Modify (73)	Training (13)			
Inadequate Resources	U.S. (113)	Find Resources (44)				
	CAPAM (32)	Find Resources (44)				
Laws, Regs.	U.S. (48)	Change Laws (27)	Political Support (19)	Persistence (15)		
	CAPAM (7)	Change Laws (57)				
Political Opposition	U.S. (21)	Pol. Support (33)	Effort (24)	Show Benefits (19)	Demo. Project (14)	
	CAPAM (6)	Show Benefits (83)	Effort (33)			
External Doubts	U.S. (70)	Consult, Co-opt (40)	Show Benefits (29)	Marketing (21)	Demo. Project (16)	Effort (16)
Reaching Target Group	U.S. (49)	Mktg (37)	Training (19)	Effort (14)	Culturally Sensitive (12)	
Affected Interests	U.S. (28)	Show Benefits (36)	Consult, Co-opt (22)	Marketing (18)		
Public Opposition	U.S. (13)	Consult, Co-opt (31)	Demo. Project (17)	Marketing (9)	Political Support (9)	

Notes:
Obstacles are as listed in Table 3.2 and tactics are as listed in Table 3.3.
N indicates the number of occurrences of each obstacle in either the US or the CAPAM samples.
The five most frequently used tactics to overcome each obstacle are listed in declining order of frequency.
Percentages for each tactic indicate the percentage of the occurrences of each obstacle for which a given tactic was used.

sample were consultation or co-optation (in 37 percent of these 98 instances), provision of training (in 26 percent of these instances), persistence (24 percent), showing the benefits of the innovation (23 percent), and establishing a demonstration project (15 percent). Similarly, the most frequent responses in the Commonwealth sample were consultation or co-optation and a demonstration of the benefits of the innovation. When the obstacle was difficulty coordinating organizations, something often faced by systems approaches, the most frequent response for both the U.S. and Commonwealth samples was consultation or co-optation. Other frequent responses for the U.S. sample were focusing all parties' attention on the most important aspects of the innovation (15 percent) and providing training (12 percent). The most frequent responses to difficulty implementing a new technology for both samples were modifying the technology to make it more user-friendly and training for those who would be using it.

The most frequent response to legislative or regulatory constraints was an attempt to change the legislation or regulations to permit the innovation (27 percent in the U.S. and 57 percent in the Commonwealth sample). Frequent responses in the U.S. sample also included building political support for the innovation (19 percent) and persistence (15 percent). Political opposition was most frequently overcome in the U.S. sample by building political support for the innovation (33 percent), persistence (24 percent), demonstrating the innovation's benefits (19 percent), and the establishment of a demonstration project (14 percent). In the U.S. sample, public doubts were most frequently overcome by consultation or co-optation (40 percent), demonstrating the benefits of the program to opponents or skeptics (29 percent), social marketing (21 percent), establishing a demonstration project (16 percent), and persistence (16 percent).

Overall, the responses to the obstacles raised show that the innovators took objections seriously and attempted to meet objectors on their own terms. They did not necessarily view opposition to change as negative or an invitation to conflict. Rather, they interpreted resistance as a challenge to communicate their message more clearly and to improve the design of their programs. Within this generally constructive approach, the specific tactics employed were tailored to each obstacle.

Obtaining Support for Innovation

In addition to asking about obstacles, the questionnaire asked applicants who their strongest supporters were. Table 3.5 shows the results for the 1995–1998 U.S. sample, as well as the CAPAM sample. (It was not coded in the earlier U.S. sample.) The table shows supporters within the agency, elsewhere in the public sector, at the political level, and outside the public

Table 3.5: Supporters of Innovations (percent)

Type of Supporter	U.S., 1990-98	Commonwealth, Advanced	Commonwealth, Developing
Direct supervisor	20	7	0
Permanent agency head	27	25	22
Middle managers	23	25	19
Frontline workers	n.a.	25	15
Other upper management, board of directors	24	23	22
Total within agency	**62**	**63**	**41**
Public sector unions	15	11	4
Other public agencies and managers	44	45	41
Total other public sector	**53**	**52**	**44**
Political head of agency	23	7	7
Head of gov't. (president, PM)	40	4	4
Other individual politicians	14	5	15
Legislative body	36	2	15
Total political	**67**	**16**	**26**
Public interest group	37	20	30
Clients of agency	36	48	41
Business lobby	39	34	37
Media	5	0	0
General public	23	9	33
Total external to public sector	**78**	**73**	**74**
N	321	56	27

Notes:
N = number of observations.
Table entries are the percentage of a given group having a particular type of supporter.
Categories in bold represent the percentage of a given group displaying one or more of the previous characteristics (e.g., Total within agency = direct supervisor or permanent agency head or middle managers or frontline workers or other upper management or board of directors.)

sector. For each of these four groups, the table shows the percentage of the total number of applications receiving support from one or more of the parties in the group.

The table shows that the innovators received support from a wide variety of sources. In general, the U.S. and Commonwealth samples look similar, with a substantial percentage of innovators in all three indicating support within their agencies, among other agencies and their managers, and from public interest groups, agency clients, and business interests. The one sharp difference is that in the U.S. sample, two-thirds of the innovations had some support at the political level, while only 16 percent of the Commonwealth sample from advanced countries and 26 percent of the Commonwealth sample from developing countries did. In part this is the result of a higher proportion of innovations being introduced at the political level in the U.S. and at the agency head and management levels in the Commonwealth samples (as shown by Table 3.7 in the next section). A second explanation might be that American legislative bodies delegate less to the public service than is the case in Commonwealth countries. Consistently, the two sources least often cited as being among the strongest supporters were public sector unions and the media. The message these results carry for future public management innovators is to consider whose support they should seek as they attempt to overcome the anticipated obstacles.

Included in the Commonwealth survey was a final question asking innovators the most important lessons they had learned and seeking their advice for would be innovators. Table 3.6 shows the results of this question in terms of the number of times a certain piece of advice was cited. The advice dealing with planning an innovation emphasizes the importance of learning ("learn from other innovators" and "learn from your mistakes") and incorporates the tension between having a clear vision ("have a clear idea of the end product," "think strategically," and "make sure program objectives reflect the organization's objectives") and improvisation ("don't be afraid to change plans based on information gathered or in response to a changing environment"). The advice regarding implementation reflects the tension between being decisive and moving quickly on the one hand ("the project manager should be task-oriented," "have a champion, take ownership," "keep the implementation team small, with decision-making power," and "implement quickly to avoid losing focus"), and recognizing the need to build wide support ("involve the stakeholders" and "keep regular, ongoing communication") on the other. The advice about process also reflects the importance of staff level innovation ("allow staff freedom to innovate"), of persistence ("be dedicated and/or persistent"), of morale ("make the project exciting for staff") and of upper level support ("get support from senior management"). The advice includes references to the constraints of operating within the public sector ("documentation is tedious but essential" and

Table 3.6: Lessons Learned by Commonwealth Innovators

Lesson Learned	Cites
Make project exciting for staff	22
Promote program, ensure positive media coverage	21
Make sure program objectives reflect organization's objectives	17
Project manager should be task-oriented	12
Involve the stakeholders	11
Keep regular, ongoing communication	11
Get support from senior management	10
Have a clear idea of the end product	9
Allow staff freedom to innovate	9
Keep implementation team small, with decision-making power	9
Think strategically, consider wider implications	7
Have a champion, take ownership	7
Be dedicated and/or persistent	7
Documentation is tedious but essential	7
Develop adequate control mechanisms, support governance structure with agreements	6
Solicit regular feedback as a motivator, demonstrate early ongoing success	5
Implement quickly to avoid losing focus	5
Learn from your mistakes, don't be afraid to change plans based on information gathered or in response to a changing environment	5
Learn from other innovators	4
Ensure that you have the necessary resources	3

Note: These lessons were based on the 83 questionnaires received from innovators in Commonwealth countries.

"develop adequate control mechanisms"). Given the frequency that resource constraints come up, it is somewhat surprising to see that the least cited piece of advice was "ensure that you have the necessary resources." While Table 3.5 showed that the media were almost never cited as being among an innovation's strongest supporters, the innovators suggest that, once a program is in place, it is important to promote it and secure positive media attention.

Who Innovates? A Challenge to Received Wisdom

The recommendations for designing and implementing innovations that were presented in the previous sections did not discuss where in the organization innovations come from. This section takes up that question. The answer to this question is important, because it bears on the issue of how to design innovative public sector organizations.

Innovation in the public sector has been frequently assumed to come from the top. There are reasonable—even systemic—grounds for the belief. In both presidential and parliamentary democracies, voters elect politicians to enact policies. While in the United States a greater proportion of senior executive appointments are made on a political basis, in many parliamentary democracies the most senior appointments in the public service are made by the politicians. This would seem to place the responsibility—and motivation—for innovation outside the public service itself. (The rationale for the system, of course, is to make the bureaucracy indirectly responsive to the public through the politicians they elect.) In addition, the existence of stringent central agency controls—to minimize corruption and ensure due process—is seen to constrain any interest in innovation public servants might demonstrate. The media's interest in exposing public sector failures (management in a fishbowl) is yet another impediment to innovation. Therefore, career public servants may not be rewarded for successful innovation and will likely be punished for unsuccessful attempts. These asymmetric incentives may well lead to adverse selection, namely, the avoidance by innovative individuals of careers in the public service, further undermining the potential for creative change from within.

That is the received wisdom. The results of all the innovation awards examined tell a different story (see Table 3.7). In the U.S., approximately 50 percent of the innovations originate from middle managers or frontline staff, 25 percent from agency heads, 21 percent from politicians, 13 percent from interest groups, and 10 percent from individuals outside government. In the sample from the economically advanced countries of the Commonwealth, the proportion from middle managers or frontline staff (82 percent) and agency heads (39 percent) was higher, while that of politicians (11 percent), interest groups (2 percent), and individuals outside government (5 percent) was lower. In developing countries, the results are also similar. Since some respondents gave multiple answers, these numbers sum to more than 100 percent.

Both CAPAM samples and the 1995-98 U.S. data separated middle managers from frontline staff. The U.S. sample found that middle managers were involved in the initiation of 43 percent of the innovations, while front-

Table 3.7: Initiators of Innovations (percent)

Initiator	U.S., 1990-98	Commonwealth, Advanced	Commonwealth, Developing
Politician	21	11	15
Agency Head	25	39	37
Middle Manager	43*	75	44
Frontline staff	27*	39	7
Middle Manager or Frontline staff	**51**	**82**	**48**
Interest group	13	2	11
Citizen	7	0	11
Program Client	3	5	0
Other	6	9	11
Total (percent)	**126**	**148**	**133**
N	321	56	27

Notes:

N = number of innovations

* The asterisks indicate that the breakdown between innovations initiated by middle managers and those initiated by frontline staff for the U.S. data was based on the 104 cases from 1995 to 1998. In the 217 cases from 1990 to 1994, these groups were coded together.

line staff were involved in 27 percent, the same frequency as politicians (27 percent) and agency heads (28 percent). The CAPAM survey showed that in the economically advanced countries, middle managers were involved in initiating 75 percent of the innovations and frontline staff in 39 percent. In the developing countries, middle managers were involved in initiating 44 percent of the innovations, a figure comparable to the 43 percent in the U.S., but frontline workers initiated only 7 percent of the innovations. The latter figure is attributable to the disinclination of developing countries to empower their frontline staff.

While these results are at variance with the traditional understanding of public sector bureaucracy, they are consistent with the conclusions of other innovation scholars. Paul Light (1998, 45) studied 26 innovative nonprofit and small public sector organizations in Minnesota and observed that "almost all of them harvested ideas up and down the organization regardless of who had the idea." Hamel (2000) presented case studies showing that the inspiration for IBM's involvement with the Internet came from two middle managers, one a programmer and the other a marketer; that the idea for the development of Sony's PlayStation video game console came from a mid-level researcher; and that the impetus for Shell to become involved in the production of renewable energy came from a mid-level planner. Peters and Waterman (1982) pointed to innovations undertaken by frontline staff, some of whom were mavericks working at "skunk works" far from central offices, often operating without a clear mandate from above and using bootlegged resources.

Hamel provides two explanations why innovations are not initiated at the top of corporate pyramids: the long years of experience predisposing those at the top to be emotionally invested in the past, and the absence of diverse points of view at the top. Given that political constituencies differ greatly in their socioeconomic characteristics and that parties of differing ideologies generally alternate power, we would expect politicians to display more diversity than senior managers in the private sector. The problem is that elected officials and political appointees often lack sufficiently detailed knowledge of their area of responsibility to innovate. On the other hand, if a public service consists of careerists right up to the top, as is the case in most parliamentary democracies, it may have the same problem Hamel finds in the private sector.

In both public and private sector organizations, the lower and middle levels contain many younger people who are close to the cutting-edge thinking they encountered in universities. They are also close to day-to-day operations and therefore in a position to apply what they have learned in an innovative way. In addition, at a time when a great deal of innovation is based on the application of new information technology, it is usually younger people who are most comfortable with it.

This finding—that innovative ideas emerge from all levels of the organization and they may be least likely to flow from the conventionally assumed sources—has important implications. If innovative ideas can come from anywhere in an organization, rather than a senior elite, then organizations will be most innovative if they can stimulate innovation throughout. This thinking is similar to that espoused by the total quality management (TQM) movement, which asserts that ensuring quality is the responsibility of everyone in a company, regardless of their position or level of formal education.

Much of the management literature on leadership deals with the exploits of those who are at the top of organizations. The research I have been conducting has demonstrated many instances of leadership by innovative public servants in middle management and on the front lines. A few examples:

- **Parks Canada's** accessibility program for seniors and people with disabilities was initiated by Robert Fern, a public servant who suffered from diabetes-related visual impairment. He moved from the field to a line position in the head office in Ottawa because of his disability. Once there, he began developing low-budget pilot programs for people with disabilities; among other initiatives, Fern taught a course at the University of Waterloo School of Architecture in which students developed designs to make the nearby birthplace of former Prime Minister Mackenzie King wheelchair accessible. The Canadian Parks Association, a non-governmental organization (NGO), took the best student design and completed the project. Fern convinced both his assistant deputy minister and Parks Canada field staff that enhancing accessibility was both desirable in itself and a good way to increase visits. When the Treasury Board—the Canadian equivalent of the Office of Management and Budget—established a program of funding pilot accessibility projects throughout government, Fern had built momentum for Parks Canada to take advantage of the program (Borins, 2000c).

- The **Texas Department of Human Services** established a Volunteer Interpretation Service to help clients with limited proficiency in English communicate with the department. The program relies on a network of volunteer telephone interpreters working from their own homes or offices. The program was developed by Sonya Meinert, a departmental caseworker, and was a finalist in the 1995 Ford-KSG awards. The application described Mrs. Meinert as "deeply empathetic with non-English-speaking people because she is a grandchild of immigrants from central Europe and witnessed the difficulties of non-English-speaking people in the U.S. in her own family." Meinert's region had a quality improvement committee with a mandate to reduce errors in eligibility determination, giving her initiative a supportive environment. The committee endorsed her proposal and she was given time to start the project. When its success was demonstrated, the position of program coordinator was created for her (Texas Department of Human Services, 1995). The site visit described her as "an organizational pro" who "has the energy of a missionary" and noted that "in the short time [the program] has existed, she has compiled excellent training materials, internal evaluation processes, and a widening base of community support." (Dunn, 1995).

- After completing a Ph.D. in 1994 in pediatric cardiology at the University of London, Dr. Victor Grech returned to Malta to practice. He established a computerized database for the entire congenital heart disease population in Malta, a total of 1,600 patients. This database was the first described in the medical literature as being used for the long-term treatment of such patients. Dr. Grech also uses the database for research, and has published prolifically in international journals. At the time of his application to the CAPAM award in 1998, the project had not been funded by his hospital or Malta's National Health Service. It came about solely because Dr. Grech spent his own money on hardware and software and his own energy on learning the necessary technology (Grech, 1999). Dr. Grech exemplifies the public management innovator who invests his own time and effort at the outset in the hope that, after the value of his concept has been proven, organizational support will be forthcoming. His application to the CAPAM award was an attempt to raise the profile of his work.

Supporting Innovation

The cases in the previous section showed the ingenuity and persistence of which frontline public servants are capable. The challenge for senior managers in the public sector is to provide incentives and support to call forth more of the innovation exemplified by Fern, Meinert, and Dr. Grech. This section starts with the premise that, rather than thinking that innovation is their responsibility alone, politicians and agency heads must encourage more innovation from the entire organization, particularly middle managers and frontline staff. What should they do to further that objective?

There has been substantial research on the characteristics of innovative organizations in the private sector. Unfortunately, that research has not been replicated in the public sector. For example, Light (1998, 212) looked for innovative public sector organizations in Minnesota, a state with a long tradition of effective government. He found 26 innovative public sector organizations, but this group consisted of 18 nonprofits and 8 small government agencies. He therefore observed that "although single acts of innovation occur in large government agencies every day, it is difficult to find many such agencies that could be described as innovating organizations. At least in Minnesota, the search for organizations that were large, governmental, and innovating produced an empty set." There will be large organizations in the public sector for the foreseeable future. The necessity is to find ways to make them more innovative.

The prescriptions that follow for making large public sector organizations more innovative are based on a number of sources: the literature about innovative private sector organizations, David Osborne and Peter Plastrik's (2000) recent fieldbook for government reinventors, Light's work on innovative nonprofits and small public sector organizations, and the handful of organizations that appear sufficiently often in the innovation awards to suggest that they have developed cultures supportive of individual innovations. Two examples of the latter are Ontario's Ministry of Consumer and Commercial Relations and the U.S. Department of Labor, in particular from 1993 to 1996, when Robert Reich was Secretary.

Support Comes from the Top

A number of innovations undertaken by the U.S. Department of Labor were recognized as finalists and winners of the Innovations in American Government Awards. These include the initiative to eradicate sweatshops by putting pressure on retailers, the Pension Benefit Guaranty Corporation's early warning program, and a program in the Occupational Safety and Health Administration to proactively identify workplace health hazards among large employers. In terms of the generic characteristics of innovations, these demonstrate process reengineering and alternative service delivery.

While middle managers and frontline staff initiated these innovations, Secretary of Labor Robert Reich played an important supportive role in a number of ways. First, he established the department's priorities, which included initiatives to improve wages and working conditions for America's lowest paid and most vulnerable workers. Second, he made a habit of consulting career civil servants, for example, in quarterly departmental town hall meetings. Third, he took every possible opportunity to recognize staff initiatives (Glynn, 1999). Forms of recognition included establishing departmental innovation awards, bringing his career public servants to meetings with political appointees, and inviting careerists whose ideas had been incorporated into legislation to White House signing ceremonies to meet the President (Reich, 1997). The roof of the Department's office building in Washington, D.C., is an ideal vantage point to watch the Fourth of July fireworks. Previous secretaries always invited political appointees and friends; Reich used these coveted invitations to reward innovative careerists.

The Defense Personnel Support Center in the U.S. Defense Logistics Agency, as discussed previously, has been energized by the threat of private sector competition. The site visit report eloquently described the role the center's top management played in supporting the reinvention efforts of middle managers. It dovetails with the discussion of the efforts of Secretary Reich at the departmental level.

> Above all, these mid-level innovators were vitally reinforced, at critical points, by support from top management. Top managers during these years pushed the envelope of what laws and regulations would allow, helped articulate a common sense of mission, gave subordinates the scope to experiment with new ideas, helped draw the connections between similar innovations to create fruitful synergies, and funded the travel, technology, and training that was essential to the realization of the ideas (Zelikow, 1995).

Rewards and Awards for Innovation

A second way of supporting innovation is by rewarding developers of successful innovations. In the private sector, the rewards for successful innovators, in particular through stock options, have been enormous. Hamel (2000, 217) observes that the energy company Enron "has typically given entrepreneurs phantom equity in the new businesses they are helping to create." Such rewards are now a necessity in the private sector because innovative individuals who are not well rewarded will either start their own businesses or move to a competitor.

The public sector traditionally has not given large financial rewards to its innovative employees. The analogue here to stock options or phantom equity would be merit pay. While some governments have adopted merit pay, the amounts are very small in comparison to the private sector. Even if innovation is not rewarded with merit pay, it could still be recognized, for example, through awards programs. In a recent study of awards and recognition in Canadian governments, I found that the number of awards has been increasingly rapidly in the last decade (Borins, 2000b). These include the following types given specifically for innovation:

- departmental or government-wide achievement awards given to groups or individuals for a number of factors, one of which can be innovation
- innovation awards given by non-governmental organizations, such as the Ford-KSG and CAPAM awards discussed earlier
- gain-sharing awards, such as financial awards given to groups or individuals for implemented cost-saving ideas or royalties given to public servants for inventions made while working for the government

The financial implications of gain-sharing awards are not large. The largest awards for cost-saving ideas are one-time awards of several thousand dollars. The standard approach the government of Canada uses for dividing royalties is 65 percent to the department and 35 percent to the inventor. The largest royalty found was $70,000, providing an annual income stream of approximately $25,000 to the inventor. Internal awards for innovation or innovation awards given by NGOs are not financial, but rather involve public recognition. That said, there is a consensus in the private-sector literature that recognition is an effective motivator (Kanter, 1988, 183) and a similar belief in the effectiveness of recognition in the public sector.

Resources for Innovation

My original study measured the frequency with which the various obstacles to innovation had been overcome (Borins, 1998, 67). While the overall success rate was 58 percent, the obstacle that innovators overcame least frequently (at only 19 percent) was inadequate resources. Following that was difficulty maintaining enthusiasm, overcome 45 percent of the time. This suggests that finding resources for public sector innovation is indeed a pressing problem.

Traditionally, the public sector has funded innovation by using budgetary slack or cost savings due to enhanced efficiency. The difficulty with these sources of funding is that they are uncertain. Budgetary control agencies have a mandate to reduce budgetary slack and recapture cost savings. If the public sector wanted to emulate the private sector's ample supply of venture capital, it would create funds that could be used to support innovation. If line agencies were to attempt to do this, they would have to convince the budgetary control agency that this is an appropriate expenditure. An alternative approach would be for the budgetary control agency to create a central fund that could be used to support innovations throughout the government.

Osborne and Plastrik (2000) provide several examples of federal, municipal, and state governments that have created central innovation funds. In some cases, such as Philadelphia and Portland, Oregon, the fund loans money to line agencies with payback terms that show an expectation of significant savings (for example, double the amount borrowed in five years in Philadelphia or a three-year payback in Portland). In 1993, the Florida Legislature established a $12 million Innovation Investment Program that funded 38 out of 163 proposals and measured returns in terms of cost avoidance, productivity gains, or new revenues.

The government of Singapore recently created The Enterprise Challenge program. Modeled after Shell Oil's development of an internal capital market for innovative ideas, the Singapore government established a fund with a two-year operating budget of S$10 million (US $5.7 million) and a mandate to fund innovative proposals for public services coming either from within government or from outside. The program's secretariat is within the public service reform and planning unit in the Prime Minister's Office. Projects are chosen by a 15-member board that includes business entrepreneurs, area experts, and senior public servants. By mid-July 2000, 104 projects had been rejected, four had been accepted, and 38 were being nurtured or evaluated (Singapore Prime Minister's Office, Public Service Division, 2000). Along similar lines, the government of Canada's executive development agency, the Canadian Centre for Management Development, is proposing a learning innovation seed fund to sponsor new ideas for service delivery, application of technology, or policy development initiatives in the Canadian federal government (Government of Canada, 2000).

These funds appear to be supporting innovation on a project-by-project basis. One could question whether that is sufficient, and some agencies might establish units whose mandate is to bring about innovation. An example of this is the Technology Department in the U.S. Internal Revenue Service, which one Ford-KSG site visit report described as:

> [having] the reputation of being a 'skunk works' in which ideas could be developed and tested without serious repercussions for failure. This was possible because executive leadership within IRS recognized that such an environment must exist within the organization to bring about innovation. (Kelly, 1997)

Public sector financial management reforms being put in place in some jurisdictions create the possibility of enhanced internal funding for innovation. Organizations are being given discretion to charge user fees and keep some of the user fee revenue for their own purposes rather than returning it all to the treasury, to retain some of the cost savings they have achieved due to increased efficiency, and to carry forward unspent balances from one fiscal year to the next.

Diversity and Innovation

Kanter (1988) argues that kaleidoscopic thinking is a good metaphor for the creative process—namely, the ability to rearrange fragments into new patterns and envision a new reality in those patterns. Hamel (2000) refers to this rethinking and reinvention in a corporate context as business concept innovation. Kanter claims that individuals who are most likely to exercise creative thinking are those who have the best kaleidoscopic vision, that is, those who can bring the richest set of ideas to a given problem. Such breadth of vision can be institutionalized by organizational and job design. Individual jobs that are defined broadly, rather than narrowly, and that give people a mandate to develop a wide range of skills and experience to use in solving problems promote creativity. Workgroups that consist of people with a wide range of backgrounds bring a great diversity of perspectives to problem solving. These approaches are at variance with the traditional public sector bureaucracy, which is characterized by narrowly defined jobs and organizations dominated by individual professions.

Learning from the Outside

The Ontario Ministry of Consumer and Commercial Relations (MCCR) has a number of very traditional transactional responsibilities, such as vital statistics, business and personal property registration, and land titles, as well as some responsibilities for marketplace regulation. In the last decade, however, it has been extraordinarily innovative in its handling of these responsibilities through the early introduction of new information technology, the establishment of teams of multi-skilled workers, a partnership with the private sector to convert land title records to a geographic information system, and industry self-regulation. It was a key player in the "Ontario Delivers" package, mentioned earlier, that has won numerous innovation awards, including the CAPAM gold award in 1998.

What is this organization's secret? When the Ontario government was running large deficits early in the decade, MCCR, like other departments, was under fiscal pressure to increase user fees and reduce costs. MCCR's creative responses came from middle management. While it had changed ministers and deputy ministers quite frequently, it had a team of assistant deputy ministers who stayed in place. One of them, Art Daniels, was notably outward looking. He was aware of best practices in the private sector, and took the lead in introducing multi-skilled work teams and electronic data interchange. He was an enthusiastic proponent of recognition programs and had served as president of the Institute of Public Administration of Canada, an organization of academics and practitioners that since 1990 has been giving an annual public management innovation award. Daniels submitted his department's innovations for the IPAC award. (Kernaghan, Marson, and Borins, 2000, 31-5). Achieving external recognition from IPAC and other awards was an effective way of motivating further innovation.

The MCCR example illustrates organizational learning from the outside. More generally, we could ask how organizations do learn from the outside. Some ways would include wide reading by individual members of the organization, attendance at conferences and workshops, bringing in outside experts or facilitators, site visits, benchmarking, and participation in professional networks (Osborne and Plastrik, 2000). A public sector organization might take a neutral stance toward such learning, leaving it to the individual to undertake. Or it could go further by encouraging learning— for example, by providing support for individuals to attend conferences and workshops, and by establishing mechanisms, such as internal seminars, to share what has been learned.

Innovation Is Everyone's Responsibility

The implication of the finding that innovations frequently come from middle managers and frontline staff is that they should be involved in the innovative process. The data on individual innovations present many examples of this, two of which are particularly compelling. The Massachusetts Department of Environmental Protection won a Ford-KSG innovation award for pioneering cross-media environmental inspection. Rather than sending several inspectors to a factory to look separately at air, water, and soil pollution, it began to send teams of cross-trained inspectors to look at a factory's impact on the entire environment. The idea was developed by Manik Roy, a member of the head office staff and a doctoral student at the Kennedy School of Government (Borins, 1998, 197).

The origin of Canada's SchoolNet program is a similar story. In the early '90s, some middle managers in Industry Canada were thinking about how the federal government could gain a presence on the rapidly evolving Internet. An undergraduate student on a work term in the government proposed an interactive website to which primary and secondary school educators could send educational materials, and SchoolNet was launched. The initiative ultimately received enthusiastic political support at both the federal and provincial levels.

These two examples show how students brought leading-edge thinking to public sector organizations. Some corporations, recognizing that being abreast of information technology is essential to their survival and that the young are closest to and most comfortable with new technology, have put in place reverse mentoring programs, whereby younger staff members help senior executives learn to use information technology and increase their understanding of its potential. In recent years, many public sector organizations have found that, as a result of downsizing, their age profile is dominated by the middle-aged, with very few employees under the age of 30. This will make it difficult for them to benefit from younger thinking. Some more forward-looking governments, such as Canada and Ontario, have established internship programs to increase the supply of bright young staff.

Experimentation and Evaluation

The process of innovation often proceeds by trial and error. Organizations undertake experiments, put in place a process for evaluating the results, and, depending on those results, expand, modify, or scrap the innovation. Traditionally, the public sector has been unwilling to do this for fear of media and opposition criticism of failures. As a consequence, it has been highly risk-averse, attempting to avoid errors by avoiding innovation. Innovative organizations, however, do not avoid errors. Rather, they become very effective at quickly correcting and learning from them.

Despite this culture of timidity with its fear of public failure, there are possibilities for public sector experimentation and learning. As embodied in Justice Louis Brandeis's famous reference to the states as "laboratories of democracy," a decentralized system of government does permit a wide variety of approaches to a given problem, and learning happens because public servants compare the results of different approaches. Some systems of government may be more supportive of experimentation than others. In parliamentary systems with disciplined majorities, it is easy for the government of the day to use its majority to introduce a comprehensive new program on a national scale. In a legislature lacking party discipline, a majority must be fashioned for each piece of legislation. Each proposal will face firm proponents, equally firm opponents, and some legislators who are undecided. Those who are undecided could be brought to support the legislation if it is introduced on an experimental basis as a pilot program. Legislative necessity may well create fertile ground for experimentation and evaluation.

The reinvention labs created under the U.S. federal government's reinventing government initiative are, of course, an example of experimentation. They were established by individual departments, usually with a relaxation of departmental and central agency controls, and with the support of the office of Vice President Gore. The objective was to replicate successful experiments (Osborne and Plastrik, 2000).

The tactics of rewarding innovation and experimentation-with-evaluation can be linked together. On the one hand, innovation awards should be given for experiments that have achieved results such as improved performance and reduced cost. On the other hand, innovation is encouraged when the costs of failure to the innovator have been reduced. Osborne and Plastrik (2000) discuss a number of ways to do this, such as celebrating honorable failures and protecting employees from punishment if their innovations do not succeed. Together, these approaches would reverse the public sector's traditional asymmetric incentives.

Conclusions and Recommendations

This study has combined two different perspectives on public management innovation, that of the individual innovator and that of the organization. It has explored the individual perspective by using the rich body of information provided by applications to the Ford-KSG awards. The CAPAM awards provided comparative data about the economically advanced and developing nations of the Commonwealth. Though the Commonwealth sample sizes are relatively small, they do suggest substantial similarities in the characteristics of public management innovations and the innovative process in both the Commonwealth and the U.S., and in advanced and developing countries.

This study has examined the characteristics of these innovations, where obstacles have arisen and support has been found. Based on what was learned from these samples, we offer the following advice to individual innovators:

1. **In planning innovations, expect to use the five key building blocks most frequently observed in our samples: the use of a systems approach; the use of information technology; process improvement; private or voluntary sector involvement to achieve public purposes; and community, citizen, or staff empowerment.** These building blocks, in turn, have several components—for example, process improvement innovations include applications of the Pareto (80-20) rule, user pay mechanisms, voluntary compliance, and alternative dispute resolution. Often innovations apply a number of building blocks together in response to a complex problem. These building blocks are flexible and scalable, and transcend policy areas and national public services or cultures.

2. **When attempting to implement your innovation, anticipate a wide variety of obstacles.** Obstacles will arise most frequently within the bureaucracy, but some may come from the political level and others from the world outside. Finding the necessary resources is the most frequent individual problem and the one least frequently resolved. The obstacles identified generate questions innovators should ask regarding, among others, program cost and the availability of resources, the program's legal mandate, the capacity of organizations expected to deliver the program, the attitudes of occupational groups that will be involved in the program, the implications of using a new technology, opposition by central agencies, difficulties reaching the target group, and public skepticism or opposition.

3. **There are many possible responses to these obstacles.** The two you are most likely to use are, broadly defined, persuasion—showing the benefits of an innovation—and accommodation of the concerns of skeptics. Each of these, in turn, has a number of aspects: accommodation includes consulting with or co-opting affected parties, providing training, compensating losers, or making a program culturally sensitive. Based on the experience of our sample of innovators, expect to use strong-arm tactics (such as attempting to have opponents removed from their positions) least frequently. Successful innovators display an ability to take objections seriously and respond appropriately. Specific sets of tactics are most likely to correspond to each obstacle.

4. **There are a wide variety of potential supporters of innovation from one's own agency, other agencies, the political level, and the world outside, and successful innovators mobilize many of them.**

5. **When asked, successful innovators gave numerous pieces of advice to potential innovators.** The advice emphasized planning and improvisation, being decisive and being inclusive of all stakeholders, persistence, and promotion of the innovation.

The data from both the U.S. and Commonwealth innovation awards showed that frontline staff and middle managers are the most frequent initiators of public management innovation. This is a surprising result, given the traditional impediments to innovation emanating from that level in the public sector. It leads to the question of how public sector organizations can be made more supportive of such innovations. There does appear to be a consensus on the characteristics of innovative organizations, whether in the private or public sectors.

This last section of the study findings provides the following advice to managers who would like to enhance the level of innovation in their organization and who have the authority to do so.

1. **An innovative culture needs support from the top.** It can come in the form of establishing organizational priorities to guide innovation, recognition for innovators, protection of innovators from central agency constraints, and granting the latitude to experiment. In this approach, those at the top of organizations, rather than initiating innovations themselves, are encouraging innovations to bubble up through the organization.

2. **Rewards to innovative individuals may include financial compensation, for example, performance-related pay and gain-sharing.** When financial compensation is constrained, awards and recognition may serve as substitutes. Awards can include those given by the department or the entire government; innovation awards given by NGOs, such as the Ford-KSG and CAPAM awards; or impromptu recognition. An example of the latter is former Labor Secretary Robert Reich inviting public servants whose ideas were incorporated into legislation to meet the President at White House signing ceremonies.

3. **Individual innovators made clear that lack of resources for innovations was a serious constraint. One response to this is to establish a central innovation fund to support innovative ideas within the public sector.** Financial management reforms also create the possibility of enhanced internal funding for innovation within all agencies.

4. **Because innovation often depends on the ability to see things differently, diversity in terms of the backgrounds and ways of thinking of an organization's members will enhance its innovativeness.**

5. **Innovative organizations are effective at seeking out information from the outside, for example, by benchmarking, making site visits, and participating in professional networks.** They are also effective at sharing this information internally.

6. **Innovative organizations draw ideas from people at all levels.**

7. **Innovative organizations are effective at experimenting and evaluating their experiments.** They recognize that failures are possible, and have lowered the cost to their staff of honorable failures. They continue with their successes and discontinue their failures.

There are some bridges between the individual and organizational perspectives to innovation. Organizations with a culture of innovation generate numerous award applications, and glimpses of the culture can be seen as a setting for each application. Similarly, innovators who succeed despite an organizational culture that is either indifferent or hostile create the possibility of a cultural transformation.

Societies throughout the world are now convinced that innovation by the private sector is essential to strong economic performance. The harder challenge is to create a public sector that is more open to innovation than has been the case. This chapter has suggested ways to do this; it will have succeeded if it strengthens the resolve or informs the thinking of a few of the public sector's future innovators.

Appendix I:
Identifying Obstacles

Identifying these obstacles in detail enables us to formulate a list of questions for innovators to ask when designing an implementation strategy.

- How much will this program cost? Can the money be found through public sector appropriations? Will user fees be possible? Are private sector donations a possible funding source?
- Will the program require any changes in current regulations or laws? If so, what is the process involved and whose support will be required?
- Which organizations will be involved in delivering the program? If multiple organizations will be involved, what are their ongoing relationships? Are they organizations that rarely deal with one another, or do they have a history of rivalry, for example, turf battles? Will they fight for control of the program or fight to avoid involvement?
- What are the occupational groups that will be involved in delivering the program? How do they define their roles? What are the status relationships among the different occupations (e.g., professionals versus paraprofessionals)? Will cooperation of different organizational groups depend on understanding one another and/or on being able to do some aspects of each other's work?
- If the innovation involves the application of a new technology, will it encounter incompatible legacy systems being used by different organizational participants? Will the technology lead to job losses, especially in unionized positions? Will users of the new technology require special training?
- Who will be the key participants in delivering the innovation? Will they be expected to go beyond what is normally expected of them in their current positions? If so, how will they be motivated?
- Innovations sometimes require help from volunteers, especially if funding is limited. If volunteers are to be used, how will they be motivated to participate and how will their efforts be rewarded?
- Will the innovation create logistical problems, for example, scheduling conflicts among different participants?
- Will public sector unions oppose the innovation because it threatens job losses or affects the working conditions of union members?
- Will middle managers oppose the innovation because it devolves responsibility to frontline staff and weakens their supervisory authority?
- Will the innovation be opposed by central agencies, for example, because it reduces their control over financial or human resource decisions?

- Will the innovation face political opposition because it is inconsistent with some politicians' values? Will it face political opposition because it will reduce their ability to allocate resources to their constituents?
- Will there be difficulties in reaching the innovation's target group— for example, because they do not use the official language, because they have special needs, or because they are unreceptive to those normally mandated to deliver the service?
- Will there be public doubt or skepticism about whether the program can work?
- Will there be public opposition to the program, for example, an application of information technology that is considered by some to be an invasion of their privacy?
- Will the program face opposition from the public because it allows public servants to operate in ways or receive compensation (for example, performance-related pay) considered to be more appropriate to the private sector than the public sector?
- Will the program face opposition from private sector firms because it regulates their activities in ways that reduce their profitability or forces them to abandon a line of business?
- Will the program face opposition from private sector firms because it introduces public sector based competition?

This list of questions— formidable as it might seem—is not intended to dissuade potential public management innovators, but is designed to alert them to the challenges faced by those who have preceded them on the road to change. While all of these questions are worth asking, only certain obstacles may be encountered in a given case.

Appendix II:
Research Methodology

The Ford-KSG awards program actively solicits applications regarding innovations in all policy areas and receives about 1,500 per year. The initial application form asks about the characteristics of the program, in particular: how it is innovative; its beneficiaries and funding sources; verifiable evidence of the program's achievements; and its replicability. From the approximately 1,500 initial applications received each year, juries of academics and practitioners with expert knowledge of the relevant policy areas choose 75 semifinalists representing each policy area in the same proportion as in the 1,500 applications. The semifinalists then complete a more detailed questionnaire, including many questions about the process of conceptualizing and then implementing the innovation. Twenty-five finalists are chosen on the basis of expert evaluation of the detailed semifinalist questionnaire. Each finalist then hosts a site visit by an expert, who files a report. Using these reports and an interview as input, a national committee chooses 10 winners. The award was changed to include the federal government in 1995.

My initial study analyzed a large sample of 217 open-ended semifinalist questionnaires completed between 1990 and 1994 when the awards program was open only to state and local governments (Borins 1998). The open-ended questionnaires were coded and quantitative results were produced. A similar procedure was applied to a sample of 104 finalists from 1995 to 1998 that included 29 federal, 44 state, and 31 local applications. The distribution of responses in the second sample strongly correlated with the first (Borins 2000a). As a consequence, results are presented for these two samples—totaling 321 questionnaires—together.

The Commonwealth Association for Public Administration and Management international innovations award competition, held in 1998 and 2000, is open to public sector organizations throughout the Commonwealth. A questionnaire that is virtually identical to the Ford-KSG semifinalist questionnaire was sent to CAPAM applicants. The Commonwealth includes several economically advanced countries (Australia, Canada, New Zealand, Singapore, the UK) and many developing countries in the Caribbean, Africa, and Asia. This questionnaire yielded a total of 83 responses, 37 in 1998 and 46 in 2000. There were 56 responses from economically advanced countries, including Canada (20), Australia (15), Singapore (14), New Zealand (3), Malta (3), and the UK (1). There were 27 responses from developing countries, including India (8), Malaysia (6), South Africa (5), Jamaica (2), and individual responses from Bangladesh, Cyprus, Ghana, Iran, the Seychelles, and Zimbabwe. These questionnaires were coded in the same way as the Ford-KSG awards questionnaires.

A similar questionnaire was also sent to applicants to the Institute of Public Administration of Canada public management innovation awards, open to public sector organizations at all three levels of government in Canada, between 1990 and 1994. The distribution of responses in the 33 questionnaires received was shown to be strongly correlated with that of the 1990-94 U.S. study (Borins, 2000c). Because the CAPAM questionnaire already includes 20 responses from Canada, I decided not to include the earlier Canadian questionnaire, to avoid over-weighting Canadian responses in the Commonwealth sample. This study uses the statistical results of the U.S. and CAPAM samples and quotes completed questionnaires—and, for the U.S. sample, expert evaluations—of the finalists. The questions discussed in this study are as follows:

1. [Asked in 1990-94 U.S. sample]. What makes your program or policy initiative innovative? Compare it with other programs currently operating in your region, state, or nationally that address the same problem. How does your approach differ? [Asked in 1995-98 U.S. sample and both Common- wealth samples]. Describe your innovation; include the specific problem it addresses, and how it has changed previous practice. (See Table 3.1.)

2. Please describe the most significant obstacle(s) encountered thus far by your program or policy initiative. How did you deal with each of the obstacles? Which implementation obstacles or difficulties remain? (See Tables 3.2, 3.3, and 3.4.)

3. What individuals or organizations are the strongest supporters of the program or policy initiative and why? (See Table 3.5.)

4. [Asked in 1998 and 2000 Commonwealth samples]. What are the most important things you have learned from initiating and/or implementing this innovation? Is there any advice you would give to a would-be innova- tor? (See Table 3.6.)

5. What individuals or groups are considered the primary initiators of the program or policy initiative? Please specify their position or organiza- tional affiliation at the time they initiated the program or policy initiative. (See Table 3.7.)

Endnotes

1. The research assistance of Dean Hennessy, Carol Hobbs, Marianna Marysheva, Marina Ninkovic, Salim Rajwani, Don Redl, and David Wolf; the editorial assistance of Beth Herst; and the support of the Innovations in American Government Awards Program and the Commonwealth Association for Public Administration and Management International Innovations Award Programme are gratefully acknowledged.

Bibliography

Bardach, Eugene. 1998. *Managerial Craftsmanship: Getting Agencies to Work Together.* Washington, D.C.: Brookings.

Borins, Sandford. 1998. *Innovating with Integrity: How Local Heroes are Transforming American Government.* Washington, D.C.: Georgetown University Press.

_____. 1999. "Trends in training public managers: a report on a Commonwealth seminar," *International Public Management Journal,* 2, 2: 299-314.

_____. 2000a. "Loose cannons and rule breakers, or enterprising leaders? Some evidence about innovative public managers," *Public Administration Review,* November/December, 60, 6: 498-507.

_____. 2000b. "Public service award programs: an exploratory analysis," *Canadian Public Administration,* Fall, 43, 3: 321-42.

_____. 2000c. "What border? Public management innovation in the United States and Canada," *Journal of Policy Analysis and Management,* Winter, 19, 1: 46-74.

California Department of Transportation, Office of Public/Private Partnerships. 1997. "AB 680 Program." Semifinalist application to Innovations in American Government Awards Program.

Centrelink. 1999. "Implementation of the Australian Commonwealth Service Delivery Agency (Centrelink)." (July 20). Questionnaire submitted to the author. Unpublished.

_____. 2000. "One-to-One Service." (May 15). Questionnaire submitted to the author. Unpublished.

Defense Logistics Agency. 1995. "National Defense on the Offense." Semifinalist application to Innovations in American Government Awards Program.

Donahue, John. Ed. 1999. *Making Washington Work: Tales of Innovation in America's Federal Government.* Washington, D.C.: Brookings.

Dunn, Nancy. 1995. "Site visit report on Texas Department of Human Services, Volunteer Interpreter Service." (June 5). Cambridge, MA. Unpublished.

Federal Emergency Management Agency. 1996. "Consequences Assessment Tool Set and Operations Concept." Semifinalist application to Innovations in American Government Awards Program.

Glynn, Thomas. 1999. Interview, November 8.

Government of Canada. 2000. *A Public Service Learning Organization,* Ottawa.

Grech, Victor. 1999. "Maltese Paediatric Cardiology Database." (May 17). Questionnaire submitted to the author. Unpublished.

Hamel, Gary. 2000. *Leading the Revolution.* Boston: Harvard Business School Press.

Industry Canada, Information Highway Applications Branch. 1998. "Canada's SchoolNet." Application to CAPAM International Innovations Awards Programme. Unpublished.

Industry Canada, Computers for Schools Program. 2000. "Computers for Schools." (July 24). Questionnaire submitted to the author. Unpublished.

Infocomm Development Authority of Singapore. 2000. "eCitizen." (May 27). Questionnaire submitted to the author. Unpublished.

Jones, Lawrence R. and Thompson, Fred. 1999. *Public Management: Institutional Renewal for the Twenty-First Century.* Stamford, CT: JAI Press.

Judicial Commission of New South Wales. 2000. "Judicial Information Research System." (May 10). Questionnaire submitted to the author. Unpublished.

Kanter, Rosabeth. 1988. "When a thousand flowers bloom: structural, collective, and social conditions for innovation in organizations," *Research in Organizational Behavior* 10, 169-211.

Kelly, John. 1997. "Site visit report on IRS Telefile." (July 15). Scottsdale, AZ. Unpublished.

Kernaghan, K., Marson, B., and Borins, S. 2000. *The New Public Organization.* Toronto: Institute of Public Administration of Canada.

Latif, Shahed. 1999. "Information technology, poverty alleviation, and village phones in Bangladesh." Unpublished.

Light, Paul. 1998. *Sustaining Innovation: Creating Nonprofit and Government Organizations that Innovate Naturally.* San Francisco: Jossey Bass.

Mechling, Jerry. 1997. "Site visit report on City of New York, Controlling Claim Costs with Imaging." (July 24). Cambridge, MA. Unpublished.

New York Police Department. 1996. "Compstat: A Crime Reduction Management Tool." Semifinalist application to Innovations in American Government Awards Program.

Ontario Public Service, Restructuring Secretariat. 1999. "Ontario Delivers." (May 13). Questionnaire submitted to the author. Unpublished.

Osborne, D. and Plastrik, P. 2000. *The Reinventor's Fieldbook: Tools for Transforming Your Government.* Jossey-Bass, San Francisco.

Pension Benefit Guaranty Corporation. 1995. "Early Warning Program." Semifinalist application to Innovations in American Government Awards Program.

Peters, T. and Waterman, R. 1982. *In Search of Excellence: Lessons from America's Best-run Companies.* New York: Harper and Row.

Province of KwaZulu-Natal, Pietermaritzburg Region. 2000. "Project Ilima." (July 5). Questionnaire submitted to the author. Unpublished.

Reich, Robert. 1997. *Locked in the Cabinet.* New York: Knopf.

Senge, Peter. 1990. *The Fifth Discipline: The Art and Practice of the Learning Organization.* New York: Doubleday.

Singapore Ministry of Education. 2000. "Teachers' Network." (May 10). Questionnaire submitted to the author. Unpublished.

Singapore Prime Minister's Office, Public Service Division, 2000. "The Enterprise Challenge." (July 20). Questionnaire submitted to the author. Unpublished.

Smith, Dennis. 1996. "Site visit report on Consequences Assessment Tool Set and Operations Concept." (July 7). New York, NY. Unpublished.

South Africa Department of Water Affairs and Forestry. 2000. "The Working for Water Programme." (June 23). Questionnaire submitted to the author. Unpublished.

State University of New York at Albany. 1995. "Center for Technology in Government." Semifinalist application to Innovations in American Government Awards Program.

Texas Department of Human Services. 1995. "Volunteer Interpretation Service." Semifinalist application to Innovations in American Government Awards Program.

U.S. Department of Housing and Urban Development, Office of Community Planning and Development. 1996. "Consolidated Planning/ Community Connections." Semifinalist application to Innovations in American Government Awards Program.

U.S. Department of Labor, Wage and Hour Division. 1996. "Eradicating Sweatshops." Semifinalist application to Innovations in American Government Awards Program.

Zelikow, Philip. 1995. "Site Visit Report on National Defense on the Offense." Cambridge,MA. Unpublished.

CHAPTER FOUR

Creating a Culture of Innovation: 10 Lessons from America's Best Run City

Janet Vinzant Denhardt
Professor, School of Public Affairs
Arizona State University

Robert B. Denhardt
Professor, School of Public Affairs
Arizona State University

This report was originally published in January 2001.

Introduction

If you have lunch at Crazy Jim's Restaurant diagonally across the street from City Hall in Phoenix, don't be surprised if you overhear city employees at the next table talking about how to do their jobs better. As implausible as this may sound, that's what happened to us. In fact, it happened more than once. The employees we overheard, of course, work for a city that is consistently recognized as the best run in the country, known for both its innovative practices and standards of excellence. In 2000, Phoenix was the only city receiving an "A" grade from a yearlong study of local government performance conducted by the Government Performance Project at Syracuse University and *Governing* magazine. In fact, the director of that project, Pat Ingraham, called Phoenix "a veritable innovation machine."

The city's accomplishments have not only been lauded in the pages of *Governing*. In 1993, Phoenix won the Carl Bertelsmann Prize for being (along with Christchurch, New Zealand) one of the two best run city governments in the world. Individual departments within the city consistently receive awards, prizes, and professional recognition. Both employees and citizens give the city extraordinarily high marks as well. In independently conducted surveys, 97 percent of employees agreed or strongly agreed that "the city is a good place to work" and 89 percent of citizens reported that they were satisfied or very satisfied with the city's performance. The city's success seems nothing short of remarkable. How has the City of Phoenix achieved this level of accomplishment and what can we learn from its experience?

The Study

Under an earlier PricewaterhouseCoopers Endowment for The Business of Government grant, we investigated how city managers can effectively and responsibly lead change (Denhardt & Denhardt, 1999). We explored this question based on case studies of three city/county managers who are especially highly regarded for their efforts in leading change. We found that in addition to managing ongoing and varied organizational change processes, these managers were also quite attentive to building a culture of innovation over time. Once ideas such as involvement and communication, quality and innovation, collaboration and engagement became embedded in the culture of the organization, people throughout those jurisdictions began to look for ways to extend these values. They became attuned to new opportunities that they previously wouldn't have recognized. We concluded that making innovation the norm, rather than the exception, is essential to the process of institutionalizing change.

Given the record of success and achievement that the City of Phoenix has compiled, it seemed an ideal setting in which to study how public administrators can create and sustain a culture that supports ongoing innovation and change. Unlike our previous work that looked at the process of leading change in new settings from the city manager's perspective, in this study we wanted to take a broader look at cultural and organizational factors that have developed over a long period of time. We wanted to examine the factors that have contributed to and sustained Phoenix's "culture of innovation," including the ways in which administrators see their roles as innovators, how they think about and respond to risk and opportunity, and how they foster innovation and creativity in others.

We explored these issues by first interviewing Phoenix's city manager, Frank Fairbanks, talking primarily about his efforts to build a culture of change. We also gathered information from the city, including the background materials that were used in the Syracuse University study, as well as surveys, reports, flyers, bulletins, new employee packets, and information provided to citizens. We then conducted approximately 30 interviews, mostly with department heads, but also with staff to the manager, mayor, and council, and with city employees. After learning of the important contribution to building the culture of innovation in Phoenix of the previous city manager, Marvin Andrews, we interviewed him as well. We then had a second interview with the current city manager in which we asked him about his approach to change and innovation and about what advice he would give others involved in trying to bring about change in local government. Drawing on our interviews and other materials, we describe here 10 lessons about organizational culture and leadership that are key to understanding the Phoenix experience. These lessons deal with cultivating leadership, building trust, empowering workers, and other factors that have contributed to organizational success. Our intent is to provide information and insights for public administrators interested in building a culture of successful innovation and change in other jurisdictions.

However, the conversations we overheard in Crazy Jim's might best exemplify the underlying theme that links these lessons together. In Phoenix, the ongoing search for new and better ways to manage and govern have developed deep, sturdy roots. This search for innovation is not just something they do, it has become who they are. The values of this culture do not rest on the surface, they are not put on for show, they are not new, nor are they simply words or symbols. These cultural roots are woven in and around the entire foundation of the City of Phoenix, becoming an integral part of how the city and the people who work there define themselves and their public service work. The offshoots of those roots can be seen in the willingness to try new things, in the creativity and energy of the employees, and in the pride people take in their work—but the roots remain underneath, so much a part of the city's character that they are largely hidden and taken for granted. And they have taken some time to grow. In order to learn from the success of Phoenix, we have concentrated on understanding this cultural foundation or "root system" for innovation and change.

These lessons and recommendations paint an overwhelmingly, some might say unrealistically, positive picture of Phoenix city government. Indeed, people in city government in Phoenix will be the first to point out that things aren't perfect. As we will discuss more fully in the sections that follow, they still feel the need to be better, to meet new challenges, and to address the problems that remain. Although things may not be perfect in the city, our purpose is to focus on the attributes of the city's organizational culture that have contributed to the city's success. On balance, we believe that the following represents a realistic picture of the organizational culture of the City of Phoenix, a picture that warrants a careful look for the lessons it can teach us.

We begin by providing some background on the city, its history, and its characteristics. We then consider the factors that emerged as important to the development of a culture of innovation in Phoenix: trust, the management of risk and opportunity, perspectives on failure and learning, organizational conditions and commitments, structural innovations, the roles of managers, and other factors. We conclude with some practical recommendations for other managers interested in the lessons we have learned from talking to some of the key people who helped create a culture of innovation in America's best run city.

Background

The City of Phoenix is a relatively new city, though one with a somewhat checkered past. Phoenix is the capital city of Arizona, the last of the 48 contiguous states to join the union (1912). The city government was established in 1881, and for the next 67 years the city experimented with various types of mayoral, commission, and manager governments. There were 27 changes of mayoral administrations between the years 1881 to 1914, and there were 31 city managers in the 35 years of commission-manager government that followed. By the late 1940s, Phoenix was in serious trouble. High crime rates and corruption plagued the city. In fact, because of widespread prostitution and venereal disease, Phoenix was declared off-limits to servicemen during World War II (Hall, 1982).

Under these circumstances, a reform movement launched in the late 1940s had few problems finding support among the media and civic groups. In 1948, voters approved a council-manager form of government that, with variations, remains the model for Phoenix city government today. Following this model, the city became much more highly professionalized, and a more effective relationship between the city's political leaders and the city administration developed. What is most striking about Phoenix today, however, is its phenomenal growth. The population grew from 107,000 in 1950 to 669,000 in 1975. During the same time period, the size of the city went from 17.1 square miles to 276 square miles. The city has continued to grow, reaching its present population of 1.2 million spread over 470 square miles, with a population increase of approximately 30,000 new residents per year. In fact, from 1990 to 1998, Phoenix experienced a 21 percent increase in population, making it the fastest growing city of its size in the nation during that time period (Morrison Institute, 2000). During this time, however, beginning in the late 1980s and extending through the early 1990s, Phoenix experienced a severe recession, wiping out numerous banking institutions, sending the housing market into a tailspin, and leaving state government in disarray.

While the economy has recovered and is currently quite strong, Phoenix battles crime problems, traffic congestion, poor air quality, and the challenges of urban sprawl just like many other American cities of its size. Yet, according to the Government Performance Project, Phoenix handles these challenges better than other cities. While the study identified a few areas where the city could improve, such as in long-term workforce planning, cost accounting, and revenue estimation, the study published in *Governing* magazine (February 2000) was nothing short of glowing in its review of the Phoenix city government. In fact, Phoenix was the only city in the study to receive an average grade of "A" across the five categories of city management studied. For a complete accounting of the city's many accomplishments and activities, the full text of the report and award application submitted by Phoenix is available at http://www.governing.com/gpp/gp0phoe.htm. Selected excerpts from Phoenix's "A" report card include:

- **Financial Management:** Rigorous is the word for every aspect of Phoenix's financial management, from contingency planning to the monitoring of contracts. When the city council makes a decision, it has in front of it information on all financial ramifications. Any programmatic change—down to an expansion of swimming pool hours—includes an analysis of the fiscal impact, which the Budget and Research Department then reviews. The city publishes a summary of its proposed budget as a 16-page newspaper insert (including a Spanish version) and distributes it widely.
- **Human Resources:** The local government in Phoenix is strikingly rich in information about its workforce and customizes training programs in accordance with the data it collects. Computer systems enable the personnel department to keep a database of information about the

effectiveness of training, a real rarity in any American city.... Phoenix uses many approaches to reward employees who do superior work, including a very strong Employee Suggestion program. Personnel evaluations are well done.

- **Information Technology (IT):** Phoenix uses what it calls a "coordinated decentralized approach" to information management. This seems to work exceptionally well, combining maximum input from agencies with a powerful central control over the general direction the city is heading in. Departmental barriers and turf fights over IT have all but faded away in Phoenix. Managers utilize the technology continually to perform their tasks better, in citywide decision making as well as in specific agencies.

- **Capital Management:** Largely because of an extraordinary capital planning process—and a vigorous effort to educate citizens—19 out of Phoenix's last 20 bond proposals have won voter approval. Departments generate five- to seven-year capital needs studies, which are carefully reviewed to make sure they're consistent with citywide plans and financial feasibility. The city generates an enormous amount of data to inform the effort. Capital needs are estimated far enough in advance to keep fees and costs from rising precipitously. Phoenix's focus on maintaining its infrastructure is also very impressive. There is a five-year facilities management plan, which includes replacement schedules for major components of infrastructure.... City policy is to fully maintain facilities and defer no maintenance costs.

- **Managing for Results:** Overall goals in Phoenix are guided by vision statements and values statements. No. 1: to produce high customer satisfaction at the lowest possible cost and in a seamless fashion. Phoenix doesn't have gargantuan strategic planning documents—"credenza ware" in the words of [Budget] Director Ceil Pettle. It does an excellent job, however, of communicating strategic vision down the line. "You ask a garbage collector how he contributes to customer service, and he can tell you," says Pettle. Getting input from citizens is a high priority. Hundreds of volunteers sit on committees to keep leaders informed on the mood of the citizenry at a given moment. Perhaps most importantly, data is used consistently to improve services. When Phoenix discovered that citizens didn't want to speak with multiple employees to get answers to easy questions ... it issued a pamphlet for every field employee with information on common problems and how to respond to them (Barrett and Greene, 2000).

The city's organizational structure looks like many other American cities, with a few exceptions. For example, most cities the size of Phoenix have a strong mayor form of government rather than Phoenix's council-manager form. The city council is made up of eight members, elected by district in nonpartisan elections. Another difference worthy of note is the longevity of its leadership. The current mayor, Skip Rimsza, took office in 1994. The current city manager, Frank Fairbanks, was appointed by the council in 1990. The previous manager, Marvin Andrews, served the city from 1976 to 1990. Many other top managers have been with the city for long periods.

The current organizational chart places citizens at the top, followed by the mayor and city council and then the city manager. The assistant city manager is second in command and then there are six deputy city managers, reporting to the manager through the assistant city manager. Each of the deputies supervises five or six city departments. Every few years these departments are moved around somewhat, so that over time the deputies supervise a different mix of departments. There is also movement and rotation among departments. Otherwise, the structure is fairly typical of similar sized cities.

Lessons Learned

Rather than chronicling the many accomplishments and innovations of the City of Phoenix, we have concentrated on understanding the culture of innovation that has served as the foundation for the creation and implementation of these innovations. We have focused on culture for two reasons. First, the impressive array of innovations and improvements successfully implemented in Phoenix has already been documented, most recently in the findings of the Government Performance Project summarized earlier. Secondly, and most importantly, we argue that *how* Phoenix planned and implemented these changes holds the answer to understanding their ability to build a culture that embraces innovation much more so than *what* they *did*. Phoenix has clearly developed what Valle would call "an adaptive organizational culture" as its core competence (Valle, 1999, p. 245). By developing this core competency, it has equipped itself to manage and embrace change on an ongoing basis.

What do we mean by organizational culture? Organizational culture has been likened to an individual's personality, the unseen force that provides identity, meaning, direction, and the basis for action (Oden, 1997). Edgar Schein (1987), whose early work brought the cultural perspective forward as a significant alternative to the prevailing structural and systems views of organizations, distinguishes three levels of organizational culture. First, there are the observable artifacts and creations of the culture including the social and physical environment, language, and day-to-day operating procedures and routines. Second, there are the values of the organization, which, when they are accepted by the members, guide and motivate behavior to reflect those values. Third, there are basic underlying assumptions or patterns of belief that are taken for granted to the point that they are not even questioned. Schein argues that it is this last category that is the core definition of culture, "a pattern of basic assumptions—invented, discovered, or developed by a given group as it learns to cope with its problems ... that has worked well enough to be considered valid and, therefore, to be taught to new members as the correct way to perceive, think, and feel in relation to those problems" (Schein, 1987, p. 9). These core assumptions are developed and become institutionalized over a relatively long period of time—from five to 15 years or more, according to some estimates (Bluedorn and Lundgren, 1993). When cultural norms become firmly rooted, they can be quite resistant to change, literally forming the identity of the organization and setting the parameters for "how things are done around here."

In the sections that follow, we talk about 10 key lessons we learned from our research and observations about the culture of "how things are done" in municipal government in Phoenix and about how that culture was established over time. To the extent possible, we have expressed these lessons using the voices of the people who work there, to provide both the information they communicated as well as the flavor of their comments. Before presenting and explaining these lessons, however, we must emphasize that while these lessons are discussed separately, they are all part of a unified, consistent, mutually reinforcing whole. Part of the success of Phoenix is that all the pieces fit together—a subject we will return to in the conclusion of this report. The city's culture of innovation is not built on any one or two or three factors. All of the following lessons or perspectives fit together to reflect and embody a consistent set of organizational and individual values and perspectives on people and innovation. As City Manager Frank Fairbanks told us, Phoenix became a city that embraced change by "evolution." It's been building "layer upon layer over many years."

So, these lessons are neither sequential, in order of importance, nor separable. They represent interdependent characteristics of a unified foundation upon which Phoenix has built a record of success over time. In other words, this cultural foundation is far more than a statement of values or principles. Rather, it has come to define the professional identity of managers, the nature of their behavior, the character of city initiatives, and the quality of service provided. It has been developed piece by piece, consistently, and over a long period. Like the proverbial "Rome," the culture of innovation exemplified in Phoenix was not built in a day. But, from the experience and perspectives of the city's administrators and staff, we can learn a number of practical lessons on how to build a culture of innovation.

Figure 4.1: The Phoenix Management Team

1. Taking Pride

Taking pride in individual, departmental, and citywide accomplish-ments seems to be a key factor fueling continued innovation and improve-ment in the City of Phoenix. In fact, one of the things that becomes immediately apparent in conversations with managers is that they take great pride not only in their city and its accomplishments, but also in their departments and in their individual work. In discussing some of the key issues emphasized during his 1976-1990 term as city manager, Marvin Andrews recalled, "We put a lot of effort into building people's pride in their job and excellence and quality." Clearly this is an emphasis that has continued to produce a number of important and positive consequences.

The fact that Phoenix has competed for a number of awards is one indi-cator of the pride managers take in their city's accomplishments. Assistant City Manager Sheryl Sculley remarked, "We want people to say about Phoenix, 'We want to be just like them.'" Citywide honors and awards emphasize and underscore for the people who work for the city that their efforts have paid off. Competing for such awards has provided an opportunity for the city to evaluate its accomplishments and take stock of its successes. Winning has provided an external "pat on the back" that further reinforces the pride that people across the organization express, creating a cycle of pride and success. As with many of the lessons discussed in this report, efforts in this regard seem to build a momentum of their own. In this case, taking pride results in quality, quality results in accomplishment, accom-plishment results in recognition, which, in turn, increases pride.

There has been a conscious effort by the city administration to view these awards as a reflection of the accomplishments of the whole city, but particular emphasis is placed on the contributions of the front-line employ-ees. The idea is to emphasize that all departments and all employees play an important and vital role in the success of Phoenix. According to Finance Director Kevin Keogh, "There's a basic emphasis on excellence, on doing an excellent job and being the best you can be in your field. But there's probably an even larger emphasis on the city as a broader organization and supporting the objectives of that organization."

That does not mean that people don't take pride in their individual departments as well. As Personnel Director Lera Riley explained, "The goal for most department heads is to have the best department of that type any-where in the country or the world. That is their goal, and there is a great amount of pride in what they're doing. There is citywide pride, but there is also pride in that department." The departments also apply for and win awards, emphasizing their expertise and success within their own field. The desire to be the best, coupled with a belief that they can be creative and successful, underlies their efforts to innovate and achieve excellence. And,

Frank Fairbanks
City Manager

Frank Fairbanks was appointed city manager by the Phoenix City Council in April 1990. He is responsible to the mayor and city council for the day-to-day management and operation of the city. He works closely with the mayor and city council, helping them formulate objectives, policies and programs.

Fairbanks joined the city in 1972 and has served as a management assistant, executive assistant to the city manager and assistant city manager. During that time, he helped develop citizen involvement and participation programs, police and fire service improvements, employee productivity, organizational development, performance measurement and the use of advanced technology.

American City and County magazine selected Fairbanks as the "1994 Municipal Leader" of the year. That same year, *Governing* magazine named him the "Public Official of the Year." While Mr. Fairbanks has been city manager, Phoenix won an international competition to be named "Best Run City in the World" by the Bertelsmann Foundation in Germany.

Prior to working with the city, he worked as a Peace Corps volunteer in the Office of the President of Costa Rica. Fairbanks has a bachelor of science degree in finance from Loyola University in Los Angeles and a master's in business administration from the University of California Los Angeles.

He is chair of the Strategic Planning Committee of the International City/ County Management Association and is active in Public Technology Incorporated, an organization which develops technological solutions to urban problems. He is a Fellow of the National Academy of Public Administration.

indeed, many specific departments in Phoenix are considered the best in their field.

Deputy managers and department heads see it as their responsibility to know what is happening in other city organizations and in the field of public administration generally. Managers told us that this occurs because in some cases it makes far more sense to adapt an innovation tested in another jurisdiction than to start from "scratch." As Aviation Director David Krietor put it, "We're pretty good at identifying what's happening out in the world, both in the public and private sectors, and adapting them to work in Phoenix." Managers also use this information to gauge the performance of their own departments not only in reference to other departments in the city, but also to what similar departments in other cities are doing and how well they are doing it. "In our annual performance plan, we are not just comparing ourselves internally, but are also looking at how we rate in our field on a national basis. I think that expectation does keep you on your toes," said Human Services Director Gloria Hurtado. Similarly, Deputy City Manager Jacques Avent commented, "We do a lot of benchmarking against a group of selected cities, our peer cities. Our people are constantly looking at that peer group and measuring ourselves against them. We don't want to come up short."

Individual pride is also a hallmark of the organizational culture of the City of Phoenix. Director of Planning David Richert pointed out, "We are an organization of a lot of different people. Not one person should stand out in that, but you all should stand pretty tall. That's what makes any team work." The emphasis is on each individual taking pride in what they do and their contribution to the team. As the city's vision and values statement reads, "We each do all we can."

This high level of individual, departmental, and citywide pride creates an interesting dynamic among managers. "We work hard at being innovative," commented Deputy City Manager Marsha Wallace. "One of the things that helps us is a little internal competition. We have several departments that are literally the best in the country, if not the world. Everyone knows it, and everyone wants their department to reach up to that level." While this competition seems to be friendly, it does seem to create an expectation that all parts of the organization will strive to be the best. Jacques Avent told us, "We have excellence awards we give out every year. You don't want your department to come up short on excellence awards. How would that look? It's a whole culture where people want to be excellent."

2. Looking Ahead and Creating New Challenges

Although pride is a key element of the City of Phoenix culture, it is pride that can be seen as balanced with, or even in tension with, a value placed on creating new challenges. In other words, when management and employees in Phoenix recognize the extraordinary accomplishments of the people in the organization, there is great celebration and pride. But with that pride, the next question is always, "What can we do to be even better?" In other words, pride is used to propel the city forward to confront new challenges.

Part of this drive to always look forward can be seen as taking root in the 1970s, when former city manager Marvin Andrews began communicating to city employees the need for ongoing change and improvement. "Things were changing extremely rapidly and would change a lot more rapidly in the future. We needed to be ready to cope with that constantly changing situation. In fact, we needed not only to not be bothered by it but to use it. Changing constantly is a good way to get new ideas and get things

Sheryl L. Sculley
Assistant City Manager

Sheryl Sculley is the assistant city manager for the City of Phoenix, the number two position in Phoenix city government and a position she has held since May 1990. She was a deputy city manager for the City of Phoenix from January 1989 to May 1990, and served as Mayor Rimsza's chief of staff in 1995. Prior to joining the City of Phoenix management team in January 1989, Sculley was city manager of Kalamazoo, Michigan, and worked for the city a total of 15 years. Sculley has worked 26 years in city management.

Sculley earned a bachelor of science degree in journalism and political science from Ball State University and a master's degree in public administration from Western Michigan University. She also graduated from Harvard University's John F. Kennedy School of Government Program for Senior Executives in State and Local Government.

Sculley currently serves on the Greater Phoenix Economic Council Board of Directors, the Downtown Phoenix Partnership Board of Directors, the Governor's Diversity Council, and the Heard Museum Board of Trustees. She served on the Valley of the Sun United Way Board of Directors for six years and is a past president of the Arizona City/ County Management Association, having served on that board for four years. Sculley is a graduate of the Phoenix Valley Leadership Program Class XII and the National Leadership America Program founded by the National Women's Resource Foundation.

done." In short, success doesn't mean the work is completed. It means you move on to the next challenge.

The idea of always looking forward to the next challenge has become an important part of the organizational culture. For example, one of the concerns among the top executives in the City of Phoenix after winning the Bertelsmann award in 1993 was that winning the award would a create a feeling of complacency, that the city had accomplished all it could and all that was left was to simply continue being excellent. Managers in Phoenix explicitly said "no" to that idea. "We have tried to approach rewards as recognition of the great work the employees are doing and reinforce innovation by employees. But we also say we need to challenge ourselves. Things aren't perfect here. We need to use rewards to challenge ourselves." We have to ask ourselves, Frank Fairbanks said with a smile, "what do we need to do to really deserve this award?"

This attitude is echoed in the voices of top management. Deputy City Manager George Flores commented, "Even though we've hit this pinnacle of success, I think there's still so much more that we could be doing. And I also think that stating that is one of the reasons why we keep pushing ourselves." Sheryl Sculley expressed a similar sentiment when she said, "We very strongly feel that while it's an honor to receive these awards, that certainly does not mean we're a perfect organization. There are always areas that we're working on for improvement, to do things better and provide an even higher level of customer service."

Yet, the message is not a negative one that suggests that the organization is not good enough. Rather the focus is on the need to move in a positive direction, to continually innovate and improve to keep up with the challenges ahead. Human Services Department Director Gloria Hurtado expressed it this way: "The environment in which we live and work is constantly changing. That doesn't allow complacency to happen." This idea has taken a firm hold in the cultural roots of this city organization. In fact, at this point, the recognition of the need to push forward and keep improving is largely taken for granted. As one manager said, "In some places, just kind of staying even is part and parcel of what you do. Here it's always been a matter of improving, of doing things better. It's something that is rooted in the organization, and it's a part of the environment."

The people who work for the City of Phoenix report feeling invigorated by this expectation and challenge. Alan Brunacini, chief of one of the most outstanding fire departments in the country, commented, "People have asked me, 'How could you have stayed in one place for so long?' I say about every 90 days I have a new career because that's how much is changing in the process." Similarly, Tammy Perkins of the Neighborhood Services Department put it this way, "It keeps managers and staff members really fresh. I've been with the city for 18 years, but I haven't ever been in a place where I've been able to kick back and say 'Yeah, I've got this job down, I know this job, and I don't have to hustle anymore.'" In fact, this seems to be part of the reason that Phoenix has been able to retain the talent in its management team. Many of the managers we talked with have been in Phoenix for 15 to 20 years. Yet none reported being bored, stagnated, or unchallenged in their jobs. In fact, it is quite the contrary. What they communicate is a sense of excitement, energy, and a delight in facing the challenges ahead.

In Phoenix, managers are expected to be generalists with a sense of the "big picture" who can unleash the creative talents of employees. One of the things the city does to foster this attitude and avoid complacency is to move both programs and people around the city organization so that people can gain new perspectives and new experiences. As people move around, they raise new questions and consider new approaches. Mark Hughes, head of public information for the city, explained: "We have a team environment here. We push responsibility downward so that we really don't spend a lot of time telling people what to do around here. We kind of let them do their

Jacques Avent
Deputy City Manager

Jacques Avent has served as deputy city manager of Phoenix since November 1992. In that role he has had oversight responsibility for the Finance Department, Personnel Department, Police Department, Public Works Department, Housing Department, Human Services Department, and Law Department, and was responsible for developing a new department of Neighborhood Services. Through the Neighborhood Services Department, Avent has had primary responsibility for all redevelopment and neighborhood revitalization programs.

Avent joined the City of Phoenix staff in 1989 as executive assistant to the City Council and then served as executive assistant to the city manager from 1990 to 1992. Prior to that, he served as vice president for public finance at Security Pacific Merchant Bank in New York for two years. Avent also was on the staff of the National League of Cities for 13 years, the last nine as director of service programs. He also served on the staff of the National Association of Regional Councils, the Metropolitan Washington Council of Governments, and the National Urban Coalition.

He currently serves as a board member of the Valley of the Sun United Way, Neighborhood Housing Services of Phoenix, Phoenix Salvation Army, Arizona Senior Olympics, and Phoenix LISC.

He is a graduate of Howard University.

thing and then we talk about how they're doing. We're coaches more than anything." As generalists, managers are not necessarily expected to be subject matter experts in the areas they supervise. According to Lera Riley, "The organization puts stronger emphasis on the well-rounded manager as opposed to assuming, for example, that we need an engineer to manage engineers." Aviation Director Krietor agreed, "There's definitely a philosophy here that comes from the top that if you're a quality manager, you will have a commitment to the city and that you will understand the big picture, so you can manage different types of organizations." For example, the personnel director came most recently from the public works department and the director of aviation was formerly in economic development. The city engineer recently moved to become the development services director and an assistant director of water service became the city engineer.

This has been a very conscious strategy on the part of top management. Riley explained, "At some point in both Andrews' and Fairbanks' tenure as city manager, they very consciously did 'fruit basket turn over.' They said they wanted to reconfigure and combine things to challenge people to be good managers as opposed to being just technical experts who had risen to management in their particular areas." In general, she continued, "We encourage people to wander around the organization and get a different perspective." This has several consequences for the style of management demonstrated in the departments across the city. First, it makes it more likely that managers will rely on the expertise of their employees. Second, as already mentioned, it helps people gain an understanding of the whole city organization and organization-wide issues. Tammy Perkins observed that as generalists, the challenge becomes one of "knowing when you need to know how much about a particular technical area, being able to learn that technical area quickly, as the issues and the policy perspectives come and go. But I think that helps us keep a bigger picture." Third, it promotes a problem solving orientation based on a broader perspective than might have otherwise been the case. As Lera Riley explained, "It forces you to look at problems and solving them based on trying to take the fundamentals of what you were doing before and asking yourself, 'How is this like other things in the organization? How are these things connected?'"

Finally, promoting a generalist management role allows people to grow and develop within the organization and enhances interdepartmental cooperation. Marsha Wallace agreed: "It keeps you on your toes and it keeps you innovative, and it allows you to look at new ways of doing things instead of being in the same job for 10 or 20 years doing things the same old way. The other thing it helps with is interdepartmental cooperation, because you really don't want to do something that has an adverse effect on another department when you know that in two months you may have that department."

3. Building Relationships and Fostering Participation

A training handout from the Fire Department reads, "The most powerful, longest term, most enduring organizational element = relationships." This statement expresses another key aspect of the values which make up the organizational culture in the City of Phoenix: that building personal relationships characterized by open communication, collaboration, and mutual respect is an important part of what makes Phoenix successful.

Early in Marvin Andrews' tenure a decision was made to build and maintain stronger relationships among the people and organizations that were important to helping the city serve its citizens. Unquestionably, one of the most important of those relationships is between elected officials and city management. Up until that time, the practice had been to have all communications with the council go through the city manager's office. This had, on occasion, led to miscommunication and frustration on the part of

George W. Britton
Deputy City Manager

George Britton is the deputy city manager responsible for Development Services, Infill Housing, Information Technology and Telecommunications, Emergency Programs, Water Services and Water Strategy. During 1994, he served as chief of staff to Mayor Thelda Williams. Prior to this appointment, he was deputy city manager with responsibility for the Human Services, City Clerk, Housing, Equal Opportunity, Fire, Engineering and Architectural Services, and Street Transportation Departments, as well as Environmental Programs and the Education Office. He came to Phoenix in 1986 as water and environmental resources manager/deputy city manager.

Prior to joining the city, he served as executive assistant to Arizona Governor Bruce Babbitt from 1980 to early 1986. As executive assistant, Britton chaired the Governor's Cabinet, oversaw state agencies dealing with finance, transportation, natural resources, environment, capital development, and health. He served as interim director of the Department of Administration in 1982 and again in 1985. Britton served on Governor Rose Mofford's transition team.

Before joining the Governor's staff, he served as the director of municipal utilities and assistant to the city manager in the City of Scottsdale, Arizona. Britton served in the Air Force Reserve from 1970 to 1978.

Britton is a member of the Governor's Water Management Commission Arizona Water Resources Advisory Board, was an advisor to the National Performance Review's Federal-State-Local Team, past chair of the State Water Quality Advisory Council, and is Vice-Chair of the Arizona Town Hall. He chaired the U.S. Environmental Protection Agency's Local Government Advisory Committee and is a member of the University of Arizona's College of Business National Advisory Board. He is a recipient of the Arizona Superior Service Award from the American Society for Public Administration and the Hispanic Network Recognition for Leadership for the New Millennium.

He received his undergraduate degree from the University of Oregon, a master's in public administration from the University of Southern California, and completed the John F. Kennedy School of Government Senior Executives in State and Local Government Program at Harvard University.

elected officials. One of the first steps Andrews took upon assuming his post was to open up communication lines between elected officials and managers in city departments. He explained that the "department heads were all seasoned professionals so I thought, I'm going to open this up as long as they keep deputy managers informed of what is happening. It worked and that's the way we continued the whole time." Andrews also made some important structural changes that have continued to the present: "I put a deputy manager in the mayor's office to act as liaison, and also put a position in the council's office as a council's assistant. Those were tough positions, but it worked out very well." These individuals worked with the mayor and council, but also with the city manager and his staff, and they became the keys to maintaining open lines of communication and information between the two parts of city government. The current city manager still credits these positions as serving as an important link and channel of communication and cooperation.

In part building on these structural arrangements, positive relationships have been cultivated over time. Today, as Deputy City Manager Jack Tevlin mentioned, "There's a very open relationship between management and the political side of the city." This relationship goes beyond structural innovations that create formal lines of communication, however. Managers in the city have cultivated a professional and personal connection with the people in the offices of the mayor and council based on mutual respect and responsiveness. "There is a close personal bond between the mayor and council and the staff of the city. Historically, the mayor and council have had a great deal of respect for the staff and vice versa, and there's an equal level of responsiveness on both sides. We try to be responsive to them, and they, in turn, have been responsive and responsible when it comes to our suggestions."

The cultivation of other relationships has been important as well. Frank Fairbanks reported, "We work very hard to build good relationships with our unions. We have put a lot of effort in communicating with them and inviting them into decisions. There is almost no significant programmatic decisions we make that we wouldn't first go to the union and talk with them about what we want to do and ask their leadership to be involved in the process. We want their input." Further, he explained, "we also encourage them, if they think they see something wrong in the organization, to just call and tell us and give us a chance to work it out."

Inside the organization, communication and personal relationships are viewed as an absolutely essential element of organizational life. City Manager Fairbanks places a great premium on communicating with and knowing city employees: "It is very important that I get a chance to talk with employees and to communicate with them. They are where the action is." For this reason, he regularly meets and talks with employees, shares his ideas and listens to theirs. Communication and listening to employees is not considered the job of the city manager alone, however. The assumption among managers is that doing their jobs well requires the cultivation of relationships characterized by open communication and cooperation. This communication, it is assumed, is not a merely a matter of memos, bulletin board postings, and pronouncements. Communication occurs in the context of a

George Flores
Deputy City Manager

George Flores began his career with the City of Phoenix 28 years ago as a management aide intern in the city manager's office. Flores was promoted to the position of deputy city manager in September of 1998 and is currently responsible to the city manager for oversight and direction of the Arts Commission, City Clerk Department, Equal Opportunity Department, Human Services Department, and Goals Compliance & Disparity Programs. Flores provides lead management support to the City Council Family, Arts and Education Subcommittee and the Mayor's Heritage Commission, and is also a member of the City Manager's Residency Committee.

Prior to this appointment, Flores was the director of the Development Services Department for 11 years. This department is responsible for issuing building permits and inspecting all private development projects within Phoenix. In this capacity, he reorganized the city's development services from six departments into a single department in order to provide a more efficient and effective approval process.

Previously, Flores served as director of the Economic Development Department for nearly two years. During that time, he managed the redevelopment efforts of downtown as well as six neighborhood redevelopment areas. The Arizona Center, the Mercado, and the French Quarter were several of the downtown redevelopment projects which resulted from programs under Flores' leadership.

In the 1970s, Flores worked in management assistant positions in the City of Phoenix as well as the cities of Scottsdale and Glendale.

Flores is active in the community and belongs to many professional organizations. He is currently the Arizona City/County Management Association (ACMA) President-Elect and has served in several capacities with the International City/County Management Association (ICMA) including president of the ICMA Hispanic Network.

Flores has received the City Manager's Excellence Award twice during his career from two different Phoenix city managers for his various management innovations.

A native of Phoenix, Flores earned his master's in public administration in 1976 and a bachelor of arts degree in 1971 from Arizona State University.

relationship. Public Works Director Juan Martin observed, "One of our philosophies is that there is no one best way to communicate. We communicate in a way that we feel comfortable with our employees." That comfort, of course, comes from building relationships and personal bonds with the people you work with. For example, as the city works to increase service integration, Gloria Hurtado said, "You can mandate service integration, and you can force people to do some things, but you won't get people to truly collaborate until they build relationships."

These relationships are enhanced by, as well as contribute to, the city's commitment to open, broad involvement in decision making. In his study of public and nonprofit organizations, Paul Light (1998) found that innovation is enhanced when organizations become more democratic and shift from centralized rules to a more participatory style. Clearly this is the case in Phoenix. When Phoenix is going to try something new or institute a change, the norm is to involve everyone who has a stake or a role to play. Marvin Andrews feels that city managers "need to encourage ideas from everyone in the city. When you get big, that gets even more difficult. That's why I tried to inculcate in the organization that ideal—that's the way things are done." Today, that is still the way things are done, and involvement includes both people inside the organization and the citizens they serve.

Employee involvement is seen not only as the best way to achieve implementation of new ideas and programs, but also as the way to develop the best programs. The first step, however, is reaching a consensus on what needs to be changed and why. "If you need to change a unit, and you can get to the point where everybody in the unit really understands why the change is occurring, and you've got a good number advocating the change, you're going to be more likely to succeed than if it comes from the top." Once the need for and willingness to change is established, involvement is the basis for designing the change. Deputy City Manager Alton Washington was more specific: "Everyone has to have a role and everyone has to have an opportunity to make recommendations and to help facilitate change in the organization. If you limit the opportunities for involvement, then you limit your ability to generate the ideas and the fixes that work."

4. Serving Citizens

Overlaid across this culture of pride, new challenges, relationships, and communication is a value on serving citizens and the public. The people we talked with evidenced a commitment to public service as the underlying purpose of everything they do: the way they challenge themselves and each other, the pride they take in their work, and their efforts to be professional, responsive, and open—all revolve around the goal of serving the public.

Jack Tevlin
Deputy City Manager

Jack Tevlin was appointed deputy city manager for the City of Phoenix in December 1991. He has responsibility for the Budget & Research, Planning, Public Transit, and Street Transportation Departments, and the education function. Prior to this, he served as chief of staff in the mayor's office in 1990, as executive assistant to the city manager from 1989 to 1990, and as executive assistant to the Phoenix City Council from 1982 to 1989. Before coming to the City of Phoenix, Tevlin served as a staff assistant for the Maricopa Association of Governments.

Tevlin received his B.A. in political science from Marist College in Poughkeepsie, New York, and his M.P.A. from Arizona State University.

This public service ethic seems to be an integral part of their professional identity. In other words, improvements are sought, innovations explored, and risks are taken for one purpose: to provide better services and be more responsive to the public. "I don't know if our good customer service is a result of our innovative tendencies, or if we've become innovative because we want to provide good customer service," Juan Martin remarked. On the other hand, maybe it doesn't really matter which one came first. In Phoenix, innovation and public service seem to go hand in hand.

City Clerk Vicky Meil expressed this public service ethic clearly when she said, "One of the things I tell my employees regularly is that they will never get in trouble if they are taking care of the customer. Ultimately that's what it's all about." Emphasis is placed on the idea that each individual works for and serves the people of Phoenix. Sheryl Sculley explained, "A groundskeeper is not just riding on the mower, but serving as an ambassador for the city. We value that and encourage it and reward it, even if it's just a note or a word of thanks." In an independently conducted employee survey, over 90 percent agreed with the statement "The people in my work group work hard to treat the customer well."

Assistant to the City Manager Ed Zuercher explained that the relationship between the city and the council is the starting place for this public service focus. He stated, "Respecting the ability of the elected officials to signal key issues and concerns from the community early on has been a key to our success." He cited the city's seamless service initiative as one example of how "professional staff can succeed because the elected officials have their fingers on the pulse of the community." Zuercher stated that the city manager "was hearing from the city council that the community was frustrated about contacting the city and getting bounced around on the phone before the right person was found to answer the question. Because of that, Frank [Fairbanks] worked with staff to develop a program to address that concern, called 'seamless service.' Now employees are trained to be *the* contact point for the citizen.... A pamphlet of information was developed for field employees to use. Most importantly, the attitude has changed that everyone needs to take ownership of an inquiry rather than passing it off."

Recognition of the need for ongoing citizen involvement permeates the entire organization. Managers do not assume that everything is okay if citizens aren't complaining. Rather, there is an active and ongoing effort to involve citizens in determining how the city will establish priorities and how it will provide services. Lera Riley commented on her experiences:

> Citizens have a stake and are involved trying to define things. There is a necessity for citizens to feel engaged in our business, helping us determine how we are going to spend money according to the priorities they establish for what they want the community to look like. I can remember going to meetings, particularly in the early '90s when resources were very, very tight. The economy was bad generally and the city had to tighten and change programs dramatically in order to bring our expenses into line with revenues. We had lots of people showing up at meetings being very clear about what their priorities were. Because things have gotten much better, the numbers of people are decreasing. But passiveness in terms of citizen involvement is not good for the city. We're doing well, but part of the reason is that we have always had an active citizenry.

Again, the belief is not only that citizen involvement helps with implementation, but that their involvement makes programs better. David Richert gave the example of the city's award-winning recycling program: "We couldn't afford it all at one time, so we went out to the people and said, 'OK, if we start it here, this is what it's going to cost and here is how we will expand the service.' Based on citizen comments, we moved the project from the south part of the city to the north. Now it's probably one of the best in the country."

Deputy City Manager Jacques Avent expressed a similar commitment to citizen involvement when he remarked, "The success of the Neighborhood Services Department is totally dependent on the ability to involve everybody else in doing the work. The reality is that a single department with limited resources can't do all the things a neighborhood needs to help them."

Managers across the organization talk about this public service responsibility. They openly reject the idea that they are the "experts" who know

Marsha Wallace
Deputy City Manager

Marsha Wallace has served as deputy city manager of Phoenix since December 1997. In that role, she has oversight responsibility for the Aviation, Personnel, and Fire Departments, and the International and Sister Cities Commission programs.

Wallace joined the City of Phoenix staff in 1980, and served as executive assistant to the city manager before being named as deputy city manager. Prior to coming to the city, she worked as a performance auditor for the State of Arizona, and a district program manager for the State Department of Economic Security.

She has a master of public administration degree from Arizona State University and a bachelor of arts degree in human development and psychology from the University of Kansas.

best about what citizens need. Rather, the citizens are considered the experts in this respect. Tammy Perkins recalls, "Traditional city government used to go out to communities, particularly low- and moderate-income communities and say, 'We know what's best for you,' and then we did it. Now the focus really is on spending time in these communities and asking the leadership what they want to do and then figuring out how we adjust and facilitate city government to provide them with the level of service that they need."

Harold Hurtt, chief of police, also emphasized that serving the public in this manner takes continual effort and attention. He places an emphasis in his department on being proactive in working with neighborhoods and staying "on the cutting edge in responding to our citizens." Similarly, David Krietor believes that serving the public and being responsive to citizens is, in large measure, what his job is about. "I spend at least four or five nights a week in some type of a neighborhood or community meeting. It's just expected that you would do that," he said. Supervisors are expected to use the public service filter in evaluating what they do and how they might do it better. As a training guide used in the Fire Department states, "Bosses must continually challenge any and every organizational activity with a standard question: 'What does what we are talking about or doing have to do with delivering service to Mrs. Smith?' Any blank looks or negative answers should produce a pause/discussion/redirection."

5. Trusting and Empowering People

People who work for the City of Phoenix trust each other. That trust is extended in every direction and is enacted in thought, word, and deed. Many point to the legacy of former city manager Marvin Andrews, who worked hard to instill this value. At one level what he did was simple. He decided that he would simply trust the people he worked with to do their best and to achieve excellent results. In practice, of course, putting that trust into action was not so simple. It required persistence and consistency. "We needed to emphasize results. To get results you help people set goals and then give them the tools and training to do their job adequately. So we embarked on a lot of training programs, particularly for new supervisors." Once trained, he trusted them to do their jobs. "A lot of other city managers thought I was crazy. They would say to me, 'You've got all these people out here and all these things going on. How do you know what's going on? You've got to keep your finger on what's happening.' To me, it's all about trust. I've got to trust my managers to do a good job and they have to trust their people to do the same thing," noted Andrews.

There is also a great deal of trust between the council and the city staff. As Ed Zuercher explained, "It is a vitally important piece of our effectiveness that there is trust between the elected body and the professional management that allows for an exchange of ideas, sharing of credit, and better, more responsive service to the community." This trust has been built up over the years and is based, again, on open communication, mutual respect, and a recognition of the contribution of each in serving the public. Today, Chief Brunacini reported, "The people who have managed this place have done an excellent job in creating systems and processes and experiences where people trust each other, and they're basically willing to change. Because of this trust, change isn't threatening to us. It's just what's next in the process." In fact, one of the sections of a training manual for supervisors in the Fire Department is entitled simply, "Build trust or go home."

This trust means that managers not only encourage innovation, but also allow people to take the reins of projects they propose. Frank Fairbanks explained that when he listens to a proposal for a new idea, "I say to myself, there is probably more to be gained in letting them make this change than in making some little, tiny improvement in it or having an argument over it. If they sense that they can put together some sort of improvement in service and all they get from management are comments about we don't like this or that doesn't work or why don't you do this another way, the energy and commitment can be lost. We really work at not being negative." This approach recognizes that giving someone freedom and control over a project may have more potential benefit for the organization in the long run than any marginal improvements a manager

Alton J. Washington
Deputy City Manager

Alton Washington was appointed deputy city manager for the City of Phoenix on June 29, 1998. In this role he currently has responsibility for the Law Department, Engineering and Architectural Services Department, and the Parks, Recreation and Library Department, as well as the Family Advocacy Center and the Office of Environmental Programs.

Prior to this appointment, Washington served the City of Phoenix for eight years as director of the Human Services Department. In this capacity, his primary duties included administrative responsibilities for 17 senior centers; employment and training programs for low-income people and meeting the labor force needs of the City's economic development efforts; education programming for pre-schoolers in the Head Start program as well as social workers in select elementary, middle, and high schools; five family service centers providing emergency assistance to needy individuals and families; program support for the homeless; and information systems support for the Human Services Department. Washington has also served Phoenix as deputy public works director for three years. In that position, he had management responsibility for telecommunications, energy conservation, contracts administration, and administrative support functions.

In addition, Washington has served in a variety of management positions at the state and local levels. He earned his bachelor of science (political science) and master's in public administration at Arizona State University. He is a member of several professional organizations including the International City/County Management Association, American Society for Public Administration, U.S. Conference of City Human Services Officials Board of Directors, Academy of Political Science, National Association of Community Action Agencies, and Arizona Community Action Association.

might make. So, in Phoenix, because you trust the people you work with, you applaud their efforts to try new approaches, even when the approach they propose is not exactly the one you would have chosen. Rather, you trust them and let them do their jobs.

Many people think of empowerment as merely a different word for delegation. In Phoenix, the attitude towards empowerment is more like that expressed by Culbert and McDonough (1985):

> Empowerment is the key to understanding trust and trusting relationships in an organization. No clear-thinking individual internalizes a system that

is not personally and professionally empowering to him or her. An organization's management can only succeed when its representatives understand this fact and comprehend what individuals need in order to feel empowered (182).

In Phoenix, empowerment is based on the assumption and expectation that each employee will internalize organizational values not only because they have an opportunity to help shape them, but also because they are empowered by them. Each employee is given the personal responsibility and opportunity to serve the public, while the organization takes the responsibility to support and to equip each person to do so. In order to empower employees, the expectation is that managers will work to ensure that people have the opportunity and freedom to do what is right and to do their jobs well. The idea that people will simply do what they are told is rejected not only as impractical, but also as destructive to the organization. And that's the city manager's view: "We don't have a world where you do what you're told when you're told. We have a world where every one of us in the city is responsible for working together to improve the community."

When everyone is willing to take responsibility, there can be many innovations going on at once. Mayor Skip Rimsza, when he was being interviewed for a story on Phoenix's "A" report card in *USA Today* (January 31, 2000) was asked about a Public Works Department test of a garbage truck that doubles its capacity by pulling a trailer. The mayor was quoted as responding, "See, I didn't know anything about that." Waving his arms in the air, he continued, "That's what I love about this city." This attitude of empowerment, coupled with trust and mutual respect, results in an environment in which managers and directors are not expected, nor are they encouraged, to control all of the decisions in their units. Deputy City Manager George Britton clarified, "One of the things this organization does is that it will adopt innovations very quickly compared to most larger organizations. And I think a lot of that is because of the distributive processes— the philosophy of distribution—of empowerment.... Decisions are made at the service level more than they're made at the central office." Part of the role of the deputy city manager, then, is to support and work with departments to ensure they have what they need to implement improvements. This not only helps departments with individual innovation projects, but also establishes a positive climate for ongoing efforts to improve. Gloria Hurtado put it this way: "We're provided with the tools and support—that keeps people innovating and doing new things."

The idea is that this sense of empowerment should permeate the entire organization. Once again, Fairbanks explained, it starts at the top, but the intent is to extend it throughout the organization. "Part of my leadership role is a responsibility to empower management. The deputies have a sense of empowerment, and through them, the department heads have a sense of empowerment. But I really spend a lot of my time communicating this with all levels by walking around the building talking to people about it. We talk about how it is up to each of us. One of the things we all say to people is that you can't leave it all up to the manager. Each one of us needs to make a difference, and the system has to allow people to make improvements."

Fairbanks also believes that empowerment is enhanced when managers interfere as little as possible. In other words, when someone is excited about an idea, has done their homework, and wants to try something, sometimes the best thing a manager can do is get out of the way. He stated, "If someone wants to innovate in a department in how they deliver services, we tend to go with it, even if we have doubts. We'll raise our concerns, and obviously if we think it would be a disaster, we wouldn't say yes. But, if someone is committed and excited, even if we're not completely sure it's such a good idea, we try to allow people to make the change so that they have the sense that they *can*." Doing so, he said, gives people a sense of empowerment to continue to try new things. In Phoenix that is the crux of the issue—they try to manage change efforts in a manner that will not only result in success, but also encourage future innovation.

6. Enacting Core Values

In the mid-1990s, the city manager asked the employees of the City of Phoenix how to make the city even more successful. Hundreds of employees responded, and from their responses a new statement of vision and values was developed. That statement now appears on every business card, as well as in reports, speeches, conversations, videos, posters, and even refrigerator magnets. As one employee said laughingly, "It's everywhere!" It states:

> We are dedicated to serving our customers.
> We work as a team.
> We each do all we can.
> We learn, change, and improve.
> We focus on results.
> We work with integrity.
> We make Phoenix better!

The elegance and simplicity of these statements may belie their importance. The purpose of the vision and values statement was to communicate and inculcate core organizational values. Importantly, however, the vision and values statement was in large measure based on the values expressed by the workers themselves. Since its development, this statement of vision has been incorporated into all aspects of city government. Reports are organized by it, speeches are written around it, departments and individuals evaluate themselves by their contribution to it. Maybe more importantly, they talk about it and they do it.

Jack Tevlin remarked on the importance of putting things in a simple and straightforward way. "One of the geniuses of Frank," he said, "is that he's a very simple communicator. And it works. Our recent employee survey demonstrated that 93 percent of our employees are aware of our vision and values." Beyond talking about it, however, managers in the City of Phoenix work to enact these values. As Chief Hurtt said, "I don't think it's old-fashioned to say we lead by example." In other words, one gets the sense in talking with managers that the statement of vision and values is more than words—in fact, more than simply what they do, it embodies who they are as managers of the City of Phoenix.

In describing the importance of Phoenix's vision and values, Lera Riley emphasized, "An important part of the message is that it's up to each of us. When we talk about vision and values, we talk about how it's our responsibility to perform well, make the community better and we do it as a team. But it's up to each one of us to do what we can." To make it work, "The whole organization needs to think like this. We've taken a fairly small list of things that say this is our organization and these are the values that we have." Each unit, department, and employee is then challenged to figure out "What am I and what is my organization doing to exemplify that? How do I fit into the whole?" The statement gets "a bunch of people talking about it, and it becomes embedded more and more," observed Riley.

Expressing and enacting values is part and parcel of being a successful manager in Phoenix. As George Flores commented, "I believe the vast majority of our managers have had positive personal values that have transcended anything of a negative nature they had to work with—or any obstacle—and that the employees below them have picked up on those things and that they work within that same spirit." Moreover, by making values explicit, Riley explained, "we tell employees about what we cherish about what they do well and what may not be as valued in the organization." In all of these discussions, however, the idea that predominates is that values are not simply a nice and tidy set of statements of principles in Phoenix. They are treated as catalysts and reinforcements for behavior and defining expressions of the culture of the city.

7. Respecting Employees and Treating Them Well

"Ultimately, successful companies and successful organizations are good to their employees, and they support, train, reward, and are nice to the people in their organization. And that's probably the most fundamental thing." This comment by Executive Assistant to the City Council Rick Naimark neatly summed up a fundamental cultural norm in the City of Phoenix: people from the top to the bottom of this organization are important, and all are respected and valued. The assumption is that the organization has become successful and will continue its success because of the effort and commitment of the employees who work there.

When Frank Fairbanks talks about the people who work for the city, his comments reflect feelings of respect and confidence. He consistently gives credit for Phoenix's success to the city's employees, he clearly believes in them, and he knows that they will do an excellent job. If they don't, then it's the organization's fault. "We have great employees here. I try to create an environment in which the employees have an opportunity to have an impact to improve service delivery. Employees want to do a good job. If you can harness their talents at the service delivery level, they're in a lot better position to make positive things happen." He went on to say, "It's important that people feel that they can make a difference and that people will support them in making a difference. We have great employees, and they'll jump at that. It's when employees feel that their supervisor won't let them change or that there will never be resources to do something differently that they stop trying."

It is clear that people who work for the city have positive feelings towards their employer as well. As noted previously, 97 percent of employees agree with the statement "The City is a good place to work." With regard to their immediate supervisors, 88 percent of employees agree their supervisor "allows me to use my judgment" and almost 80 percent agree that "we treat each other with respect." As Budget Director Ceil Pettle explained, "We feel valued and that makes us do a good job, and we're valued because we do a good job. I think it's kind of a self-feeding system. This is a great employer."

This helps create a very positive environment in which people seem to enjoy their jobs and like their work environment. As Naimark said simply, "I like coming to work every day." It seems clear that most of the people who work for the City of Phoenix like their jobs, and a significant part of those positive feelings are based on the fact that employees feel valued, respected, and listened to. Although the idea of simply "being nice" to people may seem to be an old-fashioned platitude with little place amidst the complexities and challenges of big city management, it is clearly a norm that has a significant and positive influence on the people who work for the City of Phoenix.

8. Taking Risks and Learning From Experience

When we asked what advice he would give other managers based on his experience in Phoenix, Marvin Andrews said, "Don't be afraid to take a risk, look at change as opportunity to get things done, and move forward." Clearly this remains a central value in the organizational culture in the City of Phoenix. George Britton put it simply and compellingly when he said, "Thoughtful risk—rational risk—is sort of our touchstone for survival." The assumption is that risk is an inherent part of innovation, and innovation is necessary to success. Kevin Keogh reiterated this idea. "When we are trying things, looking ahead, and anticipating how we will have to change, when we are trying to evaluate options and make informed decisions— there will be risk. There's just so much change going on, I don't know how you avoid risk."

In Phoenix, the emphasis is not on trying to avoid risk, but rather on finding ways to use risk constructively to help the organization improve and learn. So people are not only allowed, but also encouraged to try new things, even if there is risk involved. Marsha Wallace explained, "Our city managers have had a leadership style that encourages people to be inno- vative and lets them take some risks." Part of this willingness is based on trust. As Bozeman and Kingsley found in their study of risk culture in public and private organizations, "managers who trust their employees are likely to have employees who will take calculated risks" (1998, 116).

What else can an organization do to encourage calculated risk? Marvin Andrews answered, "You can encourage risk by not raising hell with people about failure, and then trying to encourage them to come up with more ideas. That isn't always the easiest thing to do. A couple of times when something failed, I had to step up and take responsibility with the council and the mayor. After a while, people get the idea that they can try some- thing out and maybe it will work and maybe it won't." Either way, they won't be abandoned or left out on a limb.

Clearly the people who work for city government in Phoenix have gotten the idea. Part of the reason is that they know they can rely on the people they work with to support them and not turn on them if things don't go as planned. "Ideas and suggestions are actively solicited and often tried," Alton Washington remarked. "That doesn't mean all change works. To me the real test is when you initiate something and it doesn't work. I've found in this setting that you don't have the recrimination that sometimes you find in other organizations." Echoing this sentiment, Ceil Pettle observed, "Because many of us have been here a long time we kind of have some information under our belts and some expertise that allows us to look for better ways of doing things and to test them. It's also never been threatening. It's never been something we've really been whacked with." City Auditor Bob Wingenroth said the message is clear: "There are probably 15 or 20 mechanisms, and subcultural messages and expecta- tions that add up to this: It's okay to take a risk and it's okay to make a mistake."

Like his predecessor, Frank Fairbanks feels strongly that the way managers respond to problems is a key factor in developing and maintaining an innovative culture. He told us, "When there are problems we work really hard not to punish people; we try to solve the problem. Sometimes it's tough, especially if you get a bad newspaper article, and especially when the newspaper article is right and fair! But when there are problems, we work really hard not to punish people and hang them out to dry. We try to solve the problem instead."

9. Recognizing and Rewarding People's Efforts

In addition to not punishing people for failure, the other side of encouraging innovation is rewarding and recognizing people when there is success. Marvin Andrews emphasized this theme during his tenure. "We worked to recognize the efforts of employees. For example, one of the things we emphasized was teamwork. We set up a quarterly program where outstanding teams were recognized. They were invited to breakfast with their families and it was videotaped and shown on the city's public television station. That went extremely well. I think they are still doing it. Someone dubbed it 'Muffins with Marv'!"

Reward and recognition of effort and accomplishment continues to be an important and visible aspect of organizational life in Phoenix. "We do a lot with rewards, celebrations, and events. We try to create a positive benefit of taking a risk so that if someone is willing to stick their neck out and it works well, there is really a big pay off. This holds for the whole organization, whether you are a police officer, a supervisor, or a middle manager," Frank Fairbanks said. In a similar vein, George Britton emphasized that positive reinforcement begins with the executive team and extends throughout the organization. "At every monthly department head meeting, if somebody has done an article or something it is recognized, it's celebrated, it's passed around and the peers see that."

Because of the positive relationship that the city offices have built with the council and council staff, people also report that they are confident that the council will recognize their accomplishments and successes as well. Bob Wingenroth stated, "Our council also supports us. People don't go to council meetings expecting to get beat up, and if we hit a home run, they pat us on the back like you wouldn't believe."

Interestingly, Frank Fairbanks thinks it is important to not only reward the people directly involved in the innovation, but also the people who facilitate those improvements and don't "get in the way" of new ideas. "Sometimes managers and supervisors can become threatened when successful innovations come from their employees—afraid they might look like they are not doing their job." So, he said, "If some employees or middle managers or supervisors in a department come up with a change and improve service, we also lavish praise on the department head, because they really did play a role by just allowing it to happen, by not obstructing it, or not being negative about the change."

10. Building a Stable Foundation and Staying the Course

For a city known as an "innovation machine" it may seem odd to talk about the importance of stability. Perhaps somewhat paradoxically, a key lesson from the Phoenix experience is that stability is critical in creating a culture that embraces change. While these two ideas can be seen as being at odds with one another, Frank Fairbanks told us, "Stability helps create an environment for change." In Phoenix, stability and constancy have, in many ways, created a firm and steady foundation from which to innovate and take chances. As Jack Tevlin claimed, "This is a very stable environment on both the management and political side." This stability is not, however, a matter of holding still. Rather, it is based on a number of elements, most particularly assuring that systems are reliable, information is available, and that people know they can rely on each other, their managers, and the organization.

Over the years, investments have been made in creating a sound and reliable system of management information, including budgetary, accounting, and performance data, that helps managers see the results of their efforts to improve and innovate. As Frank Fairbanks explained, "We have good systems—a very active auditing system, a very strong accounting system, a very strong measurement system, good personnel control, and good budgeting systems. The existence of those systems gives you the freedom to take more chances because you know you're not going to get too far out of whack." The information provided through those systems helps the city highlight problems, track progress, and identify results. Rick Naimark agreed when he said, "Resources are important to the innovation process because you have got to have the resources to create new programs and to do new things. But resources are also important because innovation is enhanced by having good information technology." Good information, he explained, allows them to innovate and monitor the results. Sound information systems and a strong budgeting process means the city can allow departments freedom in their budget to reallocate their funds and to find new ways of delivering services.

Another important piece of the stability seems to be that once people come to work for the city they tend to stay. At the risk of understatement, when 97 percent of your employees think the city is a good place to work, it bolsters recruitment and retention. This longevity is very evident at the management level. It's not that the city doesn't hire new people from outside the organization; in fact, a number of new directors from outside Phoenix were hired in recent years. But there is a core of people who have been with the city for a long time. Tammy Perkins described the effect of this long tenure. "We've known each other forever. And because all of us have moved around, we've worked with each other. So it's easier to avoid getting caught in a narrow 'silo' perspective. As we work together, it's not just about our own departments. It's about what's the right thing to do for the city." This familiarity with each other and each other's programs lends some predictability and stability to an environment characterized by change. Stability is also achieved by treating each other in a consistently professional and respectful manner.

So, perhaps one of the most fundamental lessons that can be learned from the Phoenix experience is that building a culture of innovation requires consistency, persistence, and time. As noted at the beginning of this section, the culture that has served as the basis for all the city's accomplishments was built over many years. Further, it is a culture built on many factors that are both interdependent and mutually reinforcing. Over time, these factors collectively come to define "the way we do things around here." Chief Brunacini convincingly argued that change had become a part of the institution of city government: "One of the hallmarks of Phoenix is that we have developed the approach or the philosophy that change is a process, not an event. If you hang around here very long, you see that there's just a lot of change that's going on all the time. So it becomes more of a way of life than something that you react to."

When you ask people how it all began or how the culture was established, they find it difficult to explain. They just say, "That's the way we've always done it." Bob Wingenroth said as much, "Your job is not to do what you're doing now, but is to do something better every year. When I joined this organization 20 years ago, I think that ethic was part of the place already." Marvin Andrews knew it might take a long time, but Phoenix has been able to consistently promote a set of values over time. "It takes a long time to institutionalize change. When we started some of this, some of the people I talked to said that it would take nine or 10 years to get it accepted by everybody. They told me it was a long-term thing we were getting into, and it was. It was hard from year to year to see where we were making much progress. But then when you go back five or six years, you can see that it has changed quite a bit. But changing culture is always a long-term process. It's something you just have to keep working at." Phoenix has clearly benefited from a series of managers who were willing to keep working on building and sustaining a culture of innovation.

Conclusion

Based on the lessons learned from the Phoenix experience, where does a manager interested in building a culture of innovation and a record of accomplishment begin? The short answer is that you begin everywhere at once by promoting a process of change that builds the capacity for future innovation. Remember Frank Fairbanks' remark, "There's not just one thing you do. We do a lot of things."

The Phoenix experience teaches us that the development of an innovative culture or "root system" means paying attention to core values and doing a little bit of everything all at one time, working through and with people across and outside the organization. As a model, Phoenix teaches us that in order to inculcate core values, people need to be involved in defining them in a widely shared and open process in which each individual not only has the opportunity to participate, but also to understand his or her role in promoting those values. It teaches us to examine our assumptions about people and challenges us to then act on those assumptions. It urges us to question what it means to be a manager and then take action to enhance those management skills that are most needed. It instructs us to support people, train and equip them to do a good job, and then trust them, let go, and get out of the way. It teaches us that the values of public service and citizen engagement must be at the forefront of everything we do. Finally, it teaches us that in developing and implementing improvements, we do so by involving everyone and respecting, honoring, and acting on their contributions.

The City of Phoenix has a culture that has built upon itself, as one aspect has reinforced and reflected another. For example, trusting people builds responsibility; responsibility, in turn, builds trust. Involving people and valuing them makes them more willing to participate in change. As they do so, pride and confidence grow. Their willingness to participate in change based on this pride and confidence enhances the value of their participation. Relationships built on communication, mutual respect, and personal concern foster trust and cooperation. Trust and cooperation strengthen good relationships. And so on. The complexity of these inter-relationships and inter-dependencies makes them no less clear or apparent. In this sense, the "innovation machine" has built its own momentum, fueled by pride, confidence, and trust.

In conclusion, perhaps the most fundamental and important lesson we can learn from Phoenix is that *how* you do things is every bit as important as, and perhaps in some ways more important than, *what* you do. How you do things can build the capacity for the organization and individuals to change in the future or it can undermine these capacities. Processes can leave people feeling involved, valued, responsible, and empowered. Or they can leave people feeling left out, angry, powerless, and resistant to change. It is clear that in Phoenix, when people from the manager's office to the lunchroom at Crazy Jim's talk about the "way things are done around here," they are referring to a process that features a culture of innovation, that respects and values people, that enhances their trust and confidence, and over time builds a cadre of civil servants who manage the best run city in America.

Bibliography

Barrett, Katherine and Richard Greene. 2000. "Grading the Cities." *Governing.* February.

Bluedorn, Alan and Earl Lundgren. 1993. "A Culture-match Perspective for Strategic Change." *Research in Organizational Change and Development* 7: 137-179.

Bozeman, Barry and Gordon Kingsley. 1998. "Risk Culture in Public and Private Organizations." *Public Administration Review* 58(2), 109-115.

City of Phoenix, 1999. *City of Phoenix 1999 Annual Citizens Report: We Focus on Results.*

Culbert, Samuel and John McDonough. 1986. "The Politics of Trust and Empowerment." *Public Administration Quarterly.* Summer, 171-188.

Denhardt, Robert B. and Janet Vinzant Denhardt. 1999. *Leadership for Change: Case Studies in American Local Government.* Arlington, Va.: The PricewaterhouseCoopers Endowment for The Business of Government.

Government Performance Project, 2000. http://www.governing.com/gpp/gp0phoe.htm

Hall, John. 1982. Phoenix, Ariz. In *Decentralizing Urban Policy: Case Studies in Community Development* (Paul R. Dommel and Associates, eds.) Washington, D.C.: The Brookings Institution.

Light, Paul. 1998. *Sustaining Innovation.* San Francisco: Jossey-Bass Publishers.

Morrison Institute for Public Policy, 2000. *Hits and Misses: Fast Growth in Metropolitan Phoenix.* Tempe, Ariz.: Arizona State University.

Moynihan, Donald. 2000. *Managing for Results in the Cities: Innovative Practices.* Government Performance Project. Syracuse, N.Y.: Syracuse University.

Oden, Howard. 1997. *Managing Corporate Culture, Innovation, and Intrapreneurship.* Westport, Conn.: Quorum Books.

Schein, Edgar. 1987. *Organizational Culture and Leadership.* San Francisco: Jossey-Bass Publishers.

Valle, Mathew. 1999. "Crisis Culture, and Charisma: The New Leader's Work in Public Organizations." *Public Personnel Management* 28(2), 245-257.

CHAPTER FIVE

San Diego County's Innovation Program: Using Competition and a Whole Lot More to Improve Public Services

William B. Eimicke
Director, Picker Center for Executive Education
School of International and Public Affairs
Columbia University

This report was originally published in January 2000.

Introduction[1]

San Diego County Government and the Need for Management Innovation

San Diego County is a large, multi-purpose local government encompassing most of California south of Los Angeles. The county has a long, relatively open border with Mexico, making immigration and international trade important and often politically volatile issues. About 24 percent of county residents are of Hispanic origin.

Known for its excellent climate, large military installations, and as a popular retirement destination, San Diego has become California's second largest urban area, with a county population in excess of 2.6 million. It ranks 16th in population among all metropolitan areas in the United States. The largest city in the county is the City of San Diego, with a population of 1.2 million. The county's Gross Regional Product for 1998 was estimated at $88.7 billion.

The County of San Diego was established by the State Legislature in 1850 as one of California's original 27 counties. A five-member Board of Supervisors established by the State Legislature in 1852 governs the county. At that time, the county population is believed to have been about 3,500—2,692 of whom were Native Americans. At creation, the county covered about 40,000 square miles, including the present counties of San Diego, Imperial, Riverside, San Bernardino, and portions of Inyo. Today, San Diego County covers 4,255 square miles, 65 miles from north to south and 86 miles from east to west.

Despite the region's long tradition of conservative politics and active taxpayer associations, the county government teetered on the brink of bankruptcy in 1995. A cyclical slowdown in the area economy was exacerbated by a poor decision to construct a public solid waste resource recovery plant in the northern part of the county. The plant was a major money loser from day one, and five new members of the County Board of Supervisors were forced to face the dire fiscal consequences of their predecessors' poor judgment.

The 1995-1996 county budget projected a $65 million deficit, had only a few million dollars in reserves for a $2.2 billion operating plan, and was covering both debt service and daily operating losses from the resource recovery plant. The five members of the Board of Supervisors independently reached the same conclusion regarding the fiscal crisis and what to do about. While the crisis was not of their making, they agreed to take "ownership" of the problem. Dramatic steps were needed to avert bankruptcy, but such steps were politically risky and might not work.

The supervisors essentially decided they were more concerned about their place in county history than the results of the next election. They

would use the fiscal crisis as an opportunity to comprehensively improve the county's service delivery system and decaying infrastructure, as well as its finances. They agreed on a simple but radical three-step plan:
- Pursue a market-based solution to the solid waste system crisis;
- Hire a new chief administrative officer (CAO) to get that done; and,
- Empower the CAO to overhaul the entire county government and make it run as if it were a private company.

Agreed that the solid waste system was a financial and management disaster, the supervisors decided privatization, if possible, was a critical first step in the county's fiscal recovery effort. To accomplish that objective, they sought a new CAO with the expertise, vision, energy, and leadership to bring market discipline to the operation of county government. A national search produced a pool of 229 candidates.

The successful applicant and unanimous choice of the board members sent in his resume after seeing an advertisement in *The Wall Street Journal.*

About Lawrence B. Prior III

 Lawrence B. Prior III served as Chief Administrative Officer of the County of San Diego from September 1996 to May 1999. As the chief executive for the fourth largest county in the United States, Mr. Prior managed a workforce of 17,000 employees and an annual budget of $2.39 billion.

Mr. Prior was appointed to this post by the five-member San Diego County Board of Supervisors after an extensive nationwide search. He assumed the post on September 3, 1996.

Mr. Prior brought a unique combination of private and public sector experience to his post. Before joining the County, Mr. Prior served as Vice President and General Manager for TRW Inc.'s Tactical Systems Division in Sunnyvale, California. Earlier in his TRW career, he served as Vice President of Strategic Planning, Business Development and Government Affairs for TRW's Avionics and Surveillance group based in Rancho Bernardo, California.

From 1989 to 1992, Mr. Prior served as a professional staff member to the House of Representatives' Permanent Select Committee on Intelligence, where he evaluated multi-billion-dollar technology programs. Mr. Prior also served 11 years in the United States Marine Corps as an Intelligence Officer and as an analyst for the Office of Naval Intelligence.

Born in Chicago, Illinois, Mr. Prior holds a Bachelor's degree from Loyola Marymount University and a Master of Arts degree in government from Georgetown University.

Lawrence B. Prior III was vice president and general manager of TRW's Tactical Systems Division when he applied for the CAO position. A former Marine, Prior had also worked as a congressional staff expert, so he was familiar with politics and public processes. Nevertheless, Prior intended to bring market principles and business practices to county government if he got the job.

Current board member (and board chair at the time of Prior's selection) Ron Roberts comments, "Larry was our unanimous choice because we wanted an innovator, an agent for change." The appointment was universally well received. The media characterized Prior as hands-on, high energy and a man of 12-hour days. Business groups, taxpayer associations, chambers of commerce, and the convention and visitors bureau endorsed his private sector standards and ideology, including his plan for performance-based bonuses for county managers. He was praised in the press and by county managers as well. Even union leader Mary Grillo, who was to become Prior's most ardent critic, initially approved his selection: "I think one of his biggest strengths is that he realizes county employees are our strongest asset."

The Innovation Process

Selling Solid Waste

Prior's first priority was to solve the county's solid waste crisis. The decision to build the $134 million North County Resource and Recovery Facility proved to be wrong almost from the outset, and the plant was closed only 18 months after opening to mitigate mounting operating losses. The new board members considered a variety of options to deal with the problem, including contracting out management, partnerships, and direct sale.

The mid 1990's proved to be an excellent time to sell a public solid waste system. Interest rates were relatively low, the stock market prices of the publicly traded companies in the business were high, and the solid waste industry was in a consolidation mode. The concern for consumers was mitigated by the county's continuing role as industry regulator. Eight companies responded to the county's initial solicitation and four ultimately submitted a formal bid.

Prior managed the bid and negotiation process, and received high grades in handling his first major challenge. He selected Larry Aker to head his internal "tiger team" of experts. (Aker would become the first director of the County's Competition and Reengineering Group.) Prior also hired J.P. Morgan and the law firm of O'Melveny and Myers to help oversee the financial and legal terms of the divestiture. By August of 1997, Prior had a deal with Allied Waste Management that met or exceeded all of the board's expectations.

The county received $184 million for a solid waste system that was costing it money to operate. The public liability for future losses and debt from the system were strictly limited. Provisions were made to keep user fees affordable and the county retained the power to regulate the industry. Perhaps equally important, proceeds from the sale funded an environmental trust fund, built operating budget reserves to a responsible and safe

Innovation Report Card	
Selling Solid Waste	
Criteria	**Grade**
1. Communication	A
2. Strength of Case	A
3. Implementation	A
4. Outcomes	A+
5. Sustainable	A+
Final Grade	**A**

level, jump-started the county innovation agenda, and enabled the county to finance a zero deferred maintenance infrastructure investment program. No proceeds were used as one-shot revenues to close the county's operating budget deficit. With the solid waste crisis averted and the county's fiscal affairs in order, Prior set out to achieve the board's third key objective—to make the county government run like an efficient private enterprise.

The Bonus Program

One of the tools CAO Prior used to bring private management efficiency to his new public management job was an incentive bonus program for managers. Prior was convinced—and remains so to this day—that providing significant financial rewards to his top performers and innovation allies was the only way to break through years of bureaucratic inertia and a civil service mentality.

Prior persuaded the Board of Supervisors to set aside $1.34 million for top managers and certain senior staff. However, when the first year bonus decisions were announced, a major internal and media firestorm began.

The management bonus system developed by CAO Prior provoked a violent reaction from public employee unions, which produced a fair amount of "bad press" and hurt morale among non-managers. Prior's management bonus system grew out of the performance-based pay methods he learned in the private sector. For Prior, that meant the bonuses had to big enough to make a difference to those receiving them and diverse enough to separate the

Innovation Report Card

The Bonus Program

Criteria	Grade
1. Communication	C
2. Strength of Case	C
3. Implementation	C
4. Outcomes	B
5. Sustainable	B
Final Grade	**C**

top performers from the average and the poor managers.

And it was the size and discrimination of Prior's program that made it real and extremely controversial. For the first year (1997-1998), Prior recommended and the Board of Supervisors approved performance bonuses as high as 30 percent of one's base salary. When the dust cleared, one manager's pay was cut, 40 received no bonus, and 156 received bonuses. Most bonuses were in the $5,000 to $10,000 range, but 42 received more. Prior's bonus was highest—$32,580.

While some editorial boards praised the program, union leaders were predictably outraged, and most news stories played the "Wall Street"-sized bonus angle. The worker grapevine news was also very negative, since only a few managers received relatively large rewards while the first employee raises in several years would not come until the summer of 1998. The most outspoken union leader, Mary Grillo, seized the bonus issue as a weapon against Prior personally and his innovation program generally. Her position was that bonuses pit workers against managers and require regular employees to work harder to earn big rewards for their bosses and nothing for themselves.

Prior later told an employee town meeting assembly that he did a poor job explaining the program and misjudged how it would be received. Subsequently, the maximum bonus was capped at 18 percent and a much larger group of employees are eligible for bonuses. But the relationship between organized labor and Prior, initially quite positive, never recovered.

Real pay for performance systems discriminate—there are winners and losers. This intense win/lose competition is fundamental in the private sector. The San Diego County experience raises the question of how far government can go in bringing market practices to public organizations.

The CalWORKS Competition at HHSA

The wide range of health and social service programs delivered by San Diego County comprise its largest and most critical responsibility. After a comprehensive assessment of its delivery service, the county decided to merge five separate funding and service silos into a single Health and Human Services Agency (HHSA) in late 1996. Led by Dr. Robert B. Ross (named one of the 10 Public Officials of the Year for 1999 by *Governing* magazine), HHSA managers proceeded to shape and reengineer the agency's major systems to improve customer service, cut administrative costs, speed decision-making and information flow, and emphasize prevention.

Among the strategies HHSA employed to achieve these improvements were: a regional service delivery structure; a "no wrong door" client access system; increased outreach; contracted networks for community-based service; and a managed competition program to fine-tune efficiency and effectiveness. A significant aspect of the HHSA innovation program was the commitment of the Board of Supervisors and CAO Prior to reinvest savings from management innovations into health and human service program enhancements. This public pledge to "move money to do good" seems to sustain the commitment to change in an agency that has been innovating for nearly four years.

The most interesting HHSA innovation is the CalWORKS competition. In response to federal and state welfare reform laws, the San Diego County Board of Supervisors approved a strategy plan in 1997 emphasizing private sector jobs as the goal for most welfare families. It sets out targets of 40 percent of all CalWORKS families in unsubsidized jobs, and 100 percent of able-bodied recipients in work or work-related activities by June 30, 1999.

To help achieve these goals, HHSA decided to divide the county into six regional service delivery districts and compete out approximately two-thirds of its welfare-to-work case management workload. Through the competition, the county hoped to increase community involvement, stimulate new service delivery ideas, foster partnerships and collaborations among service providers, and encourage economies and efficiencies through pay-for-performance contracts. To select its service providers, HHSA chose a Request for Proposals (RFP) process.

The competition was managed in several respects. First, two of the six districts were kept in county management, but under a new, reengineered regional organization. Second, a goal of two nonprofit and two for-profits contractors was established for the other four districts, but HHSA made clear it would look for "best value" regardless of the bidder's legal status. Providers could bid on all four districts and collaborations were encouraged, however, no bidder could manage more than two regions.

An independent board recommended the two districts assigned to the county and the Board of Supervisors affirmed their recommendation. It also approved HHSA's assessment of the RFP responses, awarding two districts to Lockheed Martin, a large national for-profit company; one district to Maximus, also a national for-profit company; and one district to Catholic Charities, a regional nonprofit organization. All three contractors have partnership

Innovation Report Card	
The CalWORKS Competition at HHSA	
Criteria	**Grade**
1. Communication	A
2. Strength of Case	A
3. Implementation	A
4. Outcomes	A
5. Sustainable	B
Final Grade	**A**

agreements and collaborations with a wide variety of community-based organizations, support service providers, and neighborhood multi-service centers.

By mid-August 1998, all four contractors and the two county organizations were fully operational and continue to operate as this report is written. All contracts were designed to be paying for performance, with the highest incentives for placement and retention of clients in unsubsidized, private sector jobs. During the start-up period and during some computer and data verification problems, contractors were paid on a cost-reimbursement basis. The shift to pay for performance began in August of 1999.

Some major milestones associated with the CalWORKS competition merit comment here. Overall, the county's welfare caseload continues to decline, dropping by 18 percent in 1998-99 and 43 percent since 1996, from 63,300 to 36,500 families in June 1999. This decline is the second largest among the state's most populous counties. Annual assistance payment costs to the county have dropped from $421 million in 1995-96 to $231 million in 1998-99.

There were 24,625 welfare-to-work participants being served by the CalWORKS providers as of June 30, 1999. At that time, 47.2 percent of the employable families reported some earnings from wages, with all regions meeting or exceeding the strategic plan target of 40 percent. Contractors identified 18,329 job opportunities for CalWORKS participants in 1998-99, up substantially from 12,966 in 1997-98.

It is too soon to make meaningful comparisons of contractor performance. An automated performance tracking system was just coming on line in September 1999 and an independent evaluation of the regions is scheduled to be completed during the fall of 1999. HHSA administrative reviews found the need for corrective action by all three contractors in the areas of documentation, record keeping and data collection. Overall performance as measured by client earnings and caseload declines is relatively uniform and positive across all six regions. By 2000-01, the county expects to have the definitive performance data required to make decisions on the re-bidding of the welfare-to-work case management services for 2001 and beyond.

The Competition and Reengineering Group Projects

On February 17, 1998, the Board of Supervisors formally approved the creation of the Competition and Reengineering Group to foster and oversee a countywide innovation effort. The group was given a $3 million budget and a strict 18-month life. Larry Aker, project manager for the solid waste system privatization, was chosen to head up the project. His top deputy and successor, Lana Willingham, was a key player in the HHSA synergy, reengineering, and competition efforts.

CAO Larry Prior championed the creation of the high level team to push departments to improve customer service and lower costs. Competition was Prior's preferred improvement tool. When competition was not possible, reengineering was applied. Prior encouraged the team to "think outside the box" and push county agencies to run their operation as if it was their own business.

Prior, Aker, and Willingham all cited Indianapolis Mayor Stephen Goldsmith's competition initiatives as their ideal type. They brought Goldsmith to San Diego, read his book on the Indianapolis experiment, talked to his staff, and applied many of the same methodologies. For example, Aker hired an outside consulting firm to help the county develop an activity-based cost accounting system to facilitate competition comparisons. San Diego also adopted Goldsmith's Yellow Pages test to choose competition targets—if there were five or more private businesses in the telephone book selling the same service as a county agency, that service was added to the group's priority list.

The group developed managed competition and cost comparison guidebooks to make sure that county teams and outside vendors were equally well informed about the services out for bid and how proposals would be evaluated. The group also provided grants to the county teams so that they could hire expert consultants to analyze costs, develop business plans, and construct a proper bid. An important part of the Competition and Reengineering Group's mission was to create as level a playing field as possible for the public-private competitions.

Remarkably, on May 26, 1999, the Final Report of the Competition and Reengineering Group was submitted to the Board of Supervisors and the group disbanded. During its short life, the group managed eight competitions and 13 reengineerings, creating nearly $35 million in annual savings. The Board of Supervisors chose to reinvest those savings to expand and improve county services or to reduce user charges. (A list of the projects and results are included in the Appendix.)

As in Indianapolis, the county faced the unexpected—and in some ways unhappy—prospect of awarding the first competition to the county team. Many senior officials had hoped that an early private contractor

Innovation Report Card

The Competition and
Reengineering Group Projects

Criteria	Grade
1. Communication	A
2. Strength of Case	A
3. Implementation	A
4. Outcomes	A
5. Sustainable	B
Final Grade	**A**

award would encourage outside interest and spur county teams to be more aggressive. The county team victory was even more surprising than the Indianapolis situation (there the road repair contract was retained by the public employees) because the County Alternative Public Defender won the contract to provide defense services for juvenile dependency cases from the private attorneys previously doing the work.

County teams won six of the other seven competitions. The only outside vendor to win a contract, California Forensic Medical Group, Inc., was selected to provide medical services in Juvenile Hall, three camps, and a work furlough facility. The contract saves the county about $3.5 million over its four and a half year term, the second largest annual savings produced from the eight competitions.

The direct savings resulting from the work of the Competition and Reengineering Group are modest compared to the proceeds from the solid waste privatization. The HHSA CalWORKS competition and synergy projects are much larger in scale and employ more "cutting edge" methodologies. Nevertheless, the group's work played a major role in the overall innovation process.

Lana Willingham, the competition group's second director, comments, "Our work was really about restoring the confidence of the public that government services are being well-run. Our commitment was to eliminate waste and use the savings to do good—move the freed-up funds to enhance critical public services. And we wanted to expand the program from a few big victories—solid waste and HHSA—to a countywide initiative that involved every department and thousands of public employees."

Our conversations with county employees, vendors, and citizens indicate that the most significant benefits of the group's work are the changes in the attitudes and behaviors of county workers. Joan Zinser, deputy HHSA administrator, told us, "The discipline of the competition and reengineering process has dramatically altered the way we do our work. County employees are much more analytical and cost-conscious, day to day. It is not an exaggeration to say that many of us now act as if we are operating in a highly competitive market atmosphere with customer service our top priority."

The Outsourcing of Information Technology and Telecommunications Services

As the Competition and Reengineering Group concluded its work, it set into motion the largest project in the county's innovation program—information and telecommunications outsourcing. The county's outdated and poorly functioning computer and telecommunications infrastructure frustrated the public, employees, vendors, and even the media. It seemed particularly problematic in a region where computer and Internet businesses were growing rapidly and public utilization of the new technologies was high compared to the rest of the nation.

The group's information and telecommunications team assessed the county's current capacity, interviewed a wide array of private vendors, and examined best practices from the public, private, and nonprofit sectors nationwide. The team recommended and CAO Prior agreed that outsourcing was the best method of securing and maintaining a state-of-the art information and telecommunications infrastructure for the county.

A Request for Statements of Qualifications (RFQ) was sent to over 150 information technology and telecommunications companies in November 1998. The county required that vendors meet the following criteria: participation in similar outsourcing contracts of at least $50 million annually; management of service bundles comparable to San Diego's needs; and corporate revenues in excess of $1 billion annually for the past three years. Thirteen responses were received and eight were deemed qualified to serve as a prime contractor for the county by the source selection committee.

As the process moved forward, three qualified vendors withdrew and several of the other candidates formed partnerships. When the Request for Proposals was issued in February 1999, three eligible bidders sought the prime contract—Computer Science Corporation (CSC), in partnership with SAIC; Electronic Data Services (EDS); and IBM, in partnership with Lockheed Martin. Final negotiations are currently underway and the county expected board approval of a contract by late 1999. The new vendor is expected to take over operations in December 1999. As this paper is being written, the CAO is expected to recommend approval of the proposal by CSC. The total seven-year cost of the contract plus related contract administration, county space, and the cost of transitioning employees is $596,674,421, or $87,218,194 less than the county estimates it would cost to provide the same services itself.

The IT outsourcing is the largest and most controversial of San Diego's innovation initiatives. The county's expert consultant estimated baseline information technology and telecommunications costs at $98.5 million annually, increasing at an annual rate of 6-8 percent. Needed infrastructure improvements are estimated at $100 million over the next five to seven years, and another $150 million will be needed for software and systems

Innovation Report Card	
The Outsourcing of Information Technology and Telecommunications Services	
Criteria	**Grade**
1. Communication	A
2. Strength of Case	A
3. Implementation	A
4. Outcomes	Incomplete
5. Sustainable	Incomplete
Final Grade	**Incomplete**

applications. This will be a very large outsourcing.

Large computer contracts have not gone well in California, with severe problems developing in the state's motor vehicles, child-welfare, and child-support systems. In April 1999, the federal government rejected the state's proposal for an automated statewide child-support system, the second time California has encountered serious difficulties with child-support automation.

Perhaps even more ominous for the county's outsourcing is Connecticut Governor John G. Rowland's decision in late June 1999 to kill his own "billion dollar" information technology outsourcing. Rowland made the project one of his top priorities and had pushed it hard for four years as a key strategy to improve government performance and save money. Public employee unions and some of their influential allies in the state legislature staunchly opposed the proposal.

The explanation was that the governor's IT staff and prime contractor, EDS (one of the finalists in San Diego) could not agree on the total cost of the project or what would be included in the basic service package. However, the state declined to open negotiations with the second place bidder, IBM (also a San Diego finalist). Connecticut will now modernize its systems using state employees and contract out with private vendors on a more selective basis. The reaction in San Diego has been muted. Lana Willingham, who now heads the IT outsourcing team, said simply, "We have the wherewithal to do this and do it well."

Public employee unions have opposed the entire innovation effort in San Diego, and the IT outsourcing has become their central focus. Unlike Connecticut, the elected members of the Board of Supervisors have resisted the political pressure and instead sought to establish programs and policies to protect public employees who are affected. On December 8, 1998, the board approved an employee transition program that encourages affected employees to accept positions with the vendor selected.

The board required that the vendor selected offer employment to all in-scope employees, and offer employees whose positions fall within the scope of the RFP at least 150 days' employment in San Diego at least equal to their existing salary plus 30 percent for benefits. The county also offered affected employees the option of a retirement credit of two years or a severance payment of 20 percent for any county employee who decides not to take the contractor offer, is laid off by the county, and does not take another county position upon layoff.

Grading the Programs

What Goes into a Successful Innovation?

Many government managers and elected officials face circumstances where incremental change will not suffice. Perhaps the situation is not as drastic as the near bankruptcy faced by the San Diego County Board of Supervisors in 1995, but nevertheless, the situation calls for more dramatic change than the traditional tools of management can produce. In such circumstances, the tools of innovation may be the answer.

Throughout the 1990s, governments around the world have used tools borrowed from the private sector and created new tools to induce substantial changes in the standard operating procedures and outcomes of the public organizations they were seeking to turn around. (See Cohen and Eimicke, *Tools for Innovators*, 1998). San Diego County officials frequently characterize their innovation program as bringing the discipline of market competition to the public sector. However, as we have described, competition-based changes represent a relatively small part of the innovation program in San Diego. Reengineering, privatization, contracting out, reorganization, benchmarking, performance management, and strategic planning have all been used to reduce costs, increase productivity, improve customer service, and "move money to do good."

Comparing the five San Diego County innovations profiled in this report, clear differences emerge in terms of the results, ease of implementation, and perception of the success (or failure) of the innovation. As we observed and assessed the five initiatives, a series of key criteria emerged. From those criteria, a simple evaluation protocol was developed to assist other public managers who might be interested in using similar innovations in their community. The criteria we used to assess the innovations are:
1. The need for innovative change is well established and communicated widely.
2. Innovation advocates make a strong case for their solution.
3. Implementation is accomplished fairly and efficiently.
4. The innovation produces meaningful, measurable outcomes.
5. The beneficial impact of the innovative change can be sustained.

Grading Box for Each Project

	PROJECT				
	Solid Waste	Bonus	CalWORKS Competition	Competition and Reengineering Group	Information Technology and Telecommunications
Criteria					
1. Communication	A	C	A	A	A
2. Strength of Case	A	C	A	A	A
3. Implementation	A	C	A	A	A
4. Outcomes	A+	B	A	A	Incomplete
5. Sustainable	A+	B	B	B	Incomplete
Final Grade	**A**	**C**	**A**	**A**	**Incomplete**

We graded each innovation on a letter grade scale according to each of the five criteria: A (outstanding results); B (better than expected); C (acceptable); D (disappointing); or F (a mistake). The five criteria grades were then averaged to create a composite indicator of success for each innovation. While completely subjective, the grades will hopefully provide some yardstick by which other governments can assess whether similar innovations are advisable in their community.

The first innovation, the privatization of the county's solid waste system, merits an **A.**

All five members of the County Board of Supervisors agreed that public management of the solid waste system was a disaster and that it was the primary cause of the county's fiscal problems. They also agreed that it was highly unlikely that a public managed system could succeed in the foreseeable future. Just as important, they were able to clearly communicate those conclusions to the media, business leaders, taxpayers groups, and the general public. Measured against the first criterion, we gave this project an **A.**

The solution was equally well considered, documented, and communicated. New CAO Larry Prior assembled a "tiger team" of top talent in-house and brought in leading financial and legal consultants to come up with the best possible terms of sale for the county. The timing was right and the media covered the process extensively and in depth. By the time the Board of Supervisors was ready to vote on the sale, they were already being praised for their vision—an **A** measured against the second criterion.

The process was accomplished through a formal RFP process. Dismissal of the only lawsuit by a losing bidder documented the fairness and objectivity of the implementation stage. The major companies in the industry submitted proposals. Another **A** for solid waste, using the third criterion.

Prior's wise decision to hire the best outside counsel and financial advisor he could find and the competitive interest in the sale produced revenues well in excess of the county's initial expectations. As a result, the solid waste transaction alone helped avert bankruptcy, balance the county operating budget, restore reserve accounts to prudent levels, fund a deferred maintenance program, and finance the development costs of the rest of the innovation program. Not only are the results measurable, they generated enough dollars and goodwill for the rest of the innovation program. We decided to give an **A+** on this criterion.

The sale of the solid waste system relieved the county of an escalating operating loss, provided a substantial cash infusion to balance the budget, fill reserve funds, and eliminate deferred maintenance throughout county government, and provided the venture capital for the rest of the innovation program. Not only have the benefits of this innovation been sustained, they have increased over time—another **A+** is earned, creating a composite grade of **A** for the solid waste privatization.

The bonus program doesn't do as well in our grading system. While bonuses may have gotten top managers behind the innovation effort, Prior himself concedes that the program was poorly explained and not marketed well. Therefore, the bonus program graded poorly against our first two criteria in particular. Overall, we gave it a grade of **C**. It must be said that the county subsequently sought to correct its mistakes, apologizing for its poor communication, expanding the number of managers and staff eligible for bonuses, and capping the maximum bonus for any individual. The program is ongoing and becoming more popular, so there are positive and negative lessons to be learned from the San Diego County experiment with incentive-based pay for public managers.

The CalWORKS competition was developed with substantial baseline research, extensive outreach, and a very formal and well-documented selection process and ongoing, widely disseminated monitoring reports. Coupled with the major reductions in the county's welfare caseloads and substantial employment earnings gains among those still receiving assistance, a grade of **A** is clearly warranted.

CAO Prior set up the Competition and Reengineering Group to spread the discipline and spirit of innovation to every county department and agency. Created by an act of the Board of Supervisors and financed by the proceeds of the solid waste privatization, the group received substantial media attention. Group members also worked closely with every county office to help develop procedures for fair and meaningful competitions.

The group's extensive outreach to county employees and private vendors, the competition and cost comparison guides they developed and the fact that most competitions were won by county agencies reinforced their well-deserved reputation for fairness and efficiency. Nearly $35 million in documented, recurring savings represent meaningful, measurable outcomes. The risk that the benefits might not be sustained while the group is in sunset are more than offset by the enormous positive impact of ending the group ahead of schedule—instead of creating a new bureaucracy to fit bureaucracy. This innovation also deserves an **A.**

Finally, the outsourcing of information technology and telecommunications services could become the county's most successful innovation. It could enable every department to work better, faster, and cheaper while saving the county more than $87 million, compared to an in-house version of the same services. However, as we write this, the contractor has not even begun operation. Therefore, we gave this innovation an overall grade of **Incomplete** at this time.

Making It Stick

What Happens When the Innovative Leader Leaves?

On May 4, 1999, the San Diego County Board of Supervisors announced that Assistant Chief Administrative Officer Walt Ekard would succeed departing CAO Larry Prior. The board moved quickly to replace Prior (who took a chief executive officer position in the private sector), deciding against the national search process they had used to find Prior. Board Chairperson Pam Slater commented, "Larry Prior is a top administrator. But if anyone can match his performance, Walt Ekard can do it."

Prior and Ekard seem to be total opposites. Prior is obviously driven and has high energy and high intensity, with an in-your-face style. He is very much a family man, but you can see him as General Patton coaching his girls' soccer club. Ekard is calm, soft-spoken, open and friendly, a consensus-oriented people person. He too is a family man, with a passion for opera and baseball (he sang the National Anthem at a San Diego Padres professional baseball game).

The board chose Prior, a man with an excellent resume but a new face to them and county government. He was hired to shake things up with his no-nonsense style and focus on "the bottom line." Ekard was chosen from inside, with a long history of government service in the county, having previously served as manager for the wealthy Rancho Santa Fe Association and as a staff advisor for several county supervisors. Ekard acknowledges the difference; "I really do have a different approach toward things. Larry was more confrontational."

About Walter F. Ekard

Walter F. Ekard is the Chief Administrative Officer for the County of San Diego. Mr. Ekard was appointed to this post by the five-member Board of Supervisors on May 4, 1999. He previously served as the assistant chief administrative officer and was the Board's "first and only choice" for the job because of his experience and strong leadership skills.

As the county's CAO, he provides policy-based program and financial decision-making support to the board and oversees the operation of 40 departments that provide a myriad of services to the region—from health and human services to criminal justice programs, land use planning, public works, parks, libraries, animal control, and voter registrar services. He also manages the allocation of personnel, capital, and budgetary resources within the county organization.

Since he began working for the County in 1996, Mr. Ekard has been a part of its dramatic transformation, including creation of a structurally balanced budget and the implementation of a general management system. Working closely with the board and the county's executive team, Mr. Ekard will continue this comprehensive effort to institute private business management practices through-out the county, stressing customer service, fiscal accountability, and teamwork. Current and future efforts will focus on ensuring that recent positive changes become a part of the culture in county government. He will also oversee the successful conclusion of an information technology outsourcing project begun in late 1998.

Mr. Ekard brings a unique combination of qualifications and experience to this post. He has worked with legislators—service as a senior policy advisor to former County Supervisor Paul Fordem (1981-1984), then as chief of staff to former Supervisor Brian Bilbray (1985-1987). He also managed the Rancho Santa Fe Association from 1987 to 1996, transforming this 70-year-old organization into a smooth-running, productive, and powerful regional influence. During his tenure with the association, he worked in a capacity much like a city manager, developing linkages between the association and other community organizations, creating a long-term strategic plan to secure needed support from local and regional government agencies, and reducing administrative staff while streamlining the budget process and privatizing certain association functions.

A native of San Diego County, Mr. Ekard received his Bachelor of Arts degree from San Diego State University and a Juris Doctor degree from the University of San Diego School of Law. He is a member of the State Bar of California and has served on a number of community boards and commissions.

However, Ekard strongly supports the entire innovation agenda, including the controversial IT outsourcing. Interestingly, Ekard finished second in the board's national search to find Prior. Prior then chose Ekard as his number two—"his strengths are my weaknesses." Prior also pushed the board to select Ekard as his replacement. Some media observers even dubbed him as Prior's "hand-picked successor." Ekard reinforced the message of continuity by appointing Helen Robbins-Meyer, whom Prior recruited from TRW, as his second in command. And he said early on, "It's my desire, and the board's desire, to leave here with the changes we have made since 1996 still in place." His top priority for 1999-2000 was to make the innovations "stick" and make the changes part of county culture.

Still, the transition from Prior to Ekard represents more than just a change in style. Ekard will not back off past changes, but he intends to consolidate past gains rather than push for even more change. Ekard's second and third priorities, a focus on employees and leveraging the benefits of their diversity, signal his desire to reduce fear and uncertainty among county workers.

The message is already getting through. Union leader Mary Grillo, who hadn't spoken to Prior in two years, credits Ekard with negotiating the July 1998 contract with her union—"Walt is someone who will meet with me and will discuss issues." While there is a better labor atmosphere, Grillo is still suing to stop the IT outsourcing and CalWORKS competition and filing a flurry of freedom of information act requests to disrupt HHSA's innovation initiatives.

Strengthening the county's health and human services safety net is Ekard's top policy priority. In many respects, this represents the true purpose of the entire innovation effort. As Supervisor Diane Jacobs said, "We inherited a fiscal crisis. Turning that around so quickly was great, but helping kids and seniors is what makes me smile." The phrase we heard so often from all the key players in the change process was "it's all about moving money to do good."

Concluding Thoughts

San Diego County is one of the larger local governments in the United States. However, its size had little to do with the innovation tools chosen or the results achieved. In that sense, the San Diego experiment has relevance for most local governments in the United States. Did competition save the county from fiscal disaster and free up nearly half a billion dollars in annual spending for new libraries and health care for poor children?

County officials concede that a healthy national economy didn't hurt their efforts. But they also point out that the county nearly went bankrupt only four years prior. In my view, the innovation initiatives made a substantial contribution to righting the county government. And there are a number of important lessons that emerge from the San Diego experiment that can help to guide other local governments considering a competition-based improvement strategy.

Strong leadership from the top is essential. The elected County Board of Supervisors were unanimous in their support for selling the resource recovery plant, hiring a strong Chief Administrative Officer to implement the sale and the entire management innovation program, and in their votes to implement the program over the next three years. The huge budget deficit created by the county's failing solid waste business helped the Supervisors to gain public support and positive media coverage for their dramatic changes. The complete success of trash privatization strengthened their political will and the public's resolve to stay the course of innovation.

Just as the board supported Prior, he too supported his managers. Prior fought hard for large performance bonuses and distributed them generously to managers throughout the county. Most promotions were selected from in-house staff, and Prior shared credit and publicity with a large number of usually invisible public managers. Similarly strong messages were sent from those managers to their top people that change was both necessary and beneficial. Performance would be rewarded.

At HHSA, multiple innovation initiatives—reorganization, downsizing, reengineering, and competition—made the work life particularly stressful. Administrator Dr. Robert Ross kept his message simple, consistent, constant, and honest—"The risk of standing pat is great. And if we are successful, the savings will be invested in programs to help people in need."

Competing out public services is difficult and not always best. The CalWORKS competition took over a year to become fully operational and it is still too soon to draw conclusions about overall contractor performance. Only one of the eight managed competitions designed by the Competition and Reengineering Group was won by an outside contractor, but the group's 15-month effort produced about $35 million in annual savings for the county. Overall, the county's innovation program used reengineering, privatization, and outsourcing more often and to achieve greater savings than it accomplished through competition.

What works well in the private sector does not always work as well in government. The management bonus system developed by CAO Prior provoked strong opposition from the union leadership, resulted in a fair amount of bad press, and hurt the morale of non-managers. Also, public employee unions will probably oppose competition and related management innovation programs. San Diego County officials learned that an extensive employee outreach and communications effort and options to layoffs can mitigate employee resistance and negative media coverage.

However, public employee union leaders may still seek to undermine these programs as a threat to their organization's survival as managers and workers begin to work more as a team.

The greatest benefit of competition may be the change in public employee attitudes and behaviors. San Diego County won seven of the eight managed competitions, and senior managers report a new atmosphere in their offices characterized by analytic thinking, a constant search for meaningful, measurable program outcomes, and an ongoing commitment to continuous improvement.

The change process has been stressful. Jobs have been redefined (often dramatically), and there are fewer employees to get the work done. Media criticisms, freedom of information requests, and lawsuits by unions make day-to-day administration much more difficult. Yet, managers and workers report a new level of energy, creativity, and effectiveness above, below, and beside them. Even with the many victories it is very clear to everyone in HHSA that the battle is far from won.

Yet the commitment to do even more at HHSA and elsewhere in county government is stronger than ever. Joan Zinser, HHSA deputy administrator in charge of their massive innovation program, comments:

> Despite the stress, we now operate more like a team. We think outcomes before action, analysis before judgment. Competition, outsourcing, reengineering, reorganization, and incentives are all tools we can use, not slogans to live by. To me, the best news for the public is we are all working harder and smarter.

Appendix:
Competition and Reengineering Group Projects

1. **HHSA Synergy, Phase 1 & 2.** Multiple reengineering efforts and welfare caseload reduction have created annual savings of $21,515,000 and a reduction of 468 full-time equivalent positions. Savings have been reinvested in expanded services to abused and neglected children, home visiting, child immunizations, mental health access for wards and dependents, and the Black Infant Health Initiative.
2. **Correctional Facilities Health Services.** An outside vendor won the managed competition, saving $795,000 annually. A total of 44 positions were replaced, but the vendor hired some of the employees. Savings represent the difference between the lower contractor price and higher employee bid. In that sense, this represents an avoidance of higher future costs rather than budget savings.
3. **Workers' Compensation Claims Administration.** Improved efficiencies were achieved through reengineered processes, elimination of unnecessary forms and paperwork, and use of performance-based outcome measures. Annual savings of $230,000 were achieved, and 4.5 full-time equivalent positions were eliminated.
4. **Office of Financial Planning.** Introduction of an Automated Budget Reporting and Analysis Support System produced more accurate spending and revenue estimates and projections. Annual savings total $300,000 with five positions eliminated.
5. **Revenue & Recovery.** Government agency won managed competition with a combination of cost savings and revenue enhancements, freeing up $575,000 annually for the county.
6. **Alternate Public Defender, Dependency.** Public agency was successful in competing to provide defense services for juvenile dependency cases, saving $235,000 annually and freeing up funding to reinvest in dependency court enhancements.
7. **El Cajon Municipal Court Pre-Arraignment Services.** The Public Defender won the managed competition to provide pre-arraignment indigent defense services, previously provided by the private bar, and was able to reduce county costs by $133,200 annually.
8. **Public Defender.** The Public Defender's Dependency Division was reengineered to enable attorneys to focus on the courtroom and legal issues while paralegals and investigators concentrate on the social welfare of the child. Three attorney positions were replaced by three legal assistants, saving $220,000 annually.
9. **Mental Health Services in the Jails.** Services previously provided by HHSA were reorganized and integrated into the Sheriff's Medical Service

System. This reengineering resulted in better coordination of health services and elimination of duplication. The sheriff was able to eliminate 13 positions, saving $500,000 annually.

10. **Air Pollution Control District.** The district reengineered business processes using automation and other systems improvements. The annual savings of $630,000 enabled the agency to reduce fees charged to businesses by $380,000, provide additional assistance to small businesses, and automate other district operations.

11. **Environmental Health.** Annual savings of $1.3 million were accomplished through reengineering, which consolidated nine divisions into four, increased management ratios from 1:5 to 1:7, and financed the creation of six new positions to improve customer service.

12. **Parks and Recreation, Fallbrook Community Center.** The Department of Parks and Recreation won the competition to operate this community center, freeing up $33,800 annually for related program enhancements.

13. **Parks and Recreation, Spring Valley Center.** The department won this competition, freeing up $30,000 for related program improvements.

14. **Public Works.** The department used reengineering to reduce staffing levels consistent with current workload and divest itself of several non-core functions. Savings of $3.2 million are being used to offset previously projected increases in sewer service fees and to finance needed capital improvements.

15. **Wastewater Management.** Reengineering and contracting of certain tasks to the City of San Diego resulted in a reduction of $74,000 in annual commercial/industrial wastewater permitting and monitoring costs.

16. **Facilities Maintenance.** The Department of General Services used reengineering to reduce the number of steps in the work order process and more efficiently deliver maintenance services through five regional operations. Annual savings of $800,000 were achieved, in part through the elimination of 27 positions.

17. **General Services Management and Administration.** The department used reengineering to consolidate six divisions into three and reduce the number of overhead support positions. Annual cost reduction of $1.3 million provided $800,000 to fund other priorities in the agency.

18. **Rental Assistance Program.** The Housing and Community Development Department reengineered its Section 8 rental assistance program using automation, reorganization, and staff reductions reflecting a reduced workload to save $500,000 annually. The savings are being used to finance low and moderate income housing initiatives.

19. **Fleet Services.** The Department of General Services won the managed competition by reducing staffing, consolidating 10 garages into six, and forming partnerships with public agencies and private vendors. The annual savings total $1 million.

20. **Probation Department.** Using reengineering, the department consolidated five divisions into three, eliminating 24 positions and downgrading 62 others. Annual savings of $2.3 million are being reinvested in frontline services to juvenile offenders and a new juvenile hall.
21. **Office of Financial Planning.** The Budget Office was restructured, consolidating 10 positions into five. Savings of $300,000 annually were reinvested in a new budgeting, projecting, and strategic planning automated system.

Endnotes

1. The author acknowledges the expert consultation and assistance of his colleague Steven Cohen and his research assistant at Columbia University's School of International and Public Affairs, Jennifer Mitchell. Patricia Frosio, Chief of Staff for San Diego County CAO Walt Ekard, provided access to the key actors and documents as well as her own insights without which this paper would not have been possible

Bibliography

Cohen, S. and W. Eimicke. *Tools for Innovators.* San Francisco: Jossey Bass Publishers, 1998.

County of San Diego. *Calworks Program Update,* July 30, 1999.

County of San Diego. *Final Report—Competition and Reengineering Group,* May 26, 1999.

Eimicke, W. "Managed Competition: Networks and Partnerships to Deliver Welfare to Work Services in Indianapolis, Indiana, San Diego and Alameda County, California." Prepared for presentation at the Annual Meeting of the American Society for Public Administration, Orlando, Florida, April 10-14, 1999.

Goldsmith, S. *The Twenty-first Century City.* Washington, D.C.: Regnery Publishing, Inc., 1997.

Gurwitt, R. "Another California High-Tech Setback." *Governing,* June 1999, p. 42.

Interviews: Much of the information reported here was gathered through a series of semi-structured interviews conducted by the author in San Diego, California. Interviews were conducted with all five members of the Board of Supervisors, their senior staff, the current and previous CAO of the county, their chief of staff, both directors and most staff of the Competition and Reengineering Group, senior staff of the Health and Human Services Agency, and a wide variety of middle management and line county staff (who spoke primarily on the condition of confidentiality). The author also reviewed confidential working papers made available by county managers and media coverage of the competition experiment between 1995 and 1999. Drafts of the report were shared with the county for comment but the author accepts full responsibility for the material presented and its interpretation.

Kucher, K. "County picks Ekard, top Prior aide, as CAO." *The San Diego Union-Tribune,* May 5, 1999, p. B-1.

Osborne, D. and P. Plastrik. *Banishing Bureaucracy.* Reading, Massachusetts: Addison-Wesley Publishing Company, Inc., 1997.

Perlman, E. "Connecticut Kills Its Billion-Dollar Outsourcing Plan." *Governing,* August 1999, p. 40.

Salamon, L. *Partners in Public Service.* Baltimore: The Johns Hopkins University Press, 1995.

Swope, C. "Paying for Performance." *Governing,* November 1998, pp. 75-79.

CHAPTER SIX

Innovation in the Administration
of Public Airports

Scott E. Tarry
Associate Professor
Aviation Institute
Department of Public Administration
University of Nebraska at Omaha

This report was originally published in March 2000.

Introduction: Innovation at Airports

Publicly owned and operated airports are an intriguing subject for those interested in the business of government. Governed by elected or appointed officials, managed by public administrators, and an integral part of the national transportation infrastructure, modern airports operate in an increasingly complex political and commercial environment. The demand for air transport services continues to increase, straining airports' ability to provide sufficient runways, gates, terminal space, automobile parking, and various amenities that passengers demand. At the same time, airlines are increasingly concerned about reducing costs, and environmentalists challenge virtually every expansion attempt. Airports that hope to succeed in such an environment must innovate. They must anticipate the future, rely less on the federal government for financial assistance, and recognize the commercial realities of today's highly competitive airline industry. In these times of rapid change in the air transport industry it is worth considering how these public enterprises respond to various challenges and opportunities.

This report details the efforts of five commercial-service airports that have successfully addressed a diverse set of challenges and opportunities through innovative management strategies. These airports are Chattanooga Metropolitan Airport, Miami International Airport, Portland International Airport, Salt Lake City International Airport, and Chicago O'Hare International Airport. They are diverse in size, the structure of their governing bodies, their missions, and their strategies. They are similar in their ability to tackle creatively myriad problems and to exploit aggressively new opportunities.

Quick Facts About Airports in this Study

Airport Name	Local/ Regional Population	Annual Departing Passengers
Chattanooga Metropolitan Airport	150,000	300,000
Miami International Airport	3.4 million	16.5 million
Portland International Airport	1.7 million	6.5 million
Salt Lake City International Airport	1.2 million	10.2 million
Chicago O'Hare International Airport	7.8 million	33.0 million

The balance of this chapter is organized as follows. The first section presents a general discussion of the role airports play in modern society and why airports are interesting cases for studying the business of government. The section also examines the various obstacles and incentives for innovation in publicly owned and operated airports. The second section provides detailed descriptive case studies of innovation at each of the five airports. Each case follows its own course, since the airports face different challenges and necessarily address them with different strategies. The information presented in each case study comes from extensive interviews conducted during site visits to each airport during the summer of 1999. The final two sections discuss lessons learned, and explore recommendations for other airports and the public sector more generally.

Airports as Public Enterprises

Airports are critical components of the national transportation infrastructure. They facilitate the movement of cargo and people by providing facilities where ground and air transportation modes intersect. This intersection of various modes of transport results in a complexity not found in other public sector enterprises. In addition to being the most used public facilities in terms of the number of people using them each day, airports are arguably the most important public facilities in terms of commerce and tourism. A city's airport provides important links to both the national and global economies.

Most commercial-service airports are publicly owned and operated by local or regional governing bodies. This structure finds its roots in the early days of air transport when airports were considered to be little different from seaports. The core business of the airport is still to provide a place for aircraft to land and take off, but myriad changes in the air transport industry, the economy, and society in general make the airport a place of constant change. In addition to well-articulated federal aviation regulations, airports must also abide by federal, state, and local statutes that deal with everything from environmental restrictions to personnel issues. At the same time, airports are expected to keep up with the needs of the highly competitive, profit-oriented airlines that utilize and pay for most of the airports' operations.

The past two decades have been a time of considerable change for America's airports. After economic deregulation of the airlines in 1978, airports faced new political, economic, and social environments. New strategies, new ideas, and new technologies were necessary for airports to keep pace with the rest of the air transport industry and the broader economy. The next section examines some of the obstacles and incentives to innovation in the airport business.

Obstacles to Innovation in Public Airports

Airports face a number of real obstacles to innovation. At this point, it is difficult to point to any one factor as the key obstacle. Rather, it is worth keeping each of the factors in mind when examining an airport, because some will matter more in specific cases. Five factors that might impede innovation are explained below. Some of these are relevant to the public sector generally, while others are specific to airports.

Public-Utility Mentality

Historically, airports operated in a fashion not much different from public utilities. In such circumstances there is little incentive to innovate since there is no market pressure and only nominal political pressure to enhance service once some basic service standard is met. Prior to regulatory reform of the airline industry in 1978, airports and airlines operated in an environment that did little to induce innovation. Since 1978 the airline industry has adjusted to its new competitive surroundings, and successful airlines now recognize the need to respond to innovations in information technologies, marketing strategies, and customer service, and to anticipate these changes and bring new technologies and strategies into their operations quickly. Airports, unlike the airlines, were not deregulated in 1978 and still operate under the regulatory framework that emphasizes maintenance of existing levels of service and performance over innovation to enhance or improve operational performance and financial efficiency. This does not mean that airports have not managed to innovate, but that the overall regulatory framework is not, by itself, likely to induce innovation.

Top-Down, Hierarchical Tradition

The traditional model for airport administration has been top down and hierarchical. Strict hierarchical or chain-of-command organizations are not likely to be fonts of innovation. Rather, they are expected to be paragons of stability and order. This model finds its roots in the function of the airport and the pool from which airport administrators have been traditionally recruited. The function of the airport, which is to facilitate the movement of passengers and cargo safely and efficiently, demands a stable and orderly environment. Hence, the core business of the airport is one that requires strict adherence to well-articulated guidelines. In such a situation, staff members are expected to follow orders and standard operating procedures. Innovation is not necessarily precluded in this environment, but the emphasis is on maintaining existing levels of performance.

It is not surprising, then, that administrators recruited into the airport business came from environments that included both substantive expertise in aviation and experience in hierarchical command structures. Although the demographics within the airport administration community are changing, top airport administrators historically followed career paths that included service in the military or the Federal Aviation Administration (FAA). Airports, not surprisingly, were interested in men who had experience and expertise in the variety of issues that confront airport administrators on a regular basis.[1] The most logical place to look for such individuals was the military, where potential administrators could be recruited from a well-trained and seasoned officer corps.

What is interesting is that even those administrators who came to their positions without military or federal government experience traditionally tended to follow the same hierarchical administrative practices as those whose careers included military and government service. The culture of the aviation community has, for a variety of reasons, always mirrored the military more than other sectors of society, most likely because the closest analogue for an airport is an airbase. The traditional language, roles, and responsibilities of airport administrators have been more akin to that of military officers than that of seaport or rail administrators.

It is important to recognize that this point focuses on general patterns of organizational structure within the airport community and says nothing about specific individuals. It is quite possible that former military officers can be successful innovators. Conversely, there is no reason to believe that administrators coming from the private sector will be successful innovators simply because of their background. The point is that the history of airport administration suggests both a culture and an organizational tradition that are not as conducive to innovation as other possible forms. While individuals can overcome these historical impediments to innovation, doing so can require considerable effort, since a number of additional obstacles remain. These obstacles are no less important, and continue to plague airports that have successfully reengineered their organizational cultures by abandoning the public-utility mentality and addressing the negative implications of hierarchical administrative structures. The good thing about contemporary obstacles is that some airports, such as those in this study, have been able to identify them and mitigate their negative impact on innovation and service improvements.

Regulatory Constraints

Regulations continue to constrain airport administrators. Safety and security issues necessitate many of these regulations, but other regulations and certain governmental policies are less easily defended. Two issues, which are explored in more detail in the case studies, involve financial autonomy and cooperation between airports and the federal air traffic controllers. Airports are currently restricted from using aviation income to fund non-aviation projects, even if the non-aviation project has direct implications for the operation of the airport. Two examples illustrate the point. The City of Los Angeles attempted to use aviation income to fund additional police officers not located on airport property. The airlines and the government agreed that this was inconsistent with the core business of the airport and that aviation income must be used for purposes more clearly relevant to the provision of air transport services.

In another example, the Port Authority of New York and New Jersey wanted to use aviation income to fund a rail link between JFK International Airport and Jamaica Station, which would give travelers better rail access and reduce ground transport congestion at the airport. The airlines fought and eventually lost a battle to prevent the Port from using aviation dollars to fund the rail link. Even though the airlines lost the battle, they have certainly not lost the war on this issue, leaving airports to struggle with the funding of projects that ultimately can improve the quality of service for the flying public, but fall outside the traditional boundaries of aviation operations.

Airports continue to grapple with their relationship with the FAA and its air traffic controllers. In a number of cases, airports have sought to alleviate their noise problems by working with the controllers to revise flight tracks to and from the airport. The idea behind these proposals is to direct inbound and outbound aircraft along specific routes over non-residential neighborhoods. Unfortunately, controllers at some airports have taken these proposals as an infringement on their authority to direct aircraft. Moreover, they have expressed their concerns about how such plans might affect workloads. Unless the controllers can be convinced that the proposals are sound, the airports will have to deal with their noise problems in ways that are more expensive and time-consuming.

Hesitancy by Airlines

It may be surprising to casual observers of the air transport industry, but the staunchest opponents of many airport initiatives are the airlines. While airports operate on revenue derived from various sources, the airlines typically fund the bulk of an airport's operating budget. They do so directly through the landing fees and passenger facility charges that are paid to the airport and indirectly through taxes and other fees that constitute the Airport and Airways trust fund. In short, the airlines keep a wary eye on any and all airport proposals. They are vigilant against any proposal that seems in excess of what is necessary for the airlines' core business.

The airlines' hesitancy stems from a perception that the airports are not accountable and must be held in check. The airlines, which operate as publicly held corporations, are accountable to their stockholders. Local and regional political bodies may monitor airports and the public may use the ballot to enforce its will upon a council or authority, but since local taxes are not typically used for airport expenses, there is little political connection between the public and the operation of the airport. In other words, the public is unlikely to be as vigilant as the airlines, since the latter pays the vast majority of the airports' bills.

Airlines are pleased when innovations improve services and reduce costs, but they tend to resist airport proposals until the airport can make a very strong case for the innovation. The case might be bolstered by evidence from other airports where the changes are already in place. Relying on evidence from other airports is problematic, however, since new ideas have to begin somewhere. Genuine innovations, by definition, have no track record and often have few analogues in other industries. In these cases, the airports must convince the airlines without the benefit of hindsight or solid empirical evidence about gains in efficiency and reductions in costs.

Inadequate Reward and Recognition Programs

One of the most basic impediments to innovation in the public sector is inadequate reward and recognition programs, which might otherwise provide monetary or other incentives for individual innovators. Many airports face this situation because their personnel policies are developed not for the dynamic commercial environment that characterizes today's public airports, but for the more routine environment of the water treatment plant or the street maintenance department.

The effect of inadequate reward and recognition programs is twofold. First, employees have little financial or professional incentive to innovate. Instead of working to develop new ways of doing business, employees are likely to continue to do their jobs as they were originally construed. Second, those employees who are successful innovators may find themselves frustrated by a system that cannot accommodate significant salary increases and rapid promotions. Such employees might recognize that their efforts and talents are more adequately rewarded in the private sector. In short, public sector reward and recognition programs, as well as traditional approaches to public sector personnel issues, may not prohibit innovation, but they may reduce its likelihood.

Incentives for Innovation

Having just argued that the deck is stacked against innovation in airport administration, it is important to recognize changes in the culture of airport administration that can make innovation more likely. Included among these changes is a move away from the public-utility mentality that historically downplayed the importance of customer service. Another significant change is that airports increasingly see themselves as part of the business world. Some airports believe that they are in competition with other airports, and most recognize that a well-managed airport can have real and significant effects on local and regional economic development. Finally, more airports are reaching the conclusion that they need to address the issue of inadequate federal funding not by complaining, but by reorganizing their processes and seeking new funding sources. The airports that have achieved some success in this effort often realize that alternative funding sources and new business practices can provide them with autonomy that they never thought possible under the traditional model of airport administration.

Fostering a Culture of Innovation

Creating a culture of innovation and change can go a long way to overcoming the obstacles that might otherwise stifle innovation. Even organizations with inadequate reward and recognition programs can foster innovation by encouraging and allowing their people to develop new ideas. Successfully implemented ideas, especially those that result in real change, can go a long way to reinforcing a new culture. Staff members may not find extra pay in their paychecks, but they and their colleagues can still take pride in knowing that their efforts are making a difference in the way the airport serves the public.

Taking Seriously the Airport's Role in Commerce

Airport authorities and other relevant political bodies increasingly recognize the impact that a well-run airport can have on local and regional economies. To the extent that these bodies are concerned about the role the airport might have on economic development, attracting new businesses, and developing new air transportation services (i.e., more flights serving more destinations), they can press the airports' administrative staff to seek new means for improving service quality. In this context, an airport becomes another tool in local and regional economic development plans. Local leaders see the airport as another means for competing against other cities for new plants, new distribution centers, and new jobs.

Some airports even consider themselves in competition with other airports. These airports reject the notion that airports merely serve the local or regional population and those travelers for whom the airport is a destination. They point to the choices that travelers have in the hub and spoke system. Passengers whose travel necessitates a transfer at a hub airport because their home airport or destination airport is not a hub itself might in fact make a choice about which hub they will travel through. A savvy traveler might choose to avoid an airport with inadequate retail and restaurant services. Such a decision costs the avoided airport revenue from concessions and aviation income. It also affects the profitability of the airline using the airport as its hub. The prospect of lower revenues and decreased service can induce an airport to innovate.

Shrinking Federal Funds and the Pressures of Privatization

Two traditional funding sources, the federal government and the airlines, are becoming increasingly problematic. Congress seems unable or unwilling to use trust fund resources to fund airport improvements, deciding instead to let the fund serve as a prop in the budget-balancing game. The result has been declining appropriations for airport improvements and the need to expand alternative funding sources. The airlines are increasingly vocal about fees and charges and demand that airports do more to reduce costs and collect revenue from other sources. The uncertain future of federal funding and the constant complaining of the airlines combine to create a significant incentive for airport administrators to innovate.

Additional pressure comes from the privatization trend. Although it seems to have lost some of its steam from several well-publicized problems in other industries, privatization is nonetheless a real prospect for the future of airport management. A number of European airports are privately managed and a handful of private management contracts exist in the United States. The prospect of privatization can serve as an incentive to innovate for those administrators who believe that they can do just as well within their current ownership/management structure.

The various obstacles and incentives to innovation in commercial-service airports are best illustrated through detailed examination of specific airports. The following five case studies highlight the diverse set of challenges and opportunities that confront airport administrators as we move into the next century.

Case Studies

It is no exaggeration to say that no two airports in America are the same. Indeed, the case studies in this project were selected to illustrate the diversity among America's commercial-service airports. Even though they provide similar services, the size, character, and function of airports are a reflection of the political, geographic, economic, and social contexts within which they exist. Politics determines who has ultimate authority over administrative decisions. Geography determines an airport's layout and myriad other operational issues. The local and regional economy determines the type and level of service, such as the mix of passenger and cargo service. Societal influences affect the way the public interacts with the airport and whether the airport is seen as friend or foe in the community. Each airport faces a unique mix of these influences, and administrators must tailor their strategies to fit within the relevant context.

However, it would be a mistake to assume that nothing can be gained from an analysis of diverse cases. Despite what often amounts to considerable differences among airports, it is still a productive exercise to see how individual airports respond to challenges and exploit opportunities. The cases described here may not match exactly the situations facing other airports, but much can be learned from the way in which the administrators in these cases identified their problems and opportunities, developed new strategies and approaches, and implemented these ideas to improve the quantity and quality of the services provided to the public. The cases do not provide cookbook solutions to any specific problems, but they do offer an intriguing slate of potential strategies for airport administrators seeking to keep up with the rapidly evolving air transport business.

Chattanooga Metropolitan Airport

Located near the Tennessee border with Georgia and about 110 miles from Atlanta, this city of 150,000 represents a number of similarly sized and situated cities that have been forced to adjust to the transformation of the American airline industry after regulatory reform in the late 1970s. The increasingly competitive airline industry's move away from point-to-point service and towards the hub and spoke system hit Chattanooga especially hard. Once served by mainline airline service to a variety of non-stop destinations, Chattanooga found itself in danger of losing the quantity and quality of air service that helped preserve its economic base. The city found itself caught in a sort of netherworld between much smaller communities, which were happy simply to have some level of commuter service, and larger cities, many of which were enjoying the fruits of having hub airports. Added to this was the fact that Chattanooga is situated near one of the largest hub airports in the world, Atlanta's Hartsfield International Airport, which is home to Delta Air Lines' Worldport.

Chattanooga's air service woes could not have come at a worse time for city leaders. After decades of being known as one of the worst polluted cities in America, Chattanooga established itself as a model for both comprehensive cleanup efforts and sustainable economic development. Poised to show the rest of the country what the city had done to fix its most glaring problems, city officials were forced to grapple with a new problem that was at once new and seemingly beyond their control. It made little sense to city officials and members of the local community to lose the air service that would allow Chattanooga to effectively link itself directly to other regions of the country and the broader global economy.

H. Hugh Davis, Jr., president of the Chattanooga Metropolitan Airport Authority and the head administrator of the city's airport, admits that the

Chattanooga Metropolitan Airport At-a-Glance

Chattanooga's population:	150,000
Departing passengers:	300,000 per year
Service:	Spoke airport with service to numerous domestic hubs
Governing structure:	Chattanooga Metropolitan Airport Authority (airport authority)
Reporting line:	Authority appointed by mayor, confirmed by council
Key administrator:	H. Hugh Davis, Jr., President, Airport Authority
Innovations:	Collaborative effort with other similarly situated airports Market research and communication

changes in the airline industry hit the community hard, leaving many Chattanoogans wondering what they had done to deserve such treatment. The frustration reached its peak four years ago when Delta pulled out of Chattanooga and turned its operations over to Atlantic Southeast Airlines (ASA). For many local residents, this represented the final indignity. Although USAirways continued to provide jet service, Delta's departure meant that Chattanooga's air service would be dominated by commuter carriers. Area political leaders wondered aloud whether the airport had done enough to maintain the level of service to which people had become accustomed.

Davis and his staff were faced with the difficult task of resolving an issue over which they had little control. The decisions by Delta and other carriers to alter service were driven by market demand. There is little doubt that if enough area residents were flying out of Chattanooga's airport, Delta or some other carrier would have maintained, or even improved, its level of service. With little more than the bottom line as a guide, the airlines collectively adjusted their levels of service to the realities of the local market.

Unfortunately, the airlines' strategies can amount to self-fulfilling prophecies for cities like Chattanooga. Consider the following cycle and set of circumstances. The airlines are concerned about the profitability of their flights to and from Chattanooga. When demand lags they reasonably conclude there is a need to reduce the number of flights, switch to smaller aircraft, or both. A likely result from such a strategy is that local travelers become increasingly disenchanted with the air service offered out of their airport. Flights are not offered with sufficient frequency, which can translate to awkward travel schedules or lengthy layovers at transfer airports.

Similarly, passengers who have come to expect a certain level of service—either in terms of the type of equipment such as jet aircraft or the quality of in-flight service and amenities—now find themselves booked on regional aircraft with a lower standard of service and fewer amenities. In the end, potential passengers begin to look for ways to avoid their local airports. As noted before, Chattanooga sits no more than a two-hour drive away from Atlanta's airport, where service frequency and quality abound. All else being equal, a two-hour drive is something most air travelers would like to avoid, but with the changes in service, more and more travelers are willing to make the sacrifice. In the end, the airlines' efforts to adjust service to demand creates a situation in which their worst projections about the local market are confirmed.

Chattanooga's airport is included in this study because it represents a model for similarly situated airports. While the airport has not been able to alter the general trends in the airline industry, it has been able to make the most of its own stake in the air transport system. Chattanooga has put together a collection of strategies that, when taken together, offer hope for airports and communities facing similar challenges.

The various strategies developed and implemented in Chattanooga are explored in some detail below. Before turning to the specifics, however, it is worth noting a central theme in what the airport has done in recent years. When asked about the most important issues facing his airport, Davis responded somewhat philosophically that he is firmly convinced that airports first need to understand who they are. In saying this, he means much more than that Chattanooga's airport should not fool itself into thinking that it can eventually become Atlanta's Hartsfield. He means that an airport must consciously consider its appropriate role in the broader air transport system and the regional economy. Instead of trying to become something it is not and will likely never be, an airport should work to do the best it can, given its specific circumstances. A sober and candid appraisal of the industry, the region, and the airport itself can provide a solid foundation from which community leaders and airport administrators can work to improve the quantity and quality of air transport services offered by their airport.

When the airlines began to reduce and alter the services offered out of Chattanooga, local officials looked to the models they knew best when confronted with economic development problems. They approached the airlines with standard chamber of commerce style appeals, which sought to convince the airlines to operate more flights out of Chattanooga because it was a dynamic city. Unfortunately, the things that might appeal to a manufacturing firm seeking to relocate a plant hardly appeal to an airline. The "dog and pony show" approach, as it is often derisively called, does little for an airline concerned almost exclusively about filling seats on its aircraft. Like in many other communities, Chattanooga leaders learned that appeals based on the quality of their city were falling on deaf ears. The task was to figure out what would get the airlines' attention.

Chattanooga's approach is best described as two-pronged. The first prong consisted of things the airport itself could do. The other prong consisted of things the airport could do in conjunction with other similarly affected airports. Instead of wringing their hands and accepting their predicament, Chattanooga officials embarked on very public campaigns to improve air service for their city.

Working With Other Airports to Address Common Problems

The most visible aspect of Chattanooga's approach was its leadership role in the National Air Service Roundtable (NASR). After raising the issue of deteriorating air service with its state's own congressional leaders, the city and its airport hosted the first NASR in February 1997. The roundtable brought together government officials, representatives from the airlines, and industry observers to discuss and debate the situation facing cities like Chattanooga. This meeting and a subsequent roundtable in Jackson, Mississippi, in January 1998 established air service issues as a national concern. Cities like

Madison, Wisconsin; Duluth, Minnesota; and Moline, Illinois, joined with Chattanooga and Jackson to seek the government's help in resolving their dilemma. Pointing to a General Accounting Office study that called these cities "pockets of pain" in the wake of regulatory reform in the airline industry, local and regional officials from around the country shared their tales of woe and explored possible solutions.

The cities involved in the roundtable found themselves in the awkward position of being between the truly neglected communities, for which the government subsidized air service, and the larger cities, which produced sufficient demand to attract desired frequencies and destinations from the airlines. While the roundtables placed the issue on the national agenda and raised the specter of a government solution, they offered no real comfort for Chattanooga and its allies. Few outside the affected cities were willing to re-regulate the industry in order to preserve or improve air services for these communities. The airlines and a vocal cadre of deregulation advocates pointed to the positive impact of deregulation and questioned the utility of a government-imposed solution.

What then did Chattanooga accomplish by engaging in the roundtables? According to Davis, the roundtables accomplished a number of things. First, they removed the sense of isolation for the cities that participated. City officials and airport staff now had a network of similarly situated airports with which to exchange ideas and information. Second, the roundtables suggested quite strongly to the airlines that they need to pay attention to the issue of air service. In the tradition of "the squeaky wheel gets the grease," Chattanooga believes that its efforts in the roundtables effectively encouraged United and American to consider it as the most desirable destination for new slots opening up at Chicago O'Hare. The result has been the development of regional jet service three times a day from Chattanooga to Chicago, a service that did not exist prior to the roundtable and may well have been prodded by the national exposure Chattanooga received in those deliberations.

Public Perceptions: Research, Communication, and Education

On the whole, however, Chattanooga was left on its own to address its air service concerns. The authority set about to work on those areas over which the airport did have some control. The primary objective in these efforts was to increase communication, not merely between the airport and the airlines, but between the airport and travel agents, the airport and the flying public, and the airport and the local business community. Three years ago, Kelly Watson was hired to head a new marketing and public relations department. According to Watson, whose background did not include airport experience, she started with research. Before creating a community relations program or a marketing campaign, the airport needed to know what people thought about the airport and air travel.

The results of Watson's research confirmed what other airport officials suspected: Public perception was based on inaccurate information about the airport and the airlines that served it. More disconcerting was the fact that frequent flyers, travel agents, and the media who covered the airport weren't much better informed. In some cases it seemed that misinformation about the airport came from people who should have known better. This is not to say that anyone was purposely trying to misinform the public, but that individuals whom the airport saw as allies in preserving existing and developing new air service were part of the problem. Watson discovered what many other airports are beginning to recognize. The public has a very poor sense of how an airport operates and what role the airport plays in the broader scheme of air transport.

Besides blaming the airport for things beyond its control, such as Delta's decision to leave Chattanooga and ASA's dreadful service record when it took over Delta's flights, the public had a number of complaints that were based more in rumor than fact. A common complaint was that the airport offered no jet service. Another complaint was that fares were always higher, and in most cases substantially higher, if one flew from Chattanooga instead of Atlanta. In both cases there was some element of truth, but the real picture was much less gloomy. The airport saw a reduction in jet service, but was never completely without it. Some fares were indeed higher, but many were comparable or in line with the additional cost associated with a trip to Atlanta to catch a flight.

The airport embarked on a comprehensive program to educate the public and open the lines of communication with all of the airport's stakeholders. Travel agents were invited to receptions at the airport and encouraged to participate in travel agent roundtable discussions with airport board members and airline representatives. For the first time, travel agents, airport officials, and the airlines were talking to each about their concerns. Watson complemented these meetings with a quarterly newsletter that provides the community with a variety of information, including a reliability report for the six airlines currently serving Chattanooga. The reports, which are also given to the media and the business community each month, provide data on cancellations and delays. Cancellation data are broken down by cause, and delay data are broken down by length of delay. The reports have had the desired effect of showing the public that the air service out of Chattanooga is quite good and improving.

Education and communication are certainly not enough if the central concern is increasing demand, so the airport works closely with carriers to coordinate events and other marketing promotions. Some carriers participate in cooperative advertising, which promotes both the airport and the airline. Supported by an airport board that understands the need for marketing, the airport is actively pursuing new business for the carriers that serve the city.

They point to their airport as a hassle-free alternative to Atlanta's busy hub airport. As traffic congestion and flight delays continue to plague their larger neighbor, Chattanooga prides itself on its accessibility.

A clear sense of where their airport fits into the broader air transport system and what really motivates airlines has helped Chattanooga overcome the myriad difficulties the airport faced four years ago. The airport is poised to take advantage of the trend towards the heavier use of regional jets and the route development possibilities that these smaller, cost-effective aircraft offer. Six airlines currently operate flights to hubs throughout the South and Midwest. Enplanements continue to increase and airlines continue to add new services. The airport is prepared to accommodate these developments with a well-designed and efficiently managed terminal that was constructed with expansion in mind.

Chattanooga has positioned itself to take advantage of what seemed until recently a real disaster for he airport and the community it serves. Instead of worrying about what it was not, and whether the government would protect it, the airport candidly assessed its predicament and set out to address it in a comprehensive manner. The airport authority worked to change both the culture of the airport and the public perception of the airport. It improved communication between the airport and its stakeholders. It educated public officials and the local business community about the airport and airline business. It looked around the country for new ideas and strategies that could put it in the best position to exploit opportunities and resolve problems. In the end, Chattanooga has air service that other cities of its size covet. It has an airport that effectively addresses the needs of the flying public and offers the airlines the flexibility to expand their service if the market demands it.

Miami International Airport

Miami is an international city well known as a tourist destination and increasingly as an important business destination for the Americas. Such popularity is not without a price, and the major concern for Miami is how to redevelop its airport into a facility that will accommodate the demands of air travelers and cargo shippers into the next century.

Like so many other major cities in America, Miami's airport is now landlocked by developed properties and communities increasingly concerned about the impact of aircraft noise. Thus, any expansion of airport capacity in Miami will take place in an increasingly difficult political, environmental, and social context. The airport administration is taking this task seriously and approaching a variety of new projects, including its $5.4 billion Capital Improvement Program (CIP), with creativity and ingenuity not often found in the public sector.

Miami International Airport At-a-Glance

Metropolitan Miami's population:	3.4 million
Departing passengers:	16.5 million per year
Service:	Hub airport with extensive international flights
Governing structure:	Miami-Dade County Aviation Department (unit of county government)
Reporting line:	Aviation Department reports to county manager, who reports to county commissioners
Key administrators:	Gary Dellapa, Director, Aviation Department Bruce Drum, Assistant Aviation Director Narinder Jolly, Architect & Facilities Manager
Innovations:	Managing $5.4 billion in capital improvements Communications Noise and environmental issues

It is impossible to talk about Miami without discussing local government. Often characterized in less than charitable terms, elected officials in Miami-Dade County have a reputation for meddling in the administration of government services, the hiring of new personnel, and the letting of contracts. Gary Dellapa, director of the Miami-Dade Aviation Department, manages Miami International Airport (MIA). Dellapa reports to Merrett Stierheim, who serves as the county's manager and in turn reports to the elected Miami-Dade Board of County Commissioners. The political framework is a critical issue in Miami, because the commissioners are very active and have a history of involving themselves in the day-to-day operations of various departments of the county government. Not surprisingly, because of its visibility and the size of the contracts that it lets, the airport is a frequent focus of the Board's attention.

Dellapa and members of his administrative staff see the airport's relationship with the airlines serving Miami as something more than the landlord-tenant relationship that has been the tradition at airports around the country. Airlines are referred to as "business partners." The change in terminology represents much more than just changing a few words. It recognizes the interdependent nature of the airport-airline relationship. Perhaps more importantly, it suggests a change in organizational culture that is increasingly apparent in the way the airport approaches its own processes and its interaction with the airlines, the media, passengers, political leaders, concessionaires, and other service providers.

Managing the Capital Improvement Program (CIP)

The $5.4 billion CIP offers evidence of the changes taking place in Miami. The project—which includes a fourth runway, new and renovated concourses, renovated and expanded terminal space, an intermodal surface transportation center, and expanded cargo facilities—was recently approved by the Board of Commissioners after stumbling through four years of political and legal problems. Hung up originally because of concerns about insufficient minority involvement in construction projects at the airport, the project was also stalled in court as five carriers sued the airport. These airlines believed that American Airlines, which operates a hub out of Miami, would gain disproportionately from the renovation and expansion. With these issues behind them, the airport now stands on the brink of one of the most ambitious airport projects in the United States.

The emerging culture at Miami is evident in the way the CIP is budgeted and managed. According to Narinder Jolly, MIA's manager of facilities, the airport has broken with traditional approaches in a number of important ways. The budget, for example, includes all known costs for over 300 projects, including the cost of environmental remediation, which has plagued other airport projects. Inflation is integrated into the cost estimates up to the midpoint of the projected construction period, giving the program managers a much clearer picture of real costs. The cost-conscious approach reflects the airport's emerging business culture. The airport is striving to show its airline business partners that it is a responsible steward of airline dollars, which will ultimately pay for the bulk of the project.

Specific innovations abound in the CIP. Jolly and his staff conducted research on cost-overruns and discovered that change orders are the most prevalent and serious culprit. A change order is required when the approved design is altered because of unforeseen technical deficiencies, environmental issues, code violations, and other unexpected problems. The task became how to reduce change orders to keep the project within budgeted limits. In an innovative use of intergovernmental cooperation, the airport convinced the county to establish an on-site office for building inspectors. The inspection process was integrated more closely into the design and planning process, which significantly reduced code violations at a stage when correcting them did not involve the cost and delays associated with change orders. Jolly also worked to bring MIA's airline business partners into the design process by integrating their ideas and concerns. By formally negotiating the design with the airline, the airport reinforced the new culture of business partnerships and developed a clear mechanism for holding the airlines accountable once a project started. The airlines were less likely, and less able, to argue for costly and disruptive design changes after construction began.

Airport officials are also making excellent use of new and existing computer technologies to more effectively manage the CIP and its numerous individual projects. In an effort to further minimize change orders related to code violations, the airport developed a Life Safety Master Plan, which carefully explored the complexities and specific needs of an airport in terms of fire safety. Airport staff used computer models to see how fires would behave in their proposed design and worked with inspectors and designers to negotiate the means by which fire safety codes could be met effectively and efficiently.

In another example of innovative use of computer technologies, MIA developed and implemented a proprietary software package called the Project Graphic Tracking System. This innovative program allows Jolly and his program managers to monitor all projects associated with the CIP. Everyone involved in the project can read the reports, which are presented numerically and graphically on the airport computer network. Individual project managers are able to write to or modify files for their own projects and do so on a regular basis. The program efficiently tracks each project's budget, payments, schedules, and changes, and will eventually include digital images of the project as well. This creative use of existing network technology and newly developed software shows that the airport is serious about managing its enormous expansion and improvement program with one vigilant eye on the bottom line and another on quality.

The CIP is designed to do much more than just expand and renovate the airport's concourses, terminals, and cargo facilities. In many ways, the program is also intended to remake the airport so that it is appropriately configured to meet the challenges of the evolving air transport industry. Key aspects of this makeover include an overhaul of the airport's retail and food/beverage programs, a move to accommodate regional jets and airline alliances, and an effort to build on MIA's already successful air cargo operations. In each case, airport officials are busy with the practical implications of the business culture that drives the airport's mission.

With decreased federal aviation funding and hesitancy by the airlines to pay any more than they absolutely have to, airports around the nation have seized on retail, food, and beverage operations as potentially lucrative revenue sources. Historically, however, airports were not built to do much more than serve as conduits for passengers and baggage. To the extent that airports offered services, they tended to be high on prices, low on quality, and short on customer service. Many observers point to Pittsburgh's efforts in the 1980s to more fully integrate a customer-oriented concessions program into its terminal and concourses as the beginning of a sea change for airports. Concessions moved from being an afterthought to an integral component of airport designs and revenue projections.

Miami has lagged behind other major airports in the area of concessions. Airport officials candidly admit that the airport has operated for years without any plan or strategy for organizing and managing this important aspect of the airport business. This is rather surprising, since MIA is a transfer point for tourists from all over the world and business travelers from around the Americas, which are both groups that typically are willing to spend considerable money at an airport.

Miami's difficulties in this area stem, in part, from its inability to proceed with major renovations until recently and the political interference of county commissioners who over the years have apparently pushed for individual concession contracts divorced from any coherent plan or strategy. The airport's current retail, food, and beverage offerings are best described as a hodgepodge of services and outlets that are poorly located, poorly managed, and not prepared to respond to customer demands. A recent report on the airport's concessions program posits that the airport can dramatically improve its performance in this area with the facilities changes proposed as part of the CIP. The report also argues that politics should be removed from the process and best practices employed in the airport's retail operations.

Getting the Word Out

Working with its airline business partners is only part of MIA's philosophy. The airport also works hard to make sure the public understands what the airport does and how it plugs in to the broader economy. Lauren Stover, who handles public affairs, came to the airport with no aviation experience. Her outsider's perspective proved to be a boon to the airport. Stover began to tackle the airport's image problems with area residents, the media, and elected officials in the region who had grown used to hearing about the airport's difficulties and considered the airport to be less than a good neighbor.

As with many other airports, MIA had not been doing a very good job of communicating with these important groups. Stover says that her first efforts to contact mayors from the municipalities surrounding the airport were not well received, because they believed that the airport was worried only about its own interests. Eventually, Stover and her colleagues were able to establish better lines of communication and develop a level of trust between the airport administration and various constituencies in the area. An important step in this direction was the airport's first media day, which gave area media representatives a chance to learn more about the airport.

Noise and Other Environmental Concerns

An emerging issue at MIA and one that is gaining momentum at many airports around the nation is noise. According to Assistant Aviation Director Bruce Drum and Jeffrey Bunting, who serves as the airport's chief of aircraft noise and environmental planning, noise is not as significant an issue at MIA as at other airports, but they are interested in dealing with the issue. A forward-looking strategy should help the airport avoid noise controversies that have confronted other large metropolitan airports. In addition to better noise monitoring and data collection on noise complaints, the airport is hoping to have aircraft use two distinct flight tracks that could minimize the impact of aircraft noise. Currently, aircraft depart and arrive on numerous tracks that expose a variety of neighborhoods and communities to aircraft noise. The airport's plan is to route all aircraft along fewer flight tracks so that aircraft will pass over less densely populated areas and do so more consistently. Unfortunately, the FAA, whose air traffic controllers are responsible for directing aircraft, has not been cooperative. Bunting points to the intransigence of the controllers as a significant obstacle to getting the noise issue at MIA under control. Discussions are ongoing, but the airport has not received much intergovernmental support for this noise abatement initiative.

An interesting example of the innovative culture that is emerging at MIA is the decision to explore unconventional ways of managing wildlife on airport property. Birds are often attracted to airports because the land offers ideal opportunities for nesting and feeding. Unfortunately, birds and aircraft don't mix very well. Collisions between aircraft and birds, called birdstrikes, can cause severe damage to aircraft. Such collisions are expensive and dangerous. It is no surprise, then, that airports and airlines are interested in reducing the probability of birdstrikes.

In an era of heightened environmental sensitivity, it is not possible merely to shoot the birds. Instead, airports have come to rely on a variety of technologies to scare the birds from the airfield. Unfortunately, birds tend to adapt to such technologies, rendering these often expensive approaches less effective. MIA is currently exploring a low-tech alternative to high-tech solutions. Working with a local breeder and trainer of border collies, a breed of exceptionally intelligent and hard-working herding dogs, the airport is exploring the use of dogs to help manage the airport's bird problem. Only time will tell if this intriguing solution will work at MIA and offer a model for other airports.

Miami International Airport is now well situated for the next century. Its comprehensive strategy for renovating and expanding the airport to meet the increasing demand for business and cargo services places MIA in a most enviable position. Getting to this place has not been easy, however, and has depended on a professional and dedicated staff that recognizes fully the changes in the airport business. From efforts to more effectively manage its $5.4 billion Capital Improvement Budget to programs that better educate the public about the airport's mission and function, the administrative staff are tackling their problems creatively and exploiting the airport's opportunities aggressively.

Portland International Airport

Portland International Airport (PDX) is part of the Port of Portland and serves Oregon's largest metropolitan area. The Port Authority governs the airport's operations and sets the tone for both the airport's mission and goals. The airport, like the communities surrounding it, seeks to balance its desire to be a full partner in the international economy with its desire to operate responsibly within the region's culture and environment. The result is an airport consistently among the front-runners in innovation. In fact, PDX is often the model upon which other airports base new programs. PDX officials proudly, but somewhat wearily, describe the many visiting delegations that come to Portland to see how the airport is tackling problems and opportunities that confront airports across the country and around the world.

Portland's innovative culture comes directly from the top. John Brockley, aviation director for the Port of Portland, describes the airport's philosophy as a private business approach within the context of federal aviation regulations. Because it is a unit within a port authority, the airport operates with fewer constraints than airports that operate as city departments. Staffing, for example, is not tied to civil service requirements or affected by political processes. The airport is able to exercise creativity and flexibility in hiring and other personnel decisions. In the rapidly changing business of airport

Portland International Airport At-a-Glance

Metropolitan Portland's population:	1.7 million
Departing passengers:	6.5 million per year
Service:	Domestic hub with international flights to Pacific Rim
Governing structure:	Port of Portland (port authority)
Reporting line:	Aviation director reports to Port's executive director
Key administrators:	John Brockley, Aviation Director Mike Cheston, Airport Manager
Innovations:	Retail and restaurant operations Public-private ground transportation project Wildlife management program Incident command system

operations, PDX has been able to recruit administrators from a variety of backgrounds. These administrators bring new perspectives, ideas, and a heightened awareness of the myriad issues that confront modern airports.

Several issues stand out when examining Portland's track record on innovation. Each example described below suggests the importance of recruiting good people, placing them in an organizational structure that is clearly focused on the airport's mission, and then letting them utilize their talents and abilities to make things work.

Shops and Restaurants With a Unique Flavor

PDX is perhaps most famous in airport circles for its innovative approach to retail operations. Like many other airports, Portland recognizes that retail operations are a critical source of revenue. Maximizing such revenue, however, is far more complicated than turning your terminal into a shopping mall. An airport's retail plan must be integrated into its central mission, which is to facilitate transportation. Portland has done a magnificent job of carefully integrating an attractive mix of retail, food, and beverage operations into its airport. Instead of detracting from the airport's primary purpose, the restaurants and shops seem to make the airport a warmer and friendlier place. Moreover, Portland's offerings give travelers a good sense that they are in the Pacific Northwest, while other airports' food and beverage operations are too often indistinguishable from generic shopping mall food courts.

Airlines appreciate retail strategies like the one employed in Portland, because they allow the airport to create an identity for itself that doesn't drain the airlines' coffers. Instead of building a monument or showpiece for which the airlines ultimately foot the bill, Portland is utilizing revenue-generating shops and restaurants to create an airport environment of which the community will be proud. In one stroke, the airport provides better service to the traveler, develops more attractive terminal spaces, and reduces the financial burden on its airline business partners. It is no surprise, then, that other airports, such as Salt Lake City and Miami, are looking to Portland as a model for their own concession programs.

Public-Private Approaches to Ground Transportation

While much of the news coverage about airport congestion deals with aircraft and flight delays, airports face a problem of similar magnitude on the other side of the terminal building. Many airports are struggling to deal with ground transportation issues. Increasing numbers of travelers mean more cars, vans, and buses on the roadways leading to the airport terminal. The impact of new runways, expanded terminals, and other improvements can be negated if travelers can't get into the airport. In this regard, Portland is not much different from other airports. PDX suffers from crowded surface transportation routes and bottlenecks that threaten to strangle the airport if not dealt with effectively.

PDX has taken an innovative approach to handling some of its ground transportation problems. Seeking to take as many vehicles off the roadways as possible and make better use of the area's rail system, the airport decided to develop a light rail link to the airport terminal. Unfortunately, federal regulations make it very difficult, if not impossible, for airports to fund rail links that can alleviate access problems to the terminal. Instead of fighting a lengthy battle to win federal approval for using airport revenues for the rail link, PDX developed an innovative land-swap arrangement with a land developer. In exchange for the land, the developer will fund and build the portion of the rail link between the airport and the region's rail system. This creative use of airport resources gives the airport autonomy to make decisions that are in the broader interest of the area and the traveling public. Until the federal government recognizes more fully the importance of ground transportation access to airports as integral to the business of air transport, Portland's innovative public-private partnership will serve as a model for other airports.

Noise Mitigation, Chemical Runoff, and Wildlife Management

Like so many other airports, PDX operates in an era of heightened environmental awareness. Various regulations, as well as public sentiment, force airports to take increasingly innovative approaches to operations that create environmental impacts. Three such issues are worth noting at Portland: noise, de-icing runoff, and wildlife management. In each case, the airport must address concerns within overlapping regulatory frameworks. Noise, for example, must be dealt with in the context of federal aviation regulations and state environmental quality statutes. Addressing one regulation may not satisfy others, and even when all regulatory requirements are met, public reaction may not be favorable. Thus, the airport must work on these issues with consideration for operational and safety requirements, the requirements of the specific statutes, and the reaction of a sometimes politically active public.

Aircraft noise has been a serious focus of the airport's attention since it conducted its Part 150 study in 1987. A Part 150 study examines the impact of aircraft noise on the surrounding community and proposes strategies to mitigate the impact. The FAA devised the Part 150 study program to facilitate increased public input in the noise process. Like many other airports, PDX responded to this initiative by creating a noise abatement advisory committee, which holds public meetings three times a year to discuss noise issues. Unfortunately, as other airports have discovered, opening up the issue to the public does not necessarily solve the problem. In Portland, the efforts of the airport to deal with noise have uncovered intergovernmental obstacles and problems.

Like Miami, PDX has suggested a reconfiguration of flight tracks that will minimize the impact of aircraft noise on surrounding communities. The idea is to take aircraft quickly and consistently away from populated areas. This is already accomplished in part by utilizing the Columbia River, which flows past the airfield. Airport officials complain, however, that attempts to further rationalize the flight tracks used by arriving and departing flights have been stymied by intransigent air traffic controllers. While the FAA is at least partly responsible for the noise regulations imposed on the airports, its own controllers often seem to ignore the issue. Instead of engaging in finger-pointing, the airport continues to work with the controllers and has turned its attention to other parts of the airport's operations that create aircraft noise.

In particular, PDX faces the double-edged sword of being home to Horizon Air's maintenance facility. Airports generally welcome having maintenance facilities on their property, since the business increases revenues. A downside to aircraft maintenance is the additional noise related to maintenance engine run-ups, which are required by FAA regulations. During a maintenance run-up, an aircraft's engines are run at extremely high levels, which results in a considerable amount of noise. The noise problem is compounded by the fact that most maintenance and run-ups are performed at night so that aircraft can return to revenue service the next day.

Ground run-ups illustrate the problem of overlapping regulatory frameworks. The FAA requires a ground run-up after maintenance, but does not consider it part of a flight. Because it is not part of a flight, it is considered industrial noise and subject to the stringent regulations of Oregon's Department of Environmental Quality. To address these more stringent requirements, the airport has worked with the airline to limit nighttime run-ups. It has also explored the possibility of building a ground run-up enclosure (GRE), which is a semi-enclosed acoustical chamber that dissipates the noise from the aircraft's engines. Mike Cheston, PDX's airport manager, and his staff have studied GREs and concluded that one can be built that will meet Portland's requirements. The airport hopes to have it in place by early 2001.

Another environmental issue is the impact of runoff from de-icing operations. Airlines use de-icing procedures to remove ice from aircraft and reduce the build-up of ice prior to departure. Airports use de-icing procedures to remove ice from aprons, taxiways, and runways, and to keep additional ice from forming. The environmental issue arises from the use of glycol, which is an effective, non-toxic de-icing solution. Unfortunately, glycol reduces the level of oxygen in water. If unprocessed glycol reaches streams, rivers, and other bodies of water, it can dangerously reduce the level of oxygen for fish and other aquatic wildlife.

Portland does not use as much glycol and other de-icers as airports in colder climates, but it uses enough to raise concerns about runoff, especially since airport property abuts two bodies of water. The Columbia River flows north of the airport and the Columbia Slough, a much smaller stream, runs to the south of the airport. As it stands, most of the offending runoff drains towards the slough. Consequently, oxygen depletion has been identified as an environmental concern. The response to this issue illustrates well the airport's willingness to work with various stakeholders and to seek innovative solutions.

Instead of selecting an approach or strategy in isolation, the airport decided to bring stakeholders together on a task force that would identify potential solutions and work to build consensus around one approach. The decision to proceed with a task force was not without risk, since bringing together individuals with divergent views and conflicting interests can result in stagnation. Fortunately, the airport was able, with the help of consultant Hal Reitmeier, to make the task force work.

The task force was divided into study groups to examine alternatives. Over 90 possible strategies were developed and studied, ranging from discharging directly into the Columbia River to comprehensive on-site treatment facilities. In the end, the task force was able to work through its internal differences and produce a workable solution. More impressive than the airport's ability to handle its runoff in a more environmentally sound way is the ability of the airport to bring divergent interests together, get them to buy in to the task force, and keep them focused on the task at hand. In the end, the airport was able to satisfy the cost- and safety-conscious airlines, the environmentally conscious activists, the regulators, and its own operations staff.

While the de-icing task force is busy trying to protect fish from the airport, the airport staff is busy trying to protect aircraft and passengers from birds and coyotes. The central issue is figuring out ways to keep birds and coyotes from colliding with aircraft. PDX employs a wildlife manager, Sharon Gordon, whose job is to develop strategies for mitigating the impact of wildlife on airport operations. Among other strategies, Gordon has embarked on two projects that will hopefully help alleviate the impact of birds. One of the attractions for birds is that airfields are ideal hunting grounds for small rodents. Airport operators unintentionally create this environment by providing perching sites on runway and taxiway signage and grass that is mowed to lengths that make spotting rodents easier. Gordon is working to maintain the airfield's operational requirements while discouraging the birds. Student interns are used to glue spikes to potential perches, and grass is now cut with the intention of minimizing its attractiveness to various bird species.

Coyotes have proven to be a more serious problem. In an effort to avoid public outrage, the airport now avoids shooting coyotes, except in the most unusual circumstances involving immediate safety concerns. The strategy now is to prevent coyotes from entering the airfield in the first place. Borrowing from sheep farmers who seek to prevent predators from attacking their flocks, the airport has reconfigured its perimeter fence. In short, the airport has buried chain-link fence to a depth of about six inches around the outside of its perimeter fence. The buried fence material prevents coyotes from digging under the vertical fence. Although the process was not without problems, the result is an airfield far more secure from runway incursions by coyotes.

Adapting Good Ideas: the Incident Command System

Borrowing ideas and adapting them to the airport's needs does not stop with wildlife management. In fact, one of the most impressive innovations in airport operations at PDX was adapted from wildfire-fighting techniques used to manage diverse operations during a crisis situation. In 1994, Portland adopted the Incident Command System (ICS) for its emergency management process. As one might expect, the idea met with some resistance since the ICS approach threatened to revise existing command structures and traditional roles and responsibilities. The fact that the concept was derived from fire fighting did little to assuage the concerns of non-firefighters, who feared its impact on their specific roles in an emergency operation.

According to Heidi Benamen, manager of communications, security, and emergency systems, implementing ICS started with about six months of breaking down barriers and traditional roles. Benamen and other airport staff spent considerable time charting 15 known events, which were then tested during a two-year period in which 18 tabletop simulations were conducted. Slowly, but surely, the new plan took shape. The real test came in 1996 when the airport was forced to deal with flooding and in 1997 when fatal injuries to construction workers shut down the airport's garage. In both cases the new system worked and skeptics were convinced that ICS was the way to go.

Since implementing ICS, Benamen has worked hard to measure its effectiveness and to improve the airport's ICS plan. With the support of various departments within the airport, each incident is thoroughly debriefed and explored so that the program is continuously improved. Success has also been gauged by the fact that people are no longer running to accident scenes without a specific purpose, resources are better managed and more effectively tracked, and staff members are increasingly comfortable in their roles. As a result of her own hard work and support from her supervisors, Benamen is now busy spreading the news about ICS to other airports throughout the United States.

PDX is an excellent example of how innovation can be fostered in the public sector. It is also a good example of how successful innovation can be shared with others. Portland has borrowed ideas and concepts liberally from within and outside the airport business. It has taken these ideas and tailored them to its specific purposes. After refining them, it gladly shares them with other airports, which fosters increased innovation, more efficiency, and better air transport services for travelers across the country.

Salt Lake City International Airport

Salt Lake City International Airport (SLC) provides air transportation services to over 2 million residents of Utah and the surrounding region. The airport itself is governed by an authority structure and operates as a department of the Salt Lake City Corporation. This structure ties the airport more closely to the city government than might be expected in a pure authority structure. While an appointed advisory board oversees the airport's operations, ultimate power rests with the mayor and city council. Thus, SLC finds itself somewhere between the pure authority structure of Portland and the county board structure found in Miami.

SLC has experienced considerable turmoil in recent years. Much of it seems to stem from the airport's success and the region's good fortune. First, the airport experienced dramatic increases in both the demand and supply of services. Economic growth in the Wasatch Front—the area west of the Wasatch Mountains and home to Salt Lake City and other growing cities— increased the demand for traffic considerably in recent years. Second, the acquisitions of Western Airlines and Morris Air by Delta and Southwest, respectively, brought two powerful and fiercely competitive carriers to SLC. Delta and Southwest subsequently developed extensive operations at Salt Lake, which strained the airport's capacity. Anxious not to lose its impressive level of air service, SLC moved to address the increased demand with an ambitious expansion plan.

With the expansion plan in place, airport officials were confronted with two unpleasant facts. First, passenger growth seemed to be slowing. Second, and perhaps more importantly, the airlines, especially Delta, began voicing their concerns that the city was planning a structure that was expensive and unnecessary. The airport's plans stumbled along as critics wondered about the need for such expensive facilities. The plan seemed to stall completely as Russell Widmar, the airport's executive director, and John Wheat, Widmar's interim replacement, both departed for positions at other airports. The airport seemed destined for disaster as administrative shake-ups and political turmoil threatened to overwhelm the airport's staff.

Managing Capital Improvements

Fortunately, the airport has been able to avoid disaster. In fact, the tumult of the past year has given the airport's administrators a chance to look carefully at the airport's expansion plans and to make decisions based on sober assessments of the air transport industry and the role SLC will play in the future. Guided by Cheryl Cook, the airport's former director of finance and administration, and Kevin Robins, who serves as the airport's director of engineering, SLC has regrouped and is ready to meet the challenges of extensive renovation and expansion.

Salt Lake City International Airport At-a-Glance

Metropolitan Salt Lake City's population:	1.2 million
Departing passengers:	10.2 million per year
Service:	Domestic hub with limited international service
Governing structure:	Salt Lake City Department of Airports (authority/department of city government)
Reporting line:	Director reports to advisory board appointed by mayor and city council
Key administrators:	Tom Troske, Director of Finance and Administration Kevin F. Robins, Director of Engineering
Innovations:	Managing capital improvements Retail and customer services

Cook and Robins shared a philosophy based on form following function following finances. In other words, instead of starting from a vague notion of wanting to build a "first class airport" or make an architectural statement, the airport starts with the business case. This is not to say that the airport wants to build a spartan or ugly facility, but that the driving forces are affordability and operational efficiency. The accountants are now much more important than the designers.

Much like their counterparts in Miami, SLC's administrative team wants to achieve firm control over the budget for the expansion. They are keenly aware of recent airport projects, namely Denver International, which experienced considerable cost overruns, with the original budget woefully out of touch with reality. To avoid a similar fate, SLC embarked on a conservative budget and planning strategy. One component of this strategy is the use of cross-functional teams to evaluate, in detail, specific aspects of the plan. The goal is to identify early on what the various operational departments of the airport need to perform their tasks. Instead of waiting to find out that a newly constructed terminal needs to be re-wired or re-plumbed, the teams identify concerns and shortcomings in the design stage, allowing problems to be addressed with pencils instead of saws and jackhammers.

The functional review process is complemented by a financial review process that involves double estimates of construction costs. The process employs both a construction contractor and a professional estimator to independently estimate the costs of the numerous projects that make up the expansion and renovation plan. Using different techniques, the estimators produce budget figures. Between the cross-functional teams and the use of independent cost estimates, the airport hopes to begin construction with a solid appreciation of how much the finished project will cost and how well it will meet the airport's needs.

The cost-conscious budgeting approach has reassured the airlines that the airport shares their concerns about making good business decisions. SLC is reinforcing this notion through a variety of other innovations. Like other successful airports, SLC recruits staff with a variety of backgrounds. For example, Ken Anderton, the airport's customer and tenant relations coordinator, came to the airport from a position with Delta Air Lines. His position was created to give the airport's many business partners a single point of contact with the administration. His airline experience gives him a perspective that would be difficult to acquire through a traditional career in the public sector.

The airport also recruits outside the air transport industry. John Buckner, Jr., joined the airport after a number of years with Nordstrom, the up-scale retailer with a reputation for customer service. Buckner serves as the airport's commercial manager and reports to Russell Pack, the deputy director of finance and administration. Buckner sees the world through the eyes of a retailer, while Pack has a wealth of experience in airport administration. The combination of Anderton, Buckner, and Pack gives the airport a diversity of experiences and perspectives that enhance the airport's ability to succeed in the increasingly important areas of commercial operations.

Retail and Customer Services: Blending Commercial and Community Interests

Bringing people like Buckner and Anderton into the administration signaled an emerging philosophy that is shared by successful airports—that is, airports must engage their customers and tenants, treat them as partners or stakeholders, and work with them to develop a comprehensive plan for the future. Just as Cook and Robin emphasized finances and function over form, Buckner and Anderton stressed the importance of the airport's transportation mission and how that mission guides their decisions.

SLC's administrators are keenly aware of what is happening at other airports. They watch the industry for things to avoid and things to emulate. Like Miami, they see Portland as a prime example for commercial operations. But they also realize that no two airports are alike. Consider, for example, an issue that other American airports are unlikely to deal with. The large population of members of the Church of Jesus Christ of Latter-day Saints in Salt Lake City and the surrounding region translates into an unusual challenge for the airport. Young adult male members of the church traditionally leave home to do mission work around the world. Unlike other travelers who may be accompanied to the airport by two or three family members, these passengers might be accompanied by as many as 20 family members and friends. The result is overcrowded gate hold areas and concourses. This is a problem that has no analogues in the United States, so SLC cannot look to any other airport for possible solutions. Airport administrators recognize this issue and understand the importance of dealing with this unique situation in its development plans.

In the end, SLC's success depends on the quality of its people and their willingness to recognize and address the legitimate concerns of the airport's business partners and customers. The airport's diverse staff is encouraged by senior management to approach creatively their opportunities and challenges. While there is no mechanism to financially reward innovative staff members, they seem to take professional and personal pride in knowing that they are contributing to something that is critical for the success of their city and region. The focus on sound business principles and a realistic understanding of what the airport means in the broader social, economic, and political context has allowed SLC to weather its recent turmoil and emerge on a course that enhances the probability of success.

Chicago O'Hare International Airport

Chicago O'Hare International Airport is run by the City of Chicago's Department of Aviation. The airport is well known for being one of the busiest airports in the world and a hub for two major airlines, American and United. Like other airports, O'Hare is straining to meet the demand from airlines and the traveling public. The State of Illinois has expressed interest in building a third airport outside the city to complement O'Hare and Midway, the city's other major airport, but city leaders and the airlines that serve Chicago have thus far successfully quashed any effort to get the project started. Both the city and the airlines argue that with appropriate improvements O'Hare and Midway can provide cost-effective solutions to the current shortage of capacity.

Three issues in particular confront the airport, and in each case it is developing innovative solutions. The first is how to meet the current needs of the airport's primary business partners, the airlines. The second, and related issue, is how to expand and improve the airport without disrupting operations. The final issue is how to deal with the issue of aircraft noise, which plagues the airport because of its size, the frequency of aircraft flights, and the airport's proximity to residential communities. In all three cases the airport is proving that a large, seemingly unwieldy department of city government can respond just as well as a small, politically autonomous organization.

The airport, according to Kate Hill of United Airlines, responds fairly well to the needs of its tenant airlines. Hill noted that the top-down governmental decision-making style has been replaced by a style that emphasizes communication and cooperation, with a clear focus on business. She noted that airlines are included in discussions about new projects from day one. This approach has eased the tension that was part of the traditional process in which the airport proposed something and the airlines fought it because they didn't want to pay for it. In recent years the airport has established credibility with the airlines by focusing on operational issues, working with the carriers to address their business needs, and being responsible stewards of the airlines' resources.

Building for the Future, Operating for Today
Construction projects are a good example of how the airport works to meld the airlines' cost-conscious approach with the airport's desire to build facilities and runways that last. The keys, according to Nonda Harris, the airport's director of development, are communication and accountability. Harris explains that the airport's construction philosophy is to "build things right the first time and build them to last." He admits that the airlines do not always agree with the airport's proposals since they are always looking for ways to save money, but when they are confronted with well-defined plans

Chicago O'Hare International Airport At-a-Glance

Metropolitan Chicago's population:	7.8 million
Departing passengers:	33 million per year
Service:	Major domestic hub with extensive international service
Governing structure:	City of Chicago Department of Aviation (unit of city government)
Reporting line:	Commissioner reports to mayor
Key administrators:	Thomas R. Walker, Commissioner, Department of Aviation Rich Monocchio, Chief of Staff, Department of Aviation Nonda F. Harris, Director of Development
Innovations:	Managing capital improvements Noise mitigation

and realistic cost estimates, they are more willing to work things out. Over the years, the airport has established credibility with the airlines by showing that this philosophy actually saves money in the long run by lowering maintenance costs and disruptions.

Harris points out that O'Hare, like most other airports, is always under construction. The perpetual cycle of construction projects means that the airport is constantly balancing the need to get work done against the need of its airline tenants to operate their flights efficiently. To keep the airport operating at peak efficiency, the administration has developed a number of innovative strategies. Construction equipment, for example, is staged at one of three substantial marshalling areas, which gives contractors efficient access to the airfield when they are permitted to work. Work is checked on a daily basis by quality control and safety inspection teams. This aggressive approach to monitoring each job ensures that the work progresses quickly and successfully with minimum disruption to the operation of the airfield. Daily construction management group meetings are held to review completed work and current plans, and adjust schedules. While such procedures might be called micromanaging, the airlines and the traveling public are better served since they rarely notice the disruption.

The constant candid communication between the airport administration and the airlines reinforces the airport's credibility. Airlines are less worried about the airport squandering resources, not considering operational issues, and interfering with the business of moving people and cargo. The credibility means that the airport can avoid some of the political and legal hassles that have stymied expansion and renovation plans at other airports, where airlines believed that their interests were not carefully considered even though they were ultimately footing the bill.

Mitigating Aircraft Noise: Technology, Cooperation, and Communication

Another issue that requires cooperation from the airlines is aircraft noise. Even though the airlines make the noise, the airport is tasked with doing something about it. O'Hare has taken an active role in mitigating aircraft noise by working with the airlines, investing in noise mitigation technologies, and carefully monitoring and studying noise so it can be dealt with efficiently and effectively.

The airport employs three different strategies for mitigating noise. First, the airport is in the process of a massive insulation program for single-family dwellings close to the airport. Second, the airport has developed a cooperative program with the airlines called "Fly Quiet," which encourages pilots to use noise abatement procedures during takeoffs. Finally, the airport has installed a ground run-up enclosure that cuts the noise from maintenance run-ups by up to 20 decibels. In each case, the airport has creatively adapted ideas and technologies to reduce the impact of aircraft noise.

The insulation program is an excellent example of innovation. Although O'Hare is not the only airport installing insulation to mitigate noise, its approach is illustrative of the innovative use of technology. Specifically, the airport, through its consultants, Landrum & Brown, employs geographic information system (GIS) software to develop and manage an enormous database of the buildings affected by noise and those involved in the insulation project. GIS allows the airport to coordinate its extensive noise-monitoring program with its insulation program. The database is used to more accurately understand the extent of the noise problem and to keep both elected officials and members of the general public informed about the insulation program.

One of the most frustrating issues surrounding aircraft noise is helping members of the public understand what produces the noise and what realistically can be done to mitigate it. Again, innovative use of technology allows the airport to bring this information to the public. Using a specially equipped van, airport officials are able to bring portable noise monitors and related computer technology to individual homes and other locations where people express concern about noise. More than just publicity that the airport is doing something, such efforts help to educate the public about noise and what the airport is doing.

The "Fly Quiet" program is a voluntary cooperative effort between the airlines, the airport, and the air traffic controllers. Designed to reduce noise during flights over the area surrounding the airport, the program designates preferred runways and preferred flight tracks that take aircraft away from populated neighborhoods and send them over industrial areas and transportation corridors, such as railroads and interstate highways. As noted earlier, Miami and Portland are hoping to implement similar plans, but are experiencing resistance from the FAA. In Chicago, the FAA and airlines signed on to the program, but participation by the airlines remains voluntary. The result is that controllers and pilots operating during peak hours at the airport tend to focus on other factors besides noise mitigation. The airport monitors each noise incident and can even identify specific aircraft as offenders, but the airport can apply little more than gentle pressure. Airport officials point to reductions in noise levels throughout their monitoring area, but also recognize that more could be done.

A final innovation, borrowed from European airports, is the use of a ground run-up enclosure, or GRE. As mentioned earlier in the Portland case study, this type of enclosure, which is an acoustical chamber large enough for a Boeing 747 and designed to dissipate noise from high-revving jet engines, has had a significant impact on noise in the neighborhoods surrounding the airport. The GRE was designed for ease of use. It is located near maintenance facilities and is large enough for all but the very largest commercial aircraft to enter and exit without the help of tugs. The ease of use and the encouragement of the airport has induced airlines to make use of the facility and considerably reduce maintenance noise. Other airports have examined O'Hare's GRE and are pursuing their own run-up enclosure projects.

Chicago O'Hare's willingness and ability to innovate suggests that innovation is not limited to small, nimble organizations. The airport has addressed a number of concerns, ranging from massive construction projects to noise mitigation, with efficiency and effectiveness that might surprise some who believe that large public enterprises are plodding and wasteful. Despite publicity about delays and other problems at the airport, it works remarkably well and is prepared to handle the challenges of air transportation in the coming years.

Lessons Learned

The cases presented illustrate many of the good things going on in America's publicly owned and operated airports. While there are obviously some innovations that are not covered and some innovative airports that are not included in the study, there are a number of lessons that can be learned from this wide-ranging survey of innovations in five diverse airport environments.

Knowing Who You Are

Whether stated explicitly as Hugh Davis did in Chattanooga or implicitly as virtually every other airport administrator did during the interviews, a central theme for successful airports is to understand who they are. In other words, airports are more likely to succeed if they recognize their role in their local political economy and the broader air transport system. Chattanooga recognizes that its best strategy is to develop as much service to as many major hubs as possible. Miami's strategy is to develop more extensive connections to the rest of the world, while Chicago's priority is to maintain its status as a major Midwestern hub, but not to forget about the importance of enhancing international air service. The key is to understand what is realistically possible given the nature of the airline industry and the broader economy, and then work aggressively and creatively to reach those goals.

Borrowing Ideas and New Technologies

Once an airport understands its mission and goals, it should look for help from other airports and industries. Each airport in this study is a successful innovator, but none has done so in isolation. Successful airports remove their blinders and look for new ideas and concepts that can help them tackle problems and exploit opportunities. Whether it is Portland borrowing concepts from wildfire fighting to help it deal more efficiently with crisis management, or Miami borrowing ideas from dog trainers to solve its birdstrike problem, successful airports are willing to look beyond standard procedures and explore solutions sometimes far removed from the aviation business. Successful airports are also eager to use new technologies to help them do their business. Miami is using proprietary software and existing computer networks to manage its capital improvement plan budget, and Chicago is using acoustical technologies to reduce the impact of aircraft noise.

Attracting Top-Quality People

The five airports examined in this study each operate in different political environments, which in turn create different constraints on personnel decisions. From Portland's authority structure, which gives it considerable autonomy on personnel issues, to Miami, which works in a much more politicized environment, top administrators have figured out that the success of their airport depends on the quality of their people. In every case, administrators have figured out how to recruit and retain quality staff. Even without significant reward and recognition programs, these administrators have been able to encourage their staffs to approach their jobs with creativity and enthusiasm. Staff at all five airports, whether they were career city officials, career airport employees, or new recruits from other sectors of the business world, exhibited a sincere interest in making their airports the best. Without fail, these individuals noted that they work hard because they believe they are making a real contribution to the success of their airport and their community. They appreciate the fact that they are working in an exciting and dynamic environment, and take considerable personal and professional pride in improving air transport services.

Communicating and Educating

No matter how well an airport is managed or how hard its staff works to improve its services, political leaders, the media, and the general public will concentrate on the airport's problems. Ironically, airports are often held responsible for things that are not within their control. Few passengers realize that security checkpoint staff are contracted by the airlines, that the airlines handle all baggage, and that the air traffic controllers and the airlines make all decisions about aircraft movements. Successful airports understand that finger pointing does not resolve problems. Instead of blasting their business partners, the airports in this study work cooperatively with airlines to resolve issues. They realize that passengers don't separate the airport from the airline in thinking about their trips. The airport's task, then, is to communicate more effectively with its airline partners and work to address issues that are of mutual concern. A secondary, and no less important, task is to educate the public about how airports operate, how they are funded, and why things work the way they do. The airports in this study make excellent use of the Internet, outreach programs, tours, and the print media to keep the public informed about the good and the bad aspects of the airport business.

Some airports have found out the hard way that the public doesn't always immediately understand why a new runway is needed, how a terminal expansion will be funded, why roads and parking garages are closed for construction, and why flights are delayed. Successful airports are open and candid. They don't treat the public with contempt. They also understand that much of what the public knows about airports comes to them through local media. Innovative airports recognize that the media is not necessarily anti-airport, but that left on its own the media will only report negative stories, such as delays and congestion. The airports in this study have top-notch public affairs people who understand the power of information and who work creatively and diligently to make sure the public and the media understand what is going on.

Partnering With Business and the Public

One of the most impressive aspects of the five airports in this study is their desire to be accountable to their business partners and other stakeholders. They recognize the interdependent relationship that exists between airports and airlines, and that airlines operate with fairly thin margins in a highly competitive market. In typical circumstances, public entities have considerable margins for error. Successful airports realize that their circumstances are not typical of the public sector and that they must operate with the same bottom-line orientation as their business partners. Establishing a track record of sound business decisions has helped each airport in this study build more cooperative and productive relationships with its airline partners and community.

Increasing Autonomy and Innovation

While all airports in this study are doing well in terms of innovation, those with less politicized governing structures tend to do somewhat better.

This is not to say that airports operating as departments of city or county governments are unable to operate efficiently. Rather it suggests that the challenges of the air transport industry are seemingly better met by governing structures that reduce local and regional politics and allow airports to operate more like their private business partners. Portland is more autonomous than any of the other airports in this study and also happens to be the most innovative. Both Miami and Salt Lake City, for example, have looked to Portland for ideas on commercial operations. In fact, Miami has been encouraged by its outside consultants to seek ways to minimize political influence in its new retail program. Decisions should be based on sound business principles and in cooperation with the airport's various business partners. The business of running the airport is too important for it to become wrapped up in political battles unrelated to the provision of air transport services.

Reducing politics and increasing autonomy are both attractive outcomes, but not without a clear appreciation that airports must remain accountable to both their business partners and the public. Political oversight is certainly one means for ensuring accountability, but it is not without significant costs. Political leaders would be best advised to find qualified airport administrators who understand fully the business of air transport and then give those administrators the autonomy to innovate. Airport administrators who are tied to traditional public sector models will be less able to react to the often fast-paced changes of the air transport industry.

Airports can prove their commitment to accountability through their actions. Miami and Salt Lake City have proven their commitment through innovations designed to more effectively manage the budgets for their expansion and renovation projects. Chicago and Portland have proven their commitment by extensively integrating the airlines, the public, and other stakeholders into their decision-making processes. In doing so, the airports have shown that they are capable of improving their operations and financial management while meeting the commercial and environmental concerns of their stakeholders.

Recommendations

Three recommendations emerge from this study. Specific innovations are not recommended since each airport faces different challenges and opportunities. Instead, the recommendations focus on three general areas where change is possible and likely to produce meaningful results.

Increase Autonomy

Elected political leaders should resist the temptation to manage their airports. They should, instead, hire qualified and experienced administrators and let them do their jobs. The rewards of innovation and effective management will increase dramatically if airport administrators are able to address the challenges and opportunities facing them without the undue interference of local and regional politics. Thus, one straightforward mechanism for achieving desired levels of innovation is to move airport business out of city and county government and place it under the control of an autonomous airport authority. The most obvious benefit of such a structure is that administrative decisions can be made with the airport and air transport as the top priorities. Administrators can focus more on how their decisions will affect the fortunes of the airport and its business partners and less on how their decisions will be interpreted by local politicians.

Measure Performance

While autonomy can effectively increase the prospects for innovation and effective management, it is not without costs. Political leaders and other stakeholders justifiably worry about accountability when administrators become more autonomous. The second recommendation, then, is that governing bodies allocate more resources and staff to performance measurement. No matter what form of governing structure, airport administrators should be required to do a better job of monitoring performance. This is especially true if administrators are to be given more autonomy, as recommended in this report.

Airport officials would be unwise to ask for more autonomy without a commitment to effective means for monitoring performance. Similarly, local elected officials would be foolish to grant autonomy without better mechanisms for measuring its impact on the operations of their airport. Airports, in general, need to spend more time and resources on performance measurement so inefficient processes can be improved and overall service quality can be enhanced. Airports must be evaluated along many more dimensions than the number of enplaned passengers and the level of fees passed along to the airlines. Large numbers of enplaned passengers and low fees do not necessarily mean that the airport is doing its best.

All too often, airport administrators point to growth in enplaned passengers, fewer complaints, and shorter flight delays as evidence of their performance. While these are certainly indicators of general trends at an airport, there are too many alternative explanations for variances in each of these indicators to accurately attribute changes to specific efforts by the airport. If airports are going to continue to improve their processes, they must begin to take seriously the issue of performance measurement.

There is good reason to be encouraged, though, since airports are showing increased enthusiasm for benchmarking and performance measurement. Airports are working with one another to establish benchmarks for airport functions and are beginning to recognize the need to collect and manage performance data on a regular basis. Unfortunately, these efforts can take considerable time and money. Airports need to recognize that if properly integrated into the normal course of operations, performance measurement can produce a solid return on investment.

Airports interested in improving the evaluation of their own operations and the impact of their improvements should seek the advice of airports that have already implemented such programs. They should also work with their industry associations, such as the American Association of Airport Executives, to learn more about benchmarking and performance measurement and how these business tools can be integrated into their operations. These tools will be invaluable for effectively gauging the impact of the many innovations that will transform airports in the next century.

Listen to Concerns and Explain What Is Being Done to Address Them

Airports and the air transport community need to redouble their efforts to communicate with the public and other stakeholders. Increased autonomy and more effective use of performance measurement techniques will go a long way to improving the delivery of airport services, but airports will continue to face an uphill battle in the media and among the public unless they do a better job of telling the air transport story more effectively. Airport administrators must provide sufficient budget and staff for public affairs, not merely to address public complaints and media inquiries, but to show the public that airports play an important role in the economy, the environment, and society.

Airport administrators should resist the temptation to rely exclusively on the economic impact of the airport to sell their case to the public. They should instead show how the airport could be, at once, an economic engine and a good neighbor. The public should understand how airports are funded, why aircraft fly when and where they do, what the airport is doing about noise, what the airport is doing about safety and security, and how a modern airport can operate without undue harm to the environment. For their part, airport administrators should understand that the public has legitimate concerns about the impact of airport operations on their daily lives and the environment.

In the end, following the first two recommendations will help achieve better results with the third. An autonomous airport administration that is empowered to innovate has a better chance of addressing the public's concerns. An airport that makes effective use of performance measurement tools will have an easier time showing the public that its concerns are not only taken seriously, but that real progress is being made towards their resolution. The ultimate result, then, will be airports that are more responsive to a variety of commercial and social demands and a public that is much more aware of the strides the airports are making towards improving both the quality of air transport and the quality of life.

Endnotes

1. The word "men" is intentional here since women have only recently made real progress in the upper ranks of airport administration.

About the Contributors

Mark A. Abramson is executive director of The PricewaterhouseCoopers Endowment for The Business of Government, a position he has held since July 1998. Prior to the Endowment, he was chairman of Leadership Inc. From 1983 to 1994, Mr. Abramson served as the first president of the Council for Excellence in Government. Previously, Mr. Abramson served as a senior program evaluator in the Office of the Assistant Secretary for Planning and Evaluation, U.S. Department of Health and Human Services.

He is a Fellow of the National Academy of Public Administration. In 1995, he served as president of the National Capital Area Chapter of the American Society for Public Administration. Mr. Abramson has taught at George Mason University and the Federal Executive Institute in Charlottesville, Virginia.

Mr. Abramson is the co-editor of *Transforming Organizations, E-Government 2001,* and *Managing for Results 2002.* He also recently edited *Memos to the President: Management Advice from the Nation's Top Public Administrators* and *Toward a 21st Century Public Service: Reports from Four Forums.* He is also the co-editor (with Joseph S. Wholey and Christopher Bellavita) of *Performance and Credibility: Developing Excellence in Public and Nonprofit Organizations,* and the author of *The Federal Funding of Social Knowledge Production and Application.*

He received his Bachelor of Arts degree from Florida State University. He received a Master of Arts degree in history from New York University and a Master of Arts degree in political science from the Maxwell School of Citizenship and Public Affairs, Syracuse University.

Sandford Borins is Professor of Public Management in the Joseph L. Rotman School of Management at the University of Toronto and Chair of the Division of Management at the University of Toronto at Scarborough. He has been a visiting professor at the Kennedy School of Government at Harvard University and the Goldman School of Public Policy at the University of California at Berkeley.

He is the author of numerous articles on public management, as well as five books, the three most recent of which are *The New Public Organization*, co-authored with Kenneth Kernaghan and Brian Marson (Institute of Public Administration of Canada, 2000), *Political Management in Canada*, co-authored with the Hon. Allan Blakeney, former premier of Saskatchewan (University of Toronto Press, 1998), and *Innovating with Integrity: How Local Heroes are Transforming American Government* (Georgetown University Press, 1998).

Professor Borins has had a wide range of professional experience. He was a member of the selection panels for the Commonwealth Association for Public Administration and Management and the Institute of Public Administration of Canada innovation awards, as well as chair of the selection panel for the Amethyst Award for Excellence in the Ontario Public Service. He was a member of the board of directors of the Ontario Transportation Capital Corporation, which developed Ontario's electronic toll highway. He is senior adviser and conference rapporteur for the Commonwealth Association for Public Administration and Management.

Professor Borins received a master's in public policy from the Kennedy School of Government in 1974 and his Ph.D. in economics from Harvard University in 1976.

Janet Vinzant Denhardt is Professor in the School of Public Affairs at Arizona State University. Her teaching and research interests lie primarily in organization theory and organizational behavior. Her book (with Lane Crothers), *Street-Level Leadership: Discretion and Legitimacy in Front-Line Public Service*, was published by the Georgetown University Press. In addition, Dr. Denhardt has published numerous articles in journals such as *Public Administration Review*, *Administration and Society*, *American Review of Public Administration*, *Public Productivity and Management Review*, and *Administrative Theory & Praxis*. Prior to joining the faculty at Arizona State, Dr. Denhardt taught at Eastern Washington University and served in a variety of administrative and consulting positions. Her doctorate is from the University of Southern California.

Robert B. Denhardt is Professor in the School of Public Affairs at Arizona State University and Visiting Scholar at the University of Delaware. Dr. Denhardt is a past president of the American Society for Public Administration, and the founder and first chair of ASPA's National Campaign for Public Service, an effort to assert the dignity and worth of public service across the nation. He is also a member of the National Academy of Public Administration and a Fellow of the Canadian Centre for Management Development. Dr. Denhardt has published 14 books, including *Theories of Public Organization*, *Public Administration: An Action Orientation*, *In the Shadow of Organization*, *The Pursuit of Significance*, *Executive Leadership in the Public Service*, *The Revitalization of the Public Service*, and *Pollution and Public Policy*. He has published over 75 articles in professional journals, primarily in the areas of leadership, management, and organizational change. His doctorate is from the University of Kentucky.

William B. Eimicke is the director of the Picker Center for Executive Education of Columbia University's School of International and Public Affairs. Dr. Eimicke teaches courses in public management, policy analysis, management for international affairs, and management innovation. He also teaches at the Universidad Externado de Colombia in Bogota, Colombia.

He is a graduate of Syracuse University (1970) and holds an M.P.A. (1972) and Ph.D. (1973) from the Maxwell School of Syracuse University. He previously taught at Syracuse University, Indiana University, Russell Sage College, the State University of New York at Albany, and Baruch College of the City University of New York.

Dr. Eimicke served as director of Fiscal Studies for the New York State Senate from 1975 to 1978, assistant budget director of the City of New York from 1978 to 1979, and deputy commissioner of the New York City Department of Housing Preservation and Development from 1979 until 1982.

He served as New York Governor Cuomo's deputy secretary for Policy and Programs from 1983 through 1985. From 1985 until 1988, he served as housing "czar" of New York State, managing the state's six housing management, finance, and regulatory agencies. In 1993, he provided housing policy and management consulting services to Vice President Al Gore's National Performance Review.

Dr. Eimicke is the author of *Public Administration in a Democratic Context* (1974) and the co-author of *Tools for Innovators* (1998), and *The New Effective Public Manager* (1995), and numerous articles on public management innovation, ethics, competition and welfare-to-work programs.

Dr. Eimicke has also served as management consultant to a wide array of public, private, and nonprofit agencies seeking to improve their performance, reorganize, develop strategic planning, and improve their productivity.

Ian D. Littman is a partner in PwC Consulting and is based in Washington, D.C. His career started with service in federal and state government, followed by over 25 years experience in consulting to the private and public sectors. During his consulting career, Mr. Littman has worked closely with over 50 federal agencies in such areas as business process engineering, change management, quality management, organizational analysis, personnel management, customer satisfaction, benchmarking, inter-governmental relations, and instructional design and training.

Mr. Littman has managed many of PwC's studies of large logistics organizations and testified before the U.S. Congress on procurement and supply issues. He is the lead partner for PwC's work with the U.S. Intelligence Community.

Mr. Littman's corporate responsibilities include membership in the firm's Senior Management Team for the Washington Consulting Practice (WCP), which consists of 3,000 professionals who serve for-profit, non-profit, and government organizations throughout the world. He co-chairs the PricewaterhouseCoopers Endowment for the Business of Government.

Mr. Littman holds a masters degree in public administration (M.P.A.) from The George Washington University, a B.A. degree from Syracuse University, and completed postgraduate and doctoral course work at the University of Southern California and Syracuse University.

Mr. Littman's book *Excellence in Government: Total Quality Management in the 1990's* (1990, second edition 1993) has been translated into five languages, sold over 35,000 copies, and is still the authoritative text on public sector quality. *Improvement Driven Government: Public Service for the 21st Century* (1995) is a comprehensive review of organizational redesign at the federal, state, and local levels. He was a contributing author to *Breakthrough Customer Service: Best Practices of Leaders in Customer Support* (1997), and a co-author of *Transforming Government Services: A Global Perspective* (1998), which describes the tools of transformation and global best practices in how to use them. He also has published articles in *Quality Progress, National Productivity Review, TQM Journal, The Federal Times, Industry Week, Government Accounting,* and other national publications.

Scott E. Tarry is Associate Professor, Aviation Institute, Department of Public Administration at the University of Nebraska at Omaha. Dr. Tarry received his B.A. from the University of Puget Sound and his M.A. and Ph.D. from the University of Michigan. His research on aviation issues has been published in *Transportation Quarterly, Public Works Management and Policy, Journal of Air Law and Commerce,* and *International Interactions.*

Prior to joining the faculty at the University of Nebraska at Omaha in August 2000, Dr. Tarry was Assistant Professor of Political Science at Southern Illinois University. He continues his research on aviation policy and airport administration while teaching in UNO's aviation administration programs.

Jonathan Walters is a staff correspondent for *Governing* magazine. Walters has been covering state and local public administration and policy for more than 20 years, writing for publications including the *Washington Post,* the

New York Times, and *USA Today.* For the past 10 years, he has been focusing on public sector management and administration with an emphasis on change management and results-based governance. Articles for *Governing* have included stories on total quality management, performance measurement, activity-based costing, performance-based budgeting, the balanced score-card, and management trends and innovation in government.

For the past 13 years, he has been directly involved in covering the Ford Foundation/Kennedy School Innovations in American Government awards. He is also the author of *Measuring Up! Governing's Guide to Performance Measurement for Geniuses and Other Public Managers.* Walters frequently speaks on a wide range of subjects related to public sector policy and administration, from performance-based governance to civil service reform.

Besides covering government, Walters is actively involved in government in his hometown of Ghent, New York, where he serves as co-chair of the planning board and as the town's freedom of information law officer. He is also active in his local volunteer fire company. Walters graduated from the University of Massachusetts, Amherst, in 1977 with a B.A. in English/Journalism.

About The PricewaterhouseCoopers Endowment for The Business of Government

Through grants for research, The PricewaterhouseCoopers Endowment for The Business of Government stimulates research and facilitates discussion of new approaches to improving the effectiveness of government at the federal, state, local, and international levels.

Research grants of $15,000 are awarded competitively to outstanding scholars in academic and nonprofit institutions across the United States. Each grantee is expected to produce a 30- to 40-page research report in one of the areas presented on pages 220-222. Grant reports will be published and disseminated by The Endowment. All the chapters presented in this book were originally prepared as grant reports to The Endowment.

Founded in 1998 by PricewaterhouseCoopers, The Endowment is one of the ways that PricewaterhouseCoopers seeks to advance knowledge on how to improve public sector effectiveness. The PricewaterhouseCoopers Endowment focuses on the future of the operations and management of the public sector.

Who is Eligible?
Individuals working in:
- Universities
- Nonprofit organizations
- Journalism

Description of Grant

Individuals receiving grants will be responsible for producing a 30- to 40-page research report in one of the areas presented on pages 220-222. The research paper should be completed within a six-month period from the start of the project. Grantees select the start and end dates of the research project.

Size of Grant

$15,000 for each research paper

Who Receives the Grant

Individuals will receive the grant, not the institution in which they are located.

Application Process

Interested individuals should submit:

- A three-page description of the proposed research
- A résumé, including list of publications

Application Deadlines

There are three funding cycles annually, with deadlines of:

- The last day of February
- The last day of June
- The last day of October

Applications must be postmarked or received online by the above dates.

Submitting Applications

Hard copy:

> Mark A. Abramson
> Executive Director
> The PricewaterhouseCoopers Endowment for The Business of Government
> 1616 North Fort Myer Drive
> Arlington, VA 22209

Online:

> endowment.pwcglobal.com/apply

Program Areas

E-Government

The Endowment is seeking proposals that examine the implementation of e-government in the following areas: (1) Government to Business (G2B); (2) Government to Citizen (G2C); (3) Government to Employee (G2E); and (4) Government to Government (G2G). The Endowment is especially interested in innovative approaches to providing information so citizens can make their own choices, complete service transactions electronically, hold government more accountable for results, and offer feedback.

Examples of previous grants in this area:
- The Auction Model: How the Public Sector Can Leverage the Power of E-Commerce Through Dynamic Pricing *by David Wyld*
- Commerce Comes to Government on the Desktop: E-Commerce Applications in the Public Sector *by Genie N. L. Stowers*
- The Use of the Internet in Government Service Delivery *by Steven Cohen and William B. Eimicke*

Financial Management

The Endowment is seeking proposals that examine specific financial management issues, such as cost accounting and management, financial and resource analysis, financial risk management and modeling, internal controls, operational and systems risk management, financial auditing, contract management, reconciliation, and overpayment recovery. The Endowment is especially interested in full costs and budgeting approaches for support services and capital assets, retirement, and other employee benefits, and other nondirect costs associated with delivering program services.

Examples of previous grants in this area:
- Audited Financial Statements: Getting and Sustaining "Clean" Opinions *by Douglas A. Brook*
- Credit Scoring and Loan Scoring: Tools for Improved Management of Federal Credit Programs *by Thomas H. Stanton*
- Using Activity-Based Costing to Manage More Effectively *by Michael H. Granof, David E. Platt, and Igor Vaysman*

Human Capital

The Endowment is seeking proposals that examine human capital issues related to public service. Human capital consists of the knowledge, skills, abilities, attitudes, and experience required to accomplish an organization's mission. It also includes an organization's ability to recruit and retain employees, as well as to undertake workforce planning and analysis.

Examples of previous grants in this area:
- Leaders Growing Leaders: Preparing the Next Generation of Public Service Executives *by Ray Blunt*
- Reflections on Mobility: Case Studies of Six Federal Executives *by Michael D. Serlin*
- Winning the Best and Brightest: Increasing the Attraction of Public Service *by Carol Chetkovich*

Managing for Results

The Endowment is seeking proposals that examine how organizations align their processes—such as budgeting, workforce, and business processes—around their strategic goals. This area also focuses on how organizations use performance and results information to make policy, management, and resource allocation decisions. The Endowment is especially interested in how different organizations work collaboratively to achieve common outcomes. The Endowment is also interested in case studies of the use of balanced scorecards, including the measurement of customer service.

Examples of previous grants in this area:
- The Challenge of Developing Cross-Agency Measures: A Case Study of the Office of National Drug Control Policy *by Patrick Murphy and John Carnevale*
- Using Performance Data for Accountability: The New York City Police Department's CompStat Model of Police Management *by Paul O'Connell*
- Using Evaluation to Support Performance Management: A Guide for Federal Executives *by Kathryn E. Newcomer and Mary Ann Scheirer*

New Ways to Manage

The Endowment is seeking proposals that examine specific instances of new ways of delivering programs and services to the public, including contracting out, competition, outsourcing, privatization, and public-private partnerships. The Endowment is also interested in innovations in the way public organizations are managed.

Examples of previous grants in this area:
- Entrepreneurial Government: Bureaucrats as Businesspeople *by Anne Laurent*
- San Diego County's Innovation Program: Using Competition and a Whole Lot More to Improve Public Services *by William B. Eimicke*
- The Challenge of Innovating in Government *by Sandford Borins*

Transforming Organizations

The Endowment is seeking proposals that examine how specific public sector organizations have been transformed with new values, changed cultures, and enhanced performance. This area also includes studies of outstanding public sector leaders.

Examples of previous grants in this area:
- Transforming Government: The Renewal and Revitalization of the Federal Emergency Management Agency *by R. Steven Daniels and Carolyn L. Clark-Daniels*
- Transforming Government: The Revitalization of the Veterans Health Administration *by Gary J. Young*
- Transforming Government: Dan Goldin and the Remaking of NASA *by W. Henry Lambright*

For more information about The Endowment

Visit our website at: endowment.pwcglobal.com
Send an e-mail to: endowment@us.pwcglobal.com
Call: (703) 741-1077

About PricewaterhouseCoopers

The Management Consulting Services practice of PricewaterhouseCoopers helps clients maximize their business performance by integrating strategic change, performance improvement, and technology solutions. Through a worldwide network of skills and resources, consultants manage complex projects with global capabilities and local knowledge, from strategy through implementation. PricewaterhouseCoopers (www.pwcglobal.com) is the world's largest professional services organization. Drawing on the knowledge and skills of more than 150,000 people in 150 countries, the practice helps clients solve complex business problems and measurably enhance their ability to build value, manage risk, and improve performance in an Internet-enabled world. PricewaterhouseCoopers refers to the member firms of the worldwide PricewaterhouseCoopers organization.